MW00610867

Praise for
The Mother of All Degrassi

"Linda Schuyler's memoir is a portrait of passion, strength, and courage — a gutsy tribute to a creative life of vision and tenacity. Her career trajectory is a road map for young women who yearn to take charge, touch people, and leave a mark. With her finger on the pulse of youth culture, Linda's dogged determination as an innovative storyteller gave birth to the whole *Degrassi* phenomenon and a homegrown entertainment platform that helped change lives."
— JEANNE BEKER, journalist, TV personality, author

"Linda cast me in my first major television role — Craig on *Degrassi: The Next Generation* — and I owe so much to her. I was blown away by her book. Linda shares the origin story of a TV show that paved the way for a young Canadian industry and countless careers. It offered encouragement to millions of fans worldwide. Written with immense honesty, her life story is filled with wisdom, comforting anecdotes, and heartbreak and is a must-read for fans of the *Degrassi* franchise."
— JAKE EPSTEIN, actor, playwright

"A triumphant pioneering story! Linda is not only the mother of all *Degrassi* but the mother of all TV where the real lives of young people shape content."
— ANNABEL SLAIGHT, C.M., O.Ont.,
co-founder of OWL magazines, books, and TV

"I thought I knew everything about the creation of this show, but *The Mother of All Degrassi* took me on a trip into the real nitty-gritty of birthing an iconic television hit. Not only a fun, exciting, emotional read but a time capsule into the early days of guerrilla television in Canada. There aren't many stories of success like Linda's, and to know that I was a small part of it gave me goosebumps. Now I know what all the adults around me were doing when I was thirteen! The circle is complete, and what a wonderful way to learn about it."

— STEFAN BROGREN, actor, director

"This book covers so many important issues contemporary to each stage of Linda's (and *Degrassi*'s) life. Linda created the role models I desperately wanted when I was a teen, and meanwhile she was living the role model life I didn't know I needed to know about and is the role model I need today as an adult."

— ANGIE KUHNLE, NetGalley reviewer, *Degrassi* fan

THE MOTHER OF ALL

A MEMOIR

LINDA SCHUYLER

Published by ECW Press
665 Gerrard Street East
Toronto, Ontario, Canada M4M 1Y2
416-694-3348 / info@ecwpress.com

Cover design: Made by Emblem
Author photo (front cover): Janet Webb / Courtesy of WildBrain / Media Commons Archives, University of Toronto Libraries
Logo & QR code (back flap): Courtesy of Kids Help Phone

Every effort has been made to contact copyright holders. The author and publisher would be glad to amend in future editions any errors or omissions brought to their attention.

"Degrassi Junior High Theme Song" (Watson/Manne)
Copyright © Fatwatson Music, Manimal Music, 1986

"Degrassi: The Next Generation Theme" (Colero/McGrath/Stohn)
Copyright © Einstein Brothers Publishing, Jim McGrath, and WildBrain Ltd., 2000. Copyright renewed. Used by permission. All rights reserved.

LIBRARY AND ARCHIVES CANADA CATALOGUING
IN PUBLICATION

Title: The mother of all Degrassi : a memoir / Linda Schuyler.

Names: Schuyler, Linda, author.

Identifiers: Canadiana (print) 20220215596 | Canadiana (ebook) 20220215766

ISBN 978-1-77041-683-3 (hardcover)
ISBN 978-1-77852-038-9 (ePub)
ISBN 978-1-77852-039-6 (PDF)
ISBN 978-1-77852-040-2 (Kindle)

Subjects: LCSH: Schuyler, Linda. | LCSH: Women television producers and directors—Canada—Biography. | LCSH: Television producers and directors—Canada—Biography. | LCSH: Degrassi television programs. | LCGFT: Autobiographies.

Classification: LCC PN1992.4.S38 A3 2022 | DDC 791.4502/32092—dc23

We acknowledge the support of the Canada Council for the Arts. Nous remercions le Conseil des arts du Canada de son soutien. This book is funded in part by the Government of Canada. Ce livre est financé en partie par le gouvernement du Canada. We acknowledge the support of the Ontario Arts Council (OAC), an agency of the Government of Ontario, which last year funded 1,965 individual artists and 1,152 organizations in 197 communities across Ontario for a total of $51.9 million. We also acknowledge the support of the Government of Ontario through the Ontario Book Publishing Tax Credit, and through Ontario Creates.

Canada Council   Conseil des arts
for the Arts   du Canada

Canadä

PRINTED AND BOUND IN CANADA

PRINTING: FRIESENS   5 4 3 2 1

MIX
Paper from responsible sources
FSC
www.fsc.org   FSC® C016245

I used to think I must be the strangest person in the world but then I thought, there are so many people in the world, there must be someone just like me who feels bizarre and flawed in the same ways I do . . . Well, I hope that if you are out there you read this and know that, yes, it's true I'm here, and I'm just as strange as you.

— REBECCA MARTIN, age 17, a *Degrassi* fan
(Quote often attributed to Frida Kahlo)

To Bruce,
Degrassi's *queer,*
queer grandfather

TABLE OF CONTENTS

INTRODUCTION

January 28, 2020.
    In a converted 1940s movie theatre, I am looking out at row upon row of upturned faces. Wilfrid Laurier University has invited me to speak to students at their Brantford campus as part of their "People Make History" series. Outside, the sun is lemon yellow and looks warmer than it is. Inside, it's Q & A time. Earlier today I gave my first talk — "Head On . . . Reflections on Life" — about my childhood as a British immigrant growing up in small-town Ontario, my teen years during the 1960s, my work as a junior high school teacher, and my long career in the film and television industry. I have just finished my second lecture, "The *Degrassi* Story," which focused on the origins and cultural impact of my life's work and passion: the *Degrassi* franchise.

    Right now, I am enjoying the conversations that have me reflecting on how my filmmaking life has simultaneously been a teaching life, spent with and for young people. For years, I shied away from identifying as a schoolteacher, wrongly thinking of it as a second-class job, an irony that isn't lost on me in this brightly lit lecture theatre. Then a student asks me if there is a simple theme that resonates through each episode and every *Degrassi* series.

I think for a moment. I've already waxed eloquently (I hope) about youth empowerment and the inclusive *Degrassi* message that "you are not alone." I've discussed *Degrassi*'s goal of being fearless about subject matter, without ever sensationalizing or trivializing. I've talked about the importance of celebrating diversity and have mentioned the cornerstone of each story: that young people make their own choices and live with the consequences. These are all ideas I have articulated many times: in boardrooms, production studios, outdoor cafés, and press interviews. But there is, I realize, something else. There is my own story that I told earlier: how, as an eight-year-old immigrant to Canada, I was mocked and tormented by my Grade 3 classmates. My plummy British accent was constantly mimicked.

"Ohhh, listen to Limey Linda — slimy, Limey Linda."

"Need to go to the loo, Lindy Loo? Ha, ha, ha!"

And worse, they would chant, "Hey, Brit girl. Yes, you, shit girl. Go back to where you came from."

Recalling these voices, I shudder slightly, even sixty-five years later. Then I think of the numerous *Degrassi* bullying stories I have told over the years: Joey with Yick and Arthur; Dwayne and Tabi with Joey; the mean girls and Spike; Spinner with Rick; Craig and his dad; Paige with Manny and Ashley; Holly J. and everyone; Bianca, Owen, and Fitz with Adam;

Me, November 6, 1956, the day we arrived in Canada.

Maya and cyberbullies; Lola and the shamers . . . the list goes on.

There's an expectant hush in the air as I collect my thoughts.

Finally I say, "I consider *Degrassi* to be probably the world's longest-running anti-bullying campaign."

★

On the drive home that night, Highway 403 is dark, the taillights of the preceding cars light my way, and I have time to think: to review the day and my life. I realize what an incredible opportunity I've had for almost forty years to tell stories for and about young people and to share these stories with audiences in Canada and around the world.

As the lights of the city begin to appear on the horizon, the volume of traffic increases. I move deftly from one lane to the other and smile to myself, recalling a time when I couldn't drive on the highway without having a panic attack. And, before that, there was a point when I was convinced I'd never get behind the wheel again when I feared I had lost my eyesight. I was twenty then and recovering from a terrifying car crash that had come close to taking my life. Following that defining moment, I made a series of choices that, by age twenty-five, convinced me that my life was nothing but a string of disappointments, accidents, and poor judgments. These feelings of failure were amplified by my being the eldest child of immigrant parents: I was expected to succeed.

Despite these early setbacks (and more to come), I managed somehow to be on stage tonight with an audience that seemed eager to hear my story. And that wouldn't have happened if, in 1974, I hadn't realized my life needed a serious reboot. For four years following my crash — more on that later — I had tried my best to be an engaging teacher for my Grade 8 students and a good wife to my high school sweetheart, but my life was on autopilot. I was stalled. As part of my fresh new start, I returned to university to complete my degree. While there, I found a small notice that I thought would change my life. Ultimately, it did. It didn't give me the immediate outcome I wanted, but, like so many pivotal moments in my life, it gave me the result I needed.

CHAPTER ONE

BETWEEN TWO WORLDS

April 1974.
I was sprawled on a moth-eaten sofa with my eyes rivetted to a portable screen. Around me, my fellow students, sitting on the floor and on various mismatched pieces of furniture, were equally enthralled. We watched shot after shot as hundreds of infantry and artillery groups marched in rigid formation to salute Hitler. The film was *Triumph of the Will*, a 1935 documentary by female director Leni Riefenstahl, part of the curriculum for our Women in Film course at a young Innis College.

Innis College, part of the University of Toronto (U of T), was situated in a once-grand Georgian house, which had been the home of Canada's first prime minister, Sir John A. Macdonald. (Rumour had it that Sir John A.'s spirit haunted the building and many students claimed to have seen the apparition of a man in a frock coat slipping quietly through the second floor.) Now, over one hundred years later, the exterior of the house remained grand, but the interior was shabby. Our film classes were held in the original living room. It had elegant proportions but had been retrofitted with a cheap wall-to-wall carpet in an off-putting shade of green. Our professors would set up the 16mm projector in the middle of the room and throw the images to the portable screen parked in

The Macdonald-Mowat House, home of Innis College from 1968 to 1976. Innis offered groundbreaking courses as well as U of T's first unisex washroom and first campus pub.

front of the defunct fireplace. Here we would watch movies, revel in the magic of celluloid, and rigorously debate the politics of film-makers and filmmaking.

Suddenly the image in front of us froze. For a moment, hundreds of Hitler Youth were stopped with their boots raised in perfect unison. Then quickly, the image evaporated, burnt by the heat of the bulb, leaving only a bright white light on the screen.

"Damn," muttered our professor, Kay Armitage, as she rushed to turn off the projector. "I'll get this spliced back together and we can finish the screening next class. Then we will have a discussion, and I assure you — it will be lively!"

As I headed out of class, my mind was swirling with what we had just watched. Evidently Riefenstahl had about thirty cameras at work and a crew of over 150 to capture the 1934 Nazi Party rally at Nuremberg, attended by over seven hundred thousand Nazi supporters. That's a huge responsibility for any director, particularly a neophyte thirty-two-year-old woman (only a few years older than me at the time). Riefenstahl's shots were crisp and innovative, and her use of music and sound highly effective. I was mesmerized by her abilities as a pioneering female filmmaker yet horrified by her message. *Triumph of the Will* was blatant propaganda that idealized Hitler and the Nazi Party. I was so deep in thought that I reached the front door without having stopped for my daily routine to check the notice board. I retraced my steps through the foyer and scanned the overcrowded bulletin board. At last, I spied a small notice that intrigued me: *TVOntario is accepting applications for summer interns.*

When I'd left my full-time teaching job a year earlier, I'd enrolled at Innis College — the only college at the time that offered courses in both cinema studies and women's studies — with the hope that I'd be positioned for a new career in the media. I had dreams of becoming a filmmaker. TV was surely cinema's sassy little sister and TVOntario hadn't even been on my radar, but I reread the application details. *This could be my foot in the door.* I took a quick glance around. No one was watching so I pulled the small poster down and shoved it in my macramé shoulder bag.

Later that night, once my application letter had been carefully drafted and redrafted, I picked up the notice to toss into the garbage — no need for competition, right? But something stopped me. The notice was a public one, not mine to destroy. It hadn't even been mine to remove. The next morning, I mailed my letter and guiltily rehung the announcement.

When the return letter arrived, I opened it warily, then threw my hands and the letter up in the air and did a happy dance in my tiny kitchen. I had a job in the media! I excitedly marked my start date on the calendar — two months away. My final classes at U of T had wrapped up, so I decided to make some money by picking up work as an occasional teacher, filling in at a moment's notice for absent teachers. All students know that an occasional teacher is prime pickings for practical jokes, name switching, tall tales, and many kinds of ad hoc misery. However, knowing that I had a new career on the horizon, I was in no mood for this and ran a tight classroom, adhering to the lesson plans and suffering no fools. As such, I became a popular supply teacher with the administration and was called to fill in on a regular basis at Earl Grey Senior Public School, an inner-city junior high school in Toronto's east end.

Barb Mackay, an enthusiastic and charming maverick, was Earl Grey's vice-principal. She took particular interest in my ability to keep a class of rambunctious adolescents in check and get some lessons taught, as well as create an atmosphere of fun. As the school year was ending and my start date at TVOntario loomed, Barb posed a question: "Would you consider returning to Earl Grey next year in a full-time position?"

Politely, but firmly, I declined the offer. I had loftier dreams.

"Well, keep us in mind if things don't work out."

As much as I liked Barb and the school, I had no intention of returning full time to the classroom. In fact, I'd never planned to be a teacher at all. In high school, we'd had little in the way of direction to help us with our post-secondary and career options. On my one mandatory visit with the guidance counsellor, he cheerfully went over the results of my aptitude test. "Well, Linda, from the results of your tests, it looks like you have two exciting career options: teacher or nurse."

I couldn't have been less enthused. In fact, I was seriously miffed. For anyone who knew me, nursing was absolutely not an option. Even though my mum — who, as a young woman, nursed the wounded through the Blitz in London — was a compassionate caregiver, I was not good with sick people. And teaching? *Really?* Could he think of anything more mundane? Why didn't he suggest astronaut, urban planner, architect, or politician instead? *He probably considers those with a Y chromosome the only ones worthy of those jobs,* I thought to myself. It didn't even occur to me then that television producer could be an option. But, in the fall of 1968, with my hippie travels abruptly ended by my violent car crash, and university application deadlines long past, I had no alternative than to enrol in teacher's college, studying for a profession that I'd scoffed at just a few short months before. With my teaching diploma, I began a four-year teaching gig in London, Ontario, and took part-time courses at Western University. Now, after a full year at the University of Toronto, I finally had my degree and *no* desire to return to classroom teaching.

Part of my Innis graduating class, 1974. No caps and gowns here — we were a rather renegade bunch.

★

I started my summer job at TVOntario with great enthusiasm. Their offices were located in the same building where the Eglinton subway stop emptied out. *Convenient,* I thought. *A very easy commute.* However, once I reported to work on my first day, I realized I wouldn't need to take public transportation again — I was given a production vehicle to drive. I was kept busy driving about the city, delivering script revisions, picking up forgotten props, and taking various directors' cars to be washed. I spent time in the art department xeroxing American money and colouring it green. Letraset signs needed to be made, and coloured pencils required sharpening. But, most importantly, I brewed and served endless pots of coffee — meanwhile constantly checking the TVOntario job postings, hopeful to find the key to my new life. Daily, my spirits started to fade — any suitable jobs were all short-term, offering minimum wage, which was not enough to support a newly separated woman.

As summer was drawing to a close, Barb's suggestion of a teaching position in the fall seemed to make sense — the prospect of a full-time salary with summers free to explore my own projects suddenly looked appealing. With hours to spare before the closing of the application deadline, I hastily submitted paperwork for a position at the Toronto Board of Education. A few days later, I was at the home of Mack White, the principal of Earl Grey, for an interview in his stunning North Toronto rose garden. Mack was engaging and the roses smelled intoxicating. I explained to Mack how I wanted to continue pursuing opportunities in the media and wondered if he was open to me trying some experimental media projects with my students. Mack responded, "I'm always open to modern teaching techniques. We can keep this dialogue going once we get the basics established."

The job was mine, but Mack was hard to read. I wasn't sure if he truly was open to the potential for media projects or was just being political, but I liked him and was willing to give it a go. I became a homeroom teacher for Grades 7 and 8 at Earl Grey, one class in the morning and another in the afternoon. I was responsible for their core subjects: basic English and math. Daily, I reminded myself that this position was only temporary, that I just needed to save enough money before taking the leap to become a freelancer somewhere in the media. But slowly, little by little, my students started tugging at my heartstrings. I'd secretly smile when Florence proclaimed during spelling dictation, "Ms. Schuyler, someone's lettin' off gas!" or when John Grove, a talented artist, flashed me an incredibly good caricature of myself as I earnestly explained quadratic equations.

Both of my classes represented a diversity that I'd not seen before. Growing up in a small town in southern Ontario, diversity was defined by which church you attended. My parents made it very clear that as a Protestant, I could not date a Roman Catholic. As a Presbyterian, I could co-mingle with United Church–goers and Anglicans. But Baptists were considered marginal, and Jews were out of the question. Using today's lens, this narrowmindedness seems ridiculous (if not much worse), but that was Paris, Ontario, in the 1950s and '60s.

What a sharp contrast to my new inner-city Toronto classroom, where every day I faced students who represented diversity not only of religion, but also of nationality and skin colour. I had students from Greece and Italy, Cyprus, Czechoslovakia, some from Jamaica and other Caribbean countries, and many from Asian countries. Most spoke two languages: English at school and their native language at home. My students appeared to integrate well into the Canadian environment during school hours, then seamlessly adapt to their parents' culture at home. I soon came to realize that these daily juxtapositions were not without tensions. I watched with great interest as my students dealt with their burgeoning adolescence while living the first- and second-generation immigrant experience. I was reminded of my early years in Canada as a British immigrant when I felt like an *other* who didn't fit in. Yet compared to the students, I'd had it very easy. On the surface, at least, I blended.

My students shared with me their lunches of curried goat, baklava, spanakopita, and lasagna. They gave me jars of homemade pickled olives, peppers, tomatoes, and beets, and, on one occasion, a bottle of homemade wine. I learned about family customs and traditions so different from my own. Kids stayed after school and shared poems they had written or played a new song on the guitar. Sometimes, they just needed to talk to someone, to vent their frustrations about their overly strict and restrictive parents. Other times, they needed a quiet and private cry. My students had stories to tell.

★

On one of my trips to the downtown administrative offices of the Toronto Board of Education, Barb Mackay introduced me to the head of the audiovisual department, the avuncular and mischievous Lou Wise. Lou had his own budget and was responsible for ordering audiovisual works (films, film strips, etc.) and audiovisual equipment. Lou and I quickly became friends and on one visit he opened his locked cupboards to show me the inventory of equipment he had amassed over the years. I couldn't believe the treasure trove inside. Not only were there the requisite 16mm projectors, slide projectors, and record players, but there was also a large supply of Super 8 cameras with accompanying editing equipment. But wait, there was more. My eyes grew wide when I noticed he also had some professional equipment — a 16mm Bolex camera, a 16mm Arriflex camera, and a Nagra sound recording system. I casually asked Lou who used this equipment. He said that he used it himself to create some of the board's own audiovisual works.

"Have others used this amazing equipment?" I asked cautiously.

"Sadly, no one has shown an interest."

Ha! I thought. *I have interest.* But I knew better than to express that just then.

I had the beginnings of a plan that I shared with Barb. With her encouragement, and within weeks of being hired in the fall of 1974, I found myself in front of my principal, Mack White, once again. I took a deep breath and started.

"With your support, I would like to make a 16mm documentary on my students as they juggle their two lives in Canada. The school board has all the necessary equipment, so we would only require a modest budget for some film stock and editing. We will use some class time as part of the English program to create a script. I'm willing to work nights and weekends, and will involve my students not just as subjects, but as crew. In their own words, my students will document their teenage lives as they juggle their school world and the reality of their immigrant home life. We'll call this *Between Two Worlds*. So . . . what do you think?"

I exhaled.

Mack remained characteristically emotionless. After a moment, he promised he would "look into it." I returned to my classroom, convinced that my idea was too outside the box, and that Mack felt I was a nuisance foisted upon him by his enthusiastic female vice-principal. I needed to reconcile myself to the reality of traditional teaching and adhere to the prescribed curriculum.

★

One grey day in early November, towards the end of a long afternoon, I was buzzed in my classroom and asked to come to the principal's office. It doesn't matter how old you get, or how experienced in life, there is something about a summons to the principal's office that conjures up feelings of wrongdoing. I checked my desk to confirm my lesson planner was up to date, found my attendance register to make sure it was correctly filled out (sometimes I'd forget), and checked my clothes and my hair. I felt like I was heading for a termination.

Mack met me with a pleasant smile, revealing nothing. "Close the door," he said. "Linda, as you know, Prime Minister Pierre Trudeau is a strong believer in multiculturalism. "

"I am aware, yes." I knew that in 1971 Prime Minister Trudeau had announced multiculturalism as an official government policy, intended to preserve the cultural freedoms and contributions of diverse ethnic groups in Canada.

"Well," Mack continued, "Trudeau's government has provided pockets of money around the country to further this agenda. As luck would have it, I have one of these pockets. I would like to fund your proposal." And then he gave me a real smile. One that said he was proud of himself and excited about this opportunity.

Holy shit. My first professional pitch. My first green light.

Then I panicked — there wasn't even a script yet. Well, I assured myself, my students and I could make that happen. But more worrying, I had no idea how to use a 16mm camera or a

Nagra, even if Lou Wise would lend them to me. I needed to call the Toronto Filmmakers Co-op.

Founded three years earlier, in 1971, and loosely based on a similar co-operative in New York City, the Toronto Filmmakers Co-op was an early gathering spot for up-and-coming Toronto filmmakers. Housed in an old Victorian house on Jarvis Street, they offered access to information on government funding, held private screenings, facilitated networking (although I don't think we called it that in those days), and offered some basic production courses. I signed up for a weekend course with cinematographer Carol Betts. Carol had distinguished herself as the first woman in Canada to make her living as a director of photography, specializing in news, sports, and documentaries — an amazing feat considering this was the mid-1970s. Even to this day, male cinematographers far outnumber women. Carol was a pioneer, a skilled craftsperson, an awesome role model, and a great teacher. In one weekend, I studied ASA, sprockets, depth of field, wide and long lenses, film stock, and emulsion. I learned how to load and unload 100-foot reels of negatives and prepare them for the lab.

I was ready to face Lou Wise.

Lou was delighted with my newfound knowledge and the fact that I actually had money to make a documentary. He furthered my education with a tutorial on his lighting package and one on the Nagra sound system. He agreed to loan me the equipment. Now it was time to share the project with my students. My classes excitedly embraced the challenge to prepare their own personal stories about living between two worlds. We collected their anecdotes and strung them together in a rough script. We brainstormed what images could support these individual stories. I gave my students crash courses in lighting and sound, as it would be their job to support me while I gathered the pictures.

Over the course of a few months we gathered footage at local ethnic festivals and events — at the Greek Orthodox Church, at Kensington Market, on the Danforth, in Chinatown, in Little Italy. I arranged for my class to take a skiing trip, and we documented some of my students experiencing skiing and snow for the first time. We shot at local hockey games, in the schoolyard, at school dances, and at the neighbourhood restaurant hangout.

Fofo, one of my Greek students, loved to be in front of the camera, but refused to take her coat off. I later realized that she didn't want her parents to see her "school" clothes. She had her own sexy image for school, and she knew her parents would not approve. She changed in the washroom every morning and afternoon. (Later, when I was developing *Degrassi Junior High*, Fofo's wardrobe would become an inspiration for the character Stephanie Kaye.)

Towards the end of the shoot, with help from Lou, I arranged for two sync sound interviews: one with Sylvia Pusey, a passionate and compassionate teacher, herself a long-time Jamaican immigrant; and the other with one of my students, Donald Hoppie, a very recent immigrant. Both interviews went well, but the end of the Donald interview wouldn't leave my head. Donald and his twin brother, Ronald, had immigrated from Jamaica a few months earlier. The Hoppie boys had never seen snow before and were delighted and awestruck when they participated in our special skiing field trip. They were charming kids who obviously came from a caring home. In my interview with Donald, I'd asked him what he liked about Canada. "I just like it here," he smiled. "My dad and mom both have jobs, and they are happy."

"Is there anything you don't like about Canada?"

"Yup — it's cold!"

"But, you seemed to have such a great time on our ski trip."

"Oh, that was fun, real fun. And cold!" He cracked a smile.

Then I asked if he had ever experienced any difficulties fitting in to his new environment at Earl Grey. As both he and his brother were forever flashing their million-dollar smiles and readily being accepted in new friend groups, I expected an upbeat answer that could sit nicely towards the end of the film. I wasn't prepared for what I got. Donald started to recount a situation that had happened a few days earlier at lunchtime. He was hanging out in the local corner restaurant with a bunch of other kids when someone called him out, used the n-word, and ordered him to shut the door. As he repeated the racial slur on camera, I asked him how the incident made him feel.

"I felt so stupid, I wanna be white," was his response.

I looked at Donald's beautiful face and couldn't reconcile how such a wonderful young man would want to be anything other than who he was.

★

I took myself back to the Toronto Filmmakers Co-op in search of an editor. Here, I met the talented Clarke Mackey, who had recently won an award for his documentary on Ontario's health-care system. Clarke and I spent hours with the footage. Back and forth. Hanging scenes in the trim bin. Naming and labelling moments. Looking for gems. Following the script, we had a basic shape for the film. We showed joyful celebrations of various students' cultures. We heard some of their challenging anecdotes about living between two worlds. And, finally, we culminated the project with a montage of students celebrating together in Canadian activities such as playing hockey, skiing, and attending a school dance. As per the script, Donald's interview came in the middle section of the film. But it gnawed at me that this didn't seem to do justice to his story.

I faced my first crisis as a documentary filmmaker. I wondered if this moment was too intimate to remain in the film. *Would Donald be uncomfortable seeing his raw words shared with others? If I keep the interview, should I leave it buried in the middle of the show, or should it be repositioned?* After much soul-searching, I decided that not only should the interview stay in the film, but it would be the very last image. This was a departure from the original shape of the script and was a pivotal moment for me. I learned, firsthand, that the editing process was, in a sense, the final draft of the script. I liked the new order; it was very powerful. But it created a deep question. By positioning the interview at the end, was I being sensational for the wrong reasons, or provocative for the right ones? I didn't want to be manipulative, as I had seen in *Triumph of the Will*, yet I wanted to raise awareness.

I sought the advice of my sage friend Sylvia.

"Leave the interview where it is," she said emphatically. "We must leave people thinking and get them talking. You've made the right choice."

With that encouragement, I shared the cut with my class, including Donald. We had a lively and raw discussion that ultimately led to the same conclusion. The picture was locked. Not only did it end with Donald, but the final image was a long freeze on his face, allowing the moment to linger.

We screened the finished project with family, friends, faculty and various members of the Toronto Board of Education in spring 1975. Even though the ending was thought-provoking, they praised the even-handedness and inclusiveness of the project. The Board quickly prepared an in-depth teacher's guide to accompany the film. Multiple copies were ordered to be distributed around the city, activating many discussions on multiculturalism and racism. Eventually, our documentary was distributed to most major school boards across the country.

Donald Hoppie in *Between Two Worlds*.

I felt like a star. My kids felt like stars. We were responsible for opening dialogue from coast to coast. It was a heady feeling for all.

*

One day, near the end of the school year, I was once again summoned to the principal's office. On this occasion, thoughts of termination did not cross my mind. I knew Mack White was happy with our project and enjoyed the positive attention coming to Earl Grey and to him.

Mack greeted me with his characteristic pleasant smile, revealing nothing. "Close the door," he said. "Linda, you know we are all very proud of you and your students for the great film you have made . . ."

Oh. I sensed a "but" coming.

"Well, we are not the only people who are proud of your work. NBC would like to air it." Mack couldn't contain his joy any longer. After a brief pause for this to sink in, Mack and I began laughing together. The Toronto Board of Education had given its permission. Our project, and our school, were going to be featured on a major U.S. television network before the end of the month. How great was this for a first-time filmmaker?

As the air date drew closer, we were told by the network that *Between Two Worlds* wouldn't be shown in its entirety, but a good number of minutes would be featured. Members of the staff gathered together for the broadcast occasion. Our film was part of a *60 Minutes*–type of show looking at race relations and racism in the U.S. and included a portion about Canada. We watched some rather unsettling interviews about the state of racism south of the border. However, we remained excited about our section. Then the announcer's voice sounded: "Coming up, after this short break, a look at racism in the North. There's a time bomb ticking in Toronto." We all looked at each other, stunned.

The commercials seemed to last forever, then finally we saw scenes from *Between Two Worlds*. Familiar footage, but in an unfamiliar order. All the balance and all the joy had been stripped from the show, leaving only the tough moments, ending with the Donald Hoppie interview. No context. No explanation.

I was devastated. I felt betrayed. My students' trust had been violated, their voices exploited. I wanted to sue. I wanted to cry. In the end, there was nothing to be done. NBC had received the correct permission to use the footage. (The copyright was owned by the Toronto Board of Education.) All the clearances were in place. There was no foul play. Just sensational editorial judgment.

Wow. I'd witnessed firsthand how context matters. I saw how the same footage, juxtaposed in a different way, could make an entirely different statement. In *Between Two Worlds*, we saw Donald as a charismatic teenager, laughing with his friends and playing in the snow. We also saw him as the vulnerable boy who had been cut by racist remarks. He came across as an engaging young man who had been deeply hurt by a spiteful comment. But in the NBC version, without context, Donald came across as a sorry victim. This difference would stay with me throughout my career. In *Degrassi*, I've constantly tried to keep our stories thought-provoking and authentic. Not sensational nor manipulative.

Despite my dismay at having my footage misused, the powers that be in the Toronto Board, and even in my own school, did not share my outrage. They continued to bask in the glow of a national U.S. broadcaster being interested in the material. My project had succeeded on many levels. As time went on, and the school year yielded to summer holidays, the sting of the NBC experience started to fade. I reflected on how lucky I'd been to work in a school where the principal and vice-principal were supportive of my ideas and projects. And how blessed I was to have such amazing students.

★

Years later, after I had left teaching, Barb revealed to me that it was a serendipitous day when I'd arrived as an occasional teacher at Earl Grey. The year before, she and Mack had been specifically dispatched to Earl Grey, as Barb put it, "to happy up the domain of an old-school martinet who had ruled Earl Grey with the four Rs of education — reading, 'riting, 'rithmetic, and RULES!" The neighbourhood had been changing: immigrant families, low-income housing projects, and group homes were moving in beside ambitious yuppies and proud gay couples. Earl Grey needed to be part of the change, and Barb and Mack were carefully staffing their faculty to meet these evolving times. One of their first hires, the year before me, was a young man with energy and fresh ideas, Bruce Mackey. Bruce, a born teacher with a cocky attitude and

Vice-principal Barb Mackay and her husband, Malcolm (Mac), play prospective home buyers in an episode of *The Kids of Degrassi Street*. The real estate agent is played by writer Yan Moore.

large personality, had rocked the rigid rule of his previous principal. But Bruce was exactly who Barb and Mack wanted on their team. It was no surprise that in a very short time, Bruce and I became friends.

I met Bruce at lunch in the staff room at Earl Grey. It was my first day as a full-time teacher, and I was still feeling disappointed that my job at TVOntario had not turned into a new career. I was also trying to come to terms with my new "separated status." Plus, I was tired — I had walked for over an hour and a half that morning. The transit workers were on strike and I'd had no other way to get to work. Feeling cranky, I distanced myself from the other teachers by burying my head in a novel. But Bruce Mackey would not let my book stop him from trying to strike up a conversation. When he found out that I had walked to work, he insisted that from that afternoon on, until the end of the strike (which would turn out to be a record twenty-three days), he would pick me up and drop me off daily. And he did. Every morning,

Bruce would pick me up at my modest beach house (waiting to be sold as part of my divorce settlement) in his 1970 red Mustang.

As the school librarian, Bruce embraced my *Between Two Worlds* project. He gave me tremendous support, both professionally and personally, and became my driver, cheerleader, and general assistant.

After the NBC airing of *Between Two Worlds*, Bruce and I enjoyed a beer on the patio of the Red Lion, a popular hangout of ours in a rambling old Victorian mansion just up the street from the Toronto Filmmakers Co-op. I shared with Bruce how so much of my life had changed in the previous two years, mostly for the good. But, regardless of the changes, I couldn't shake the fact that I was a failure. Bruce already knew about my first failed attempt at university, my aborted international travels and my ongoing divorce, but he had no idea how my parents had responded to the disintegration of my young marriage. I told him about the night I'd called them with the news that Brian and I were separating. They rushed to Toronto in record time, as if by getting there immediately they could change the outcome. After they hugged me and we shed a few tears, they told me that I had made a sacred vow before God, and divorce was a sin. Yikes. I'd known that my folks would be disappointed, but I wasn't ready to hear that God also saw me as a failure.

"So, you see," I said to Bruce, "it's pretty hard to come back from a sense of failure when you have let down your high school sweetheart, your parents, yourself, and . . . God."

Bruce looked at me as if to say, *You done now?* He took a swig of beer and started in.

"Shooler," as he affectionately called me, "you are so not a failure. First, I met your parents the night of the premiere of *Between Two Worlds*. They looked and sounded like very proud parents to me! And, secondly, I've been with you. I've watched you work. I see what you've done for your students. You've given them a platform to let their voices be heard. You've become their champion."

"Hmm, I have to admit, that does feel good." I nodded and started to smile.

Bruce laughed. "Damn right you should feel good!"

"I'm not a disappointment." I chuckled as I took a swig of beer.

"What did you say?" Bruce asked mockingly. "I didn't hear you."

"I'M NOT A DISAPPOINTMENT," I shouted back, turning heads from adjacent tables.

"Totally not a disappointment." Bruce stood up and spoke loudly to those around us. "This young lady just made a killer documentary and she's going to do more. Cheers," he said, as he raised his glass to slight applause and bemused smiles.

"And," Bruce laughed as he sat down, "tonight we're going to celebrate your current success. We're going dancing."

"But I'm enjoying being here at the pub," I protested.

"Nope, we're leaving," Bruce said. "You deserve some fun, and . . . you might even learn a little bit more about me!" He winked.

That night, at Chaps, while line dancing and laughing, I let the joy of my first film wash over me. Bruce encouraged me to keep dancing. He was happier than I'd ever seen him before.

My new bestie, Bruce, and me.

He brazenly sidled up to various folks, challenging them to dance faster and longer. It was almost as though he were in a trance.

At some point, well after midnight, I saw Bruce at the far end of the bar, intimately chatting with another man. I signalled that I was getting a cab. I thought he might disengage and offer to drive me, but no, he sent me an air kiss and waved me goodnight.

As I settled into bed for the night, my head spun. I knew that over the last few months I'd done some good work — not just for Earl Grey and my students, but for me as well. I felt as though I was finding my voice, and it wasn't about me. I realized that by listening and observing, I could give a voice to others. I wanted to do more.

As I drifted off to sleep, I thought about Bruce and the message he had sent me. In his unique way he had confirmed to me his unspoken sexuality. Through him, I was about to get a window into the tumultuous world of the 1970s and '80s gay scene in Toronto.

CHAPTER TWO

My Queer, Queer Education

B *ang-bang.* Someone was pounding on my front door. With one eye half open, I checked the clock: 3:14 a.m. Seriously? *Bang-bang-bang.*

With both eyes wide open, I grabbed my housecoat and cautiously approached the door of my one-bedroom apartment. I'd moved there a couple of years ago, after my ex-husband and I had sold our beach home as part of the divorce settlement. My apartment was on the ground floor of a detached house in the west end. The dwelling had been divided into three units. I knew both my fellow neighbours were home because I'd heard them each return at different times this Saturday night: the drug-addicted ophthalmologist shortly after midnight, and the shy, stooped-shouldered university student, just before 2 a.m. We had a code. If I hit the ceiling or floor with a broom in a particular manner, they would come. We were not close, but we looked out for each other.

Bang-bang-bang-bang.

I peered through the small window in the top of the old oak door and saw him. Actually, at first, I didn't really see *him* — I saw blood. Blood on the forehead. Blood over the left eye. Blood running down the cheek.

Then I saw more. Tears in both eyes. A mouth pinched in pain. And I knew who it was. I opened the door and all five-foot-seven of Bruce fell into my arms, sobbing. I hugged him. Somehow, we manoeuvred our way into the living room and turned on the lights. The sight was not pretty. "We're going to the ER," I said.

"No, we're *not*. You know I can't do that."

"I can't fix this."

"Yes, you will. You always do."

I was now in my third year of teaching at Earl Grey, and Bruce and I were close friends. I had become well aware of his various weekend trysts. We headed to the bathroom, pulled out the first-aid kit, and began the cleanup. I am not a nurse, but I did my best. Once I got most of the blood off, it didn't look so bad. Though there would be some swelling around the eye, the superficial cuts would heal soon. But Bruce's tears . . . I couldn't remove those. His tears were not about the pain from his bleeding head, they were about the pain of a double life. He told me he'd been beaten up. He and his one-night stand, both high on poppers, had had sex in his car. The scene had turned ugly, from sex to violence propelled by their mutual self-contempt.

The next Monday morning, I marched my homeroom class into the library for their scheduled session. The librarian, Mr. Mackey, was sporting a vibrant black eye. "Silly me," he laughingly shared with my class, "I had an argument with my kitchen door. The door won!" Bruce and I exchanged surreptitious looks that didn't go unnoticed by our students. For the next forty minutes, Bruce was the consummate librarian. He introduced my class to new authors. He read a passage from a YA book that had them mesmerized. He challenged them to pair their personalities with potential books. As the students roamed through the library, he watched carefully. He wanted each student to have a meaningful and positive experience. He was one fine teacher — captivating, endearing, and charming. The kids loved him and so did I. As my students left the library, heading back to our homeroom, they could not hold back from editorializing on their teachers. What they saw was two young,

Bruce channeling his inner educationalist while playing a teacher in *The Kids of Degrassi Street.*

fun, and single teachers who obviously shared a connection. They stroked their index fingers together indicating that they knew that "Mr. Mackey and Ms. Schuyler are in loooove!" Giggle, giggle!

★

Bruce had been brought up by hard-living, tax-paying, blue-collar workers in Toronto's east end. He was the middle of three brothers. As teenagers they would often be found together in front of the television set watching sports, swigging beer, and screaming obscenities at various officials. Upon leaving secondary school, both his brothers would pursue lives in the trades. Bruce was different. He went to university and got a degree in education. He spoke French fluently and playfully butchered many other languages. He was considered the "queer one" of the family. (Little did they know how queer this "queer one" really was.) Bruce was boisterous and fun, enjoyed his beer and sports, and always insisted everyone have a good time. He described himself to me as a "queer queer."

Bruce also had a closeted side. Although he admitted his sexuality to a few close friends, he was not out at work, nor to his family, and had no intention of ever coming out to either.

He couldn't — the times wouldn't allow it. When Bruce and I would part company on a Friday or Saturday night, I knew the night was not over for him. The weekend was short and he needed to pack in as much partying as he could. This would often mean a trip to one of the city's bathhouses for a quick hookup, or a stroll through High Park, cruising near the bushes.

Our birthdays being just six days apart, Bruce and I shared a zodiac sign. We would joke with each other that, as Aquarians, it was our job to change the world. We'd laugh, but both secretly hoped, in our own small ways, we could do just that. Bruce and I would sometimes combine our birthday celebrations, but on the evening of February 5, 1981, a Thursday, we decided to celebrate Bruce's birthday a day early. He had plans for the weekend that he didn't want to share. I got the sense that he might be seeing someone. I really don't remember much of that birthday celebration. More than likely, it included a few beers at the Red Lion.

But I remember the next day, vividly.

Having left teaching a couple of years earlier, I was at work in my home office. Bruce called me from the school phone, and in a hoarse whisper said, "Shooler? Have you seen the news? It's terrible. The police, they raided the baths. It's a travesty." Then he added in an even quieter voice, "I was supposed to meet someone there, tonight."

I rushed out to get a newspaper. And there, on the front page of the *Toronto Star*:

POLICE ARREST HUNDREDS IN STEAMBATHS

Metro policemen, many armed with crowbars and hammers, swooped down on four downtown Toronto steambaths last night and charged 253 men with being found-ins at bawdy houses.

The raids galvanized the gay community. The following night over three thousand protesters, gay and straight, gathered at the corner of Yonge and Wellesley Streets to march to Toronto Police

52 Division and eventually to Queen's Park. They chanted, "No more shit!" and "Fuck you, 52!"

Back in December 1967, a young, edgy justice minister (soon to become prime minister), Pierre Elliott Trudeau, had spoken his now famous words: "There is no place for the state in the bedrooms of the nation." He also went on to say, "What's done in private between two adults doesn't concern the Criminal Code." Toronto police thought differently. In June, two more bathhouse raids occurred, and twenty-one more men were charged.

Bruce no longer visited the baths. He did, however, continue his midnight cruises in High Park. Until that ended abruptly in 1985.

★

On the morning of Wednesday, June 26, Bruce arrived at my office early. It was the first day of his summer holidays. He held a folded *Globe and Mail* newspaper. His manner was agitated, and his face grave. "Read this," he said, as he angrily shoved the paper at me.

"'Theft Likely as Motive for Killing,'" I read.

"Go on," he insisted. "Who was it that was killed? Who? Read on and see who. *Read on.*"

> Kenneth Zeller, 40, was found slumped over in the front seat of his car at 12:25 a.m. on Sunday. An autopsy revealed that Mr. Zeller, a librarian at Williamson Road Public School, died of a fractured skull.

Okay, I still wasn't sure what to make of it other than Bruce must know this guy. "You're not getting it, Shooler," he said with mounting frustration. "He was gay-bashed. Had his skull kicked in because he's a faggot."

In the article, Staff Sergeant Ken Cenzura was quoted as saying, "We believe that a group of four or five white males are responsible." He urged witnesses to come forward. No mention of gay bashing. I questioned Bruce's allegation.

"Don't be so naïve," Bruce chastised.

I didn't think I was being naïve; I was just responding to the newspaper facts. I still had a lot to learn about the gay world and the media. But Bruce knew the truth. He knew from the growing chatter, fear, and anger mounting in the gay community at Church and Wellesley. He knew, because he lived in fear that that could have been him.

Months later, when the five teenage killers were each sentenced to nine years in prison, the press coverage would finally talk about a motive other than theft. *The Globe and Mail* reported, in part:

> The night of June 21, 1985: It is the last day of school and the longest day of the year. Eight friends from a Toronto neighbourhood, all under 18, decide to celebrate. They get some beer, borrow a truck and set off. People in a park overhear them planning a visit to High Park, to "beat up a fag" and "get money from a queer."

And, finally, it was there, in black and white.

By this time, I not only had left teaching, but had produced several episodes of *The Kids of Degrassi Street* and was now developing the proposal for what would become *Degrassi Junior High*. I wanted desperately to reflect some of Bruce's journey through dramatic storytelling. When *Degrassi Junior High* hit the air on CBC in the late 1980s, we were applauded for our frank and fearless storytelling: we tackled teen pregnancy, suicide, racism, and abortion. Many called us "gutsy" and "groundbreaking." I was proud of the response but knew we didn't do justice to gay and lesbian storytelling. Yes, we did a storyline with Snake's older brother coming out to his parents, and another where Caitlin questions her sexuality — both considered bold at the time for a teenage audience — but they didn't capture the anguish that I saw in Bruce. The times weren't ready. It wouldn't be till 2003 in *Degrassi: The Next Generation* that we really cracked our storytelling for the

LGBTQ+ community. It would take me partnering with a young and ambitious writer, Aaron Martin, to finally tell a story that would do justice to the horror of Kenneth Zeller's death, and the pain that was Bruce's.

Over time, the *Degrassi* writing team broke other critical LGBTQ+ storylines that would have done Bruce proud: stories exploring the sexuality of young people — some gay, some lesbian, some questioning, some bi, some gender fluid, and some trans. One of our boldest LGBTQ+ storylines, and one I wish I could have shared with Bruce, was that of Adam Torres (played by Jordan Todosey).

We first introduced Adam in season ten of *Degrassi: The Next Generation* as one of the guys. Audiences soon find out he is a trans male (a male who has been born with a biologically female body). This comes to light when his mother says to him, "Please be Gracie and wear a dress for your grandmother's visit."

A lot of research preceded the actual script. We consulted with various members of the LGBTQ+ community and in particular, Nick Adams from GLAAD. Nick, himself a trans male, headed up the Outreach and Education Department for GLAAD (then the Gay & Lesbian Alliance Against Defamation) based in L.A. He was very enthusiastic about our storyline. He had been advocating to see a trans story on television for years. It would be another couple of years before he would be consulted on Laverne Cox's character, Sophia Burset, in *Orange Is the New Black*.

Degrassi: TNG's "My Body Is a Cage" was written by Michael Grassi. Michael had joined the writing department only two years earlier as our story coordinator. In this junior position, he quickly took the opportunity, somewhat shyly, to pitch himself as a writer and secured himself two credits in his first year. By the time he approached us with the pitch for the trans male storyline, he had seven writing credits and his confidence was growing. His sensitive, warm, and respectful script for "My Body Is a Cage" went on to win a Peabody Award. When we received the award in New York, the citation from the judges read in part: ". . . this

Clare (Aislinn Paul, left) and Eli (Munro Chambers, right) play supportive friends to our trans male, character Adam (Jordan Todosey, centre).

episode neither sensationalizes nor trivializes the subject matter." I think that is my favourite citation ever. It embodies everything I want from my show regardless of the subject matter. That episode was also nominated for a Primetime Emmy in 2012. We didn't win that night but came away with an even better prize. At the opulent afterparty, "My Body Is a Cage" served as an introduction to Chaz Bono — not just an introduction but a commitment, facilitated by our publicist Iain Christiansen, to do a guest spot in an upcoming Adam storyline.

A few short months later, along with cast members and writers, we entertained Chaz in our lakeside garden. It was one of those magical beach evenings where we enjoyed a barbecue and shared stories. I was particularly fascinated with Chaz's tales about his mother, Cher. Their relationship had been through some rocky times during Chaz's journey, first as a lesbian (a "very bad lesbian," as Chaz readily points out), and later, when he identified as Chaz. At this point, Chaz said his mother went "ballistic" and they needed to take some time apart. Now, as he was planning his top and

Aislinn, Munro, and Jordan, friends in real life, pose on the red carpet for the 2011 Emmy Awards.

bottom surgery, he and Cher had found a good place. "Oh yeah," he laughed, "she still gets my pronouns mixed up, but I know she doesn't mean harm. The most annoying things now are the corny messages she sings on my answering machine!"

Bruce was a huge Cher fan. I thought about him that night and how much he would have liked to have been a guest at our barbecue. Apart from the sheer joy Bruce would have experienced from meeting Chaz, he would have been so proud of all my *Degrassi* LGBTQ+ storylines. Unfortunately, with the exception of the early episodes in *Degrassi Junior High* and *Degrassi High*, he didn't see any of them. He died in 1997 from pancreatic cancer, days after his fifty-ninth birthday.

★

I was shattered by Bruce's death. Not only did I mourn the loss of my best friend, I mourned what he had lost as well. After the death of his parents, whom he loved dearly, Bruce took an early retirement from teaching. After fifty-plus years of living a double life, of clandestine meetings at baths and parks, of self-contempt and shame . . . *Bruce was out.*

When I got married for the second time, in 1995, I asked Bruce to be my maid of honour. He thought it was a saucy ask and happily agreed. The wedding took place at home, on our lakeside lawn, the same location where we'd later hold Chaz's party. Bruce bought a special Armani jacket for the occasion. I don't think I had ever seen him look more handsome. He had a glow about him that radiated from deep within. He was finally at peace with himself and his sexuality.

Bruce's happiness was short-lived. A few months later, he got his cancer diagnosis. Just before Christmas of 1996, Bruce invited a dozen of his closest friends for dinner at his country home in

Brighton. This charming, historic town, built on the shores of Lake Ontario, is only a few short kilometres from where my husband and I now have our beloved farm. In fact, it was Bruce who introduced me to this picturesque part of Eastern Ontario. I would often accompany him on weekend visits to his parents, who lived in the house that Bruce would eventually inherit. On such visits, his mother would say, without fail, "Come on now, you two. When are you goin' to get hitched?" Bruce and I would share a sly smile.

My radiant maid of honour.

Christmas dinner was hard work for Bruce. He had shrunk in size and stature and had hollowed cheeks, the telltale sign of heavy doses of chemotherapy. When chemo hadn't worked, Bruce underwent a wicked multi-hour Whipple surgery to remove part of his pancreas. When that didn't work, he tried various holistic remedies. He was in his final days and knew it. When we left that night, during a gentle snowfall, Bruce gave a personalized gift to each of us. Mine was a ceramic spoon holder that his mother had made years earlier, and a cutting from his jade plant. Over the years, the spoon holder has disappeared but today, over twenty years later, I still have the jade plant. I've shared many jade clippings with friends, and most recently I gave one to my stepson Max when he moved into a new apartment.

After Christmas, Bruce was moved to palliative care in Belleville, the closest facility to Brighton. Bruce assigned powers of attorney to me and our friend Nancy Sinclair, and we were on call 24/7. We made frequent urgent drives from Toronto to Belleville. We were his queer, queer family, as his immediate family had yet to accept his sexuality. On our last visit, Nancy and I stopped before entering the hospital room and watched from the window. There, on either side of Bruce, were both of his baseball hat–wearing "bohunk" brothers, as Bruce liked to call them. They awkwardly each held one of Bruce's hands. Nancy and I observed the family and backed away quietly. That was the last time we would see our friend Bruce.

My last Christmas with Bruce. I cry every time I look at this picture.

★

I miss my Bruce deeply. I miss looking in the mirror with him and stretching our cheeks, wondering what we would look like with a facelift. I miss sharing recipes, gossip, and gardening tips. I miss our trips to auction sales and antique dealers. I miss his bluster and butchered attempts at foreign languages. I miss his smile and his Aquarian passion. I even miss his judginess — and Bruce could be very judgmental.

In the late 1970s, when I had a new man in my life, Bruce certainly let me know that he did not approve. From the moment he first met Kit Hood, Bruce said, "Be careful, Shooler."

You cheeky bitch, I thought, *you're jealous!*

CHAPTER THREE

WHY PLAYING WITH TIME

In the summer of 1975, it was hot. It was humid. The city had declared a heat alert, and I was desperately trying to stop my bare leg from touching the stranger beside me in the crowded Queen streetcar, one of those early models before they installed air conditioning. In my cut-off jeans and crumpled army shirt, I was sweating, and of course, it was the first day of my period. I'd spent most of the day curled up in bed with cramps. So annoying. So inconvenient. I nervously counted the stops to make sure I wouldn't miss mine. I reminded myself, *Get off at the Sherbourne Street stop. Walk south to Britain Street.*

There, waiting at the corner, was my good friend Wendy Watson. I took one look at Wendy and thought, *How does she do this?* She was wearing a bright yellow linen-cotton-blend pantsuit, immaculately pressed, no creases. Not a single strand of her shoulder-length curly hair was out of place, and of course, as always, she was early. She stood in stark contrast to our surroundings. On one corner was the Armory, a greasy spoon on another, and a number of pawnshops with security bars on the windows dotted either side of the street. Water spat from an air conditioner over the door of a convenience store where a ceramic bust of Elvis, covered with dead flies, sat in its crowded window. "Okay," I said. "Let's go find this fancy film guy."

Wendy's and my journey to Britain Street had begun a number of months earlier. She and I were both teaching for the Toronto Board of Education and juggling our interests in film and music during our summer months. Wendy, who had helped with *Between Two Worlds* by providing narration and moral support, called me one day to say, "I just heard on the radio, Paul Hoffert and his band, Lighthouse, are running a music camp this summer for young students. We should film it." Lighthouse, a popular Canadian band with a big sound — including a rock rhythm section, a jazz horn section, and a classical string section — had been formed in 1968 by vocalist/drummer Skip Prokop and keyboardist Paul Hoffert. They'd topped the charts with a number of hits, including "One Fine Morning" and "Sunny Days." I loved their sound and was intrigued by their interest in running an educational camp for young aspiring musicians.

Wendy and I had met years earlier when we both taught in London, Ontario, and lived in the same apartment building. She was married to a young medical student at the time. I'll never forget the day she asked if I could come up to her apartment. There, with tears flowing down her cheeks, she said simply, "Dave's having an affair." I'd never heard these words before in real life. They sounded like something from a soap opera. But this wasn't scripted, this was real, and Wendy was devastated. At this point in my life, I was still stoically trying to make my own marriage work and had little in the way of comfort to offer Wendy. I did, though, become a sounding board for her as she and Dave began the messy process that would eventually lead to divorce. When Brian (my then-husband) and I moved to Toronto, Wendy and I lost touch. It was a random day in 1974 when I was walking home from Innis College and ran into her on the street. After her divorce, she had returned to her music studies at the Royal Conservatory in Toronto and to teaching. She and I started having regular coffee sessions. It was then her turn to listen to me as I navigated the disintegration of my own young marriage.

Wendy and I have shared many laughs and tears over the years.

Wendy's Lighthouse venture appealed to me for more than just their great music and the innovative camp. I was fresh off the success of *Between Two Worlds* and anxious to make a second documentary. While Wendy gathered more information on Lighthouse's summer plans, I explored the possibility of the Toronto Board of Education financing my second film. I found it surprisingly easy to raise a modest budget and got permission to use Lou Wise's 16mm equipment package. We finalized all the necessary clearances from Lighthouse, and we were ready to load up my car and rock 'n' roll.

A few months earlier, for $400, I had bought a ten-year-old Acadian that I'd affectionately named Rust Bucket 2 (RB-2) in honour of the original rust bucket Acadian that my mum and I had shared when I was a teenager. My first road trip with RB-2 was when I visited my parents for Canada Day. Dad was the popular mayor of Paris, Ontario, a position he would hold for almost twenty years. He and Mum would be appearing in the local Canada Day parade, riding in a vintage convertible. As "The Mayor" was needed for official duties earlier, I offered to drive Mum to the parade.

RB-2's engine was relatively reliable (it had only been driven by one elderly woman), but the body work was challenging. There were times when the rust buildup made it impossible for me to open the driver's door. I'd solve this by scooching across the bench seat and exiting via the passenger door. As I pulled up near the start of the parade to let Mum off, her passenger door wouldn't open. She pushed. And pushed again. Still nothing. I tried my door. Nope, wouldn't open.

This was awkward.

"Wait a minute," I optimistically said. "I'll just drive to a side street." There, a block and a half from the start of the parade, I rolled down the window on my driver's side, manoeuvred one leg out the window, and unceremoniously climbed out of the car. Glancing about, I casually walked to my mother's side, put my foot against the back panel, and pulled — hard — on the passenger door. After a few attempts, I liberated the First Lady of Paris. With her eye on the clock, she adjusted her hat, pulled on her white gloves, gave me an amused smile, and headed off to join Dad in the Cadillac. *She's a trouper*, I thought as I watched Mum walk away. I then turned my attention back to RB-2. *Please get Wendy and me safely to Collingwood*, I pleaded silently.

The day of our departure, I pulled RB-2 into the loading dock at the Toronto Board of Education, and we filled her with the familiar lights, tripod, Nagra, and Bolex from Lou's office. This time, I added the Arriflex to our equipment package. I didn't know how to shoot sync sound (sound and pictures married together) but had hired a cameraman for the weekend who would film the interviews. We headed north to Collingwood, where the Lighthouse camp would take place in the ski chalets of Blue Mountain Resort. The drive should have taken only a couple of hours, but I periodically needed to pull over to stop RB-2 from overheating.

It was early evening when we approached Blue Mountain. There, about a kilometre out, RB-2 died and refused to restart. Knowing we were close, Wendy and I locked the car and started the walk to the main office, situated in an old farmhouse. As we marched up the long drive, we could hear noodling on guitars and the soft sound of singing and laughter. The young men on the porch caught sight of us, put down their instruments, and came to ask if they could help. We explained about our car difficulties. "No problem," they replied cheerfully. "We can help. We're just killing time waiting for the film crew."

"Oh, of course. Hmm . . ." Wendy and I looked at each other wondering how to say it. "Well, you see, we *are* the film crew."

A subdued silence followed, along with some raised eyebrows. To their credit, once over their suprise, the guys were most helpful. RB-2 was pushed to the chalet that we had been assigned for the week. We unloaded the gear and settled in to prepare for our shoot.

The next morning, I was excited to meet Phil Earnshaw. Phil, a recent graduate from York University's film program, had landed himself a job as a cameraman for Global News. Phil and I, through the facilitation of a mutual friend, had negotiated a deal over the phone for him to come to Blue Mountain for the weekend to shoot my sync sound material. Phil had a friend drive him to Collingwood. As I greeted him at the car, Phil asked if I could give his friend gas money.

More money? I thought. *The nerve of this guy. I've already agreed to pay him fifty bucks to work the weekend.* I held my tongue and reluctantly handed over some cash, wondering how I was going to pay for repairs on my own car. I showed Phil to his room in our chalet, not sure if I was going to like him or not.

Over the course of the next couple of days we had a blast. The band was so much fun and Paul Hoffert was a real gentleman. There was a loose and lovely feel to the camp that Phil on Arri, Wendy on Nagra, and I on Bolex worked tirelessly to capture. When Sunday evening came around and Phil was getting ready to return to the city for his real job, I realized that we still had at least one more sync interview to film. "No problem," Phil said. "You can do it!" With that, Phil settled in to give me a lesson on the Arriflex. It was a much larger and heavier camera than the Bolex and used 400-foot loads rather than the 100-foot ones I'd been used to. Patiently, Phil opened the Arri and showed me how the inner mechanisms operated. "Great. Now keep all that in your head while your hands do the work in the dark," he coached.

Phil brought out the black bag, had me put my hands in either side, and feel my way to open the film canister, load it in the magazine, unload it, and return it to the empty cannister. Then next morning, Phil was gone, but certainly not gone for good. Despite our rocky introduction, Phil and I have worked together for over forty years. He has an easy professionalism about him that belies his passion. Among other collaborations, he became the DOP (director of photography) for all *The Kids of Degrassi Street* episodes, and director for many *Degrassi Junior High*, *Degrassi High*, and *Degrassi: The Next Generation* episodes, winning multiple awards for his work. I now think of Phil fondly as a brother.

The next few days at Blue Mountain were . . . challenging. Wendy and I were a crew of two. She continued collecting the sound while I operated the Arriflex. I'd cue her to roll sound, then I'd start the camera rolling. I'd dash in front of the camera with the clapper board to slate the scene, then back behind the camera to get focus. Once settled, I'd try to remember all my questions for the interview. A bit crazy, but, by the end of the week, we felt good. Our subjects, Lighthouse, had been great hosts, good sports, and just genuinely a lot of goofy fun.

Director Phil Earnshaw and me on the set of *Degrassi Junior High*.

It was now time to return to Toronto.

After a few days of rest and some tinkering under the hood, I was able to get RB-2 running again. Wendy and I and Lou's equipment spluttered our way back to Toronto. The car finally died, for good, outside my apartment. And that was why I was taking public transportation the day I met Kit Hood.

★

It was only a short walk south from the streetcar stop to Britain Street. It turned out that "street" was a bit of a misnomer — it was really more of an alley. We consulted the paper once again. Yup.

"Number 43 Britain Street. Go to the basement. Room 6." Down the creaky stairs we encountered the receptionist, barely visible behind piles of papers, sound boxes, film cans, and delivery slips. We asked for Kit Hood. "Well, I don't work for him, but you can find him down that hall," she gestured.

Along a windowless corridor we passed closed doors with various sounds emanating from within. I'd heard so much about the brilliant Kit Hood, I couldn't believe I was going to meet him. We located Room 6 and knocked.

"Come in," said a warm voice with a distinct British accent. We found award-winning director and editor Kit Hood, leaning back, with his hands behind his head and his feet resting casually on his rented Steenbeck (a flatbed editing machine). He wore denim overalls with a beige turtleneck sweater (yes, even in the heat), and sported a well-trimmed beard and large, metal-rimmed glasses.

"Pardon me." Kit gave us an impish grin, as he quickly removed his feet and offered us a seat. Wendy and I looked at each other and shared an unspoken thought: *He's cute!* But seriously, we needed to get down to business. We were here to interview him for our new project.

Kit had begun his film career in his native England, editing for Walt Disney Productions. Kit recognized he had little room for advancement at Disney and, with his young family, had immigrated to Canada. Upon arrival in Canada in 1968, Kit found work in various commercial houses. He gained a stellar reputation as quick, witty, and creative and garnered the awards to support this. But Kit wanted to do more than polish sixty-second commercial spots to sell products. He wanted to tell stories about the human condition. A year before we met, Kit had left the lucrative world of ad agencies and had holed himself up as an independent filmmaker and editor, operating from the small space he rented from the production company, Hobel-Leiterman.

Phil Hobel and Doug Leiterman were movers and shakers in the world of Canadian television. From their modest offices, they produced the documentary series *The Fabulous Sixties* followed by *Here Come the Seventies*. These shows, produced on minimal budgets, were magnets for young filmmakers wanting to get a foot in the door. Before this, Doug had made his mark at CBC, where he and Patrick Watson produced the edgy and controversial newsmagazine *This Hour Has Seven Days*. I was sixteen when this show came on air. Sundays, after supper, I would go to our local church for a young people's gathering. After that, many would go out for coffee and cherry Cokes. Not me. I raced home to watch Patrick Watson and Laurier LaPierre recount the news of the week with droll wit and raised eyebrows, while Dinah Christie commented satirically through song. I loved this show. And now I was in the offices of one of the creators!

This building not only housed the office of Doug Leiterman, but also was the administrative base for Beryl Fox, his wife. Beryl was an influential filmmaker, having made a name for herself with the groundbreaking *The Mills of the Gods: Viet Nam*, shot entirely on location in Vietnam while war raged. She went on to produce feature films, most notably 1981's *Surfacing*.

Also housed in the same building at 43 Britain Street was the young equipment rental company, PS Production Services, owned by Doug Dales. Doug was a techie who loved amassing equipment. Over the years, he would build this business from its modest beginnings to offices throughout Canada and the world. Doug was always there for the independent filmmakers. As my business grew, he repeatedly gave me good deals to keep my productions afloat. Elsewhere in the eclectic Britain Street building, I would later discover, was The Mixing House. This sound facility, owned and operated by George Novotny, would provide the sound services for multiple episodes of *Degrassi*. But on that stifling day in August, when Wendy and I walked into 43 Britain Street for the first time, we had no idea about the rich and vibrant community we were about to join.

★

After Wendy and I shared our Lighthouse adventures with Kit, he told us he was interested in being our editor and would get back to us with a quote. And he did. Wow, if I thought Phil Earnshaw had been audacious asking for more than $50, Kit's request left me speechless.

Wendy and I met for crepes the next morning to recover from the sticker shock. I had done some checking the night before and found that Kit's quote was, in fact, very modest by current industry standards. We knew we needed someone good to help us through the footage; we had miles of it, and no real plan. We also acknowledged his great reputation . . . and let's not forget that he wasn't hard on the eyes.

Eventually, I agreed to Kit's price. I knew that my modest Toronto Board of Education budget wouldn't cover it all, but I could cover the rest myself. From my previous experience with *Between Two Worlds*, I knew the importance of the editing room and a good editor.

By the time Kit had a rough picture edit in place, it was late September and I had returned to teaching. I'd head to the editing room after school and we'd spend hours together wrestling with the footage. This was taking longer than either of us expected, and one day Kit's contract was up. Embarrassed, I had to explain that I couldn't afford to pay him for any more of his time. Kit looked at me with his impish smile: "You've got me hooked, Linda. Let's do what it takes to get it done. You can pay me the remainder when you make a sale." *Wow, what a gentleman,* I thought. This was an extraordinary gesture, and one that made me realize that we had each other's trust.

Kit and I persevered to give the film shape. We mixed the show, conformed the negative, and pulled prints. We had a small premiere at the Toronto Board of Education office. People were polite. I made a modest sale to TVOntario. But there would be no national distribution as there had been for *Between Two Worlds*. I had to admit, *Blue Mountain Crude* was okay at best. I was disappointed for myself, but more disappointed for Paul and Lighthouse, who had so graciously accepted us into their lives.

By this time, Kit and I were missing our daily sessions in the editing room and looked for excuses to continue meeting. When we did get together for drinks, we'd talk endlessly about the films we would like to make. Kit revealed how great he'd felt making his first documentary, *The Wayward Cell*, a moving story of a woman fighting breast cancer. I shared with him my success with *Between Two Worlds*. We talked about how gratifying it was to see a film you've made appear on television and have an impact on people's lives. We joked, "We could change the world together!" Within six months of our first meeting, despite Bruce's warnings, Kit and I moved in together. We had great plans to become full-time filmmakers, but, for immediate financial reasons, I continued to teach and Kit remained a freelance editor. We found a loft-style apartment above a greasy spoon at the corner of Queen and Carlaw in Toronto's east end, only minutes away from my school. We converted one of the bedrooms into an editing suite. Kit had amassed assorted trim bins, a couple of splicers, and an old Moviola (an upright editing machine), that he'd bought from one of his previous employers. "I bloody broke my wrist on this thing," Kit told me.

I looked at the machine. "It really doesn't look that dangerous," I offered up.

"Oh, it wasn't the Moviola's fault. It was mine. I was so pissed off with my ad agency, I hit the machine — hard." He gave me a wry smile.

"Whoa!" I laughed. "Remind me to never piss you off!"

"I can't imagine that ever happening," smiled Kit as he gave me a gentle kiss on the forehead.

★

As Kit's freelance career grew, he confided that the Moviola was a bit of a hindrance. Owning a Steenbeck, a flatbed like he had rented for *Blue Mountain Crude*, would make him much more competitive. We researched our options and figured we needed about $8,000 to get a new one from Germany. As luck would have it, we had just received approval for an $8,500 grant from the Ontario Arts Council for a children's film we proposed to make. As we wouldn't be ready to shoot the film for another year or more, it seemed logical to use these dollars to buy a Steenbeck — then with the money Kit made from editing, we should be square well before production. This was my first experience with managing cash flow. It wouldn't be my last.

We took the calculated risk and ordered the machine. But there was a hitch: to bring the Steenbeck tax-free from Germany, we needed a manufacturer's licence. The thing about a manufacturer's licence was that you had to have manufactured something to be eligible. Kit and I had both made our own films, but the copyright on these was retained by others. We weren't sure how to proceed — until we devised a game plan. We would screen Kit's documentary *The Wayward Cell*. The head credits clearly stated that this was a film by Kit Hood and credited him as producer, director, and editor. It wasn't until the very end that the copyright notice appeared in the name of Hobel-Leiterman. H-L had financed the film to include in one of their television series. We would find a credible way to stop the film just before the end.

We booked a meeting with the government inspector, as late in the afternoon as possible, knowing they didn't work after 5 p.m. We explained that I was a schoolteacher and the earliest I could be home was four o'clock. This would give us enough time to engage in some small talk, go over our paperwork, and start the film running by 4:30 p.m. — running time was thirty minutes.

The appointed day came and started according to plan. Just as the film was at about the twenty-seven-minute mark, almost to the credit roll, I excused myself from the editing room. All of a sudden, the power went out. I re-entered the room, wearing an apron, and offered many apologies. "I thought I'd get an early start on supper," I said, playing dumb. "I fear the electric frying pan must have blown a fuse. Give me a sec, and I can get it fixed." The bureaucrat looked at his watch: 5:05 p.m. "No, I really should get going," he said. "I've seen most of the film and congratulations,

Kit and me at work on our new Steenbeck.

it's very good. We are fine from our end. You should get your licence within thirty days."

And with that, he left. Kit and I roared with laughter. Our plan had worked.

★

We juggled so many projects in those early days. We won a contract to shoot a short documentary for the Ontario Women's Federation and another with the Canadian Council of Christians and Jews on multiculturalism. From his time in advertising, Kit landed us a modest account to adapt toy commercials originally produced in the States for Canadian broadcast. In order to make them comply with Canadian regulations they needed extra disclaimers at the end — "Batteries not included," "Each sold separately" — superimposed on a beauty shot of the toy. The problem was, where to shoot the beauty shots?

"It's simple," said Kit. "Let's use your classroom. It's stocked with all sorts of film equipment, including the Bolex." (Yes, the Bolex was now stored permanently in my cupboards.)

"Might be pushing it," I cautiously said. Then Kit smiled and winked, and it was all over.

As my students would leave at the lunch bell, Kit waited patiently at the door carrying a cardboard box of toys. We'd pull the blackout drapes, set up our little homemade green screen, put up lights, and fire up the Bolex. By the time the lunch period was over, Kit had his box repacked and the film safely in its cannister. The blackout drapes were reopened, and I was ready for my next class.

★

One night at home, I was marking papers when Kit came into the room excitedly. "Guess what, there's a seventy-two-year-old guy playing piano at the Roxy, trying to break a marathon record for the *Guinness Book of World Records*. We should check it out." I wasn't so sure. I had academic deadlines. Kit said he'd go and do a recce. Later that night, he came home — pumped.

"It's extraordinary. The guy is old. He keeps playing and playing. When he needs a washroom break, he hops onto a miniature toy piano and continues playing. And the best part? . . . He just failed!" I looked questioningly at Kit, not sure why this was a good thing.

"You're not following," Kit spat out. "He wants to make another attempt later this summer. This is a friggin' unique opportunity! We can film it."

Part of the fun of living with Kit was how intense and excited he could get about things — it was contagious. I became truly convinced that the most exhilarating documentary we could make would be about a seventy-two-year-old pianist visiting from New Zealand. Before I knew it, I was in deep.

As school wound down for the summer, my relationship with aging pianist Jimmy Montecino heated up. Somehow, I had become his manager and had negotiated a gig for him at the 1976 Canadian National Exhibition (CNE) in late August. Kit had arranged to have a mobile float built that would travel to various locations around the CNE, as Jimmy played continuously for his official marathon attempt. We applied for, and received, a $7,000 Canada Council grant. At least a government agency thought this might be a film.

We hired the brilliant Mark Irwin as our cinematographer. I would do B-roll on the Bolex. And the loyal, ever-game Wendy was up for gathering the sound, even though two days earlier she had broken her foot and was limping in a cast.

On the first day, the weather was beautiful, and spirits were high. Kit and Mark were thrilled with the images we were getting. As evening fell, the lights on the midway came up. A full August moon began to rise and a gentle breeze blew in off the lake as Jimmy kept playing. There was a sense that we were all onto something special.

Day two started off well, but, as night came, the temperature dropped drastically. I went into management mode. "Jimmy can't stay out all night in these temperatures," I said to the CNE executives. "We need an indoor overnight location."

Running back and forth between the administration offices and our float, through the midway, clowns, and weight guessers, I finally got administration to concede that the whole float could be moved into the Better Living Centre once the CNE was closed for the night. The float had to be removed before opening time in the morning. It was very surreal to see a senior citizen playing piano, nonstop, on a float against the backdrop of ladies' leather purses, La-Z-Boy chairs, and the latest samples of linoleum floors. The following night the float was moved to the Agricultural Hall, where Jimmy played all night for the disinterested cows and bulls.

By about the one hundred–hour mark, things started to deteriorate, badly. Mark was done his contract, so any further shooting was up to me. Jimmy's playing had been reduced to hands randomly slapping the keyboard. Kit's usually precise direction had become rambling and incoherent. Then Jimmy collapsed. Paramedics arrived and Jimmy was whisked off in an ambulance. I crumpled to the sidewalk, exhausted. Kit did the same.

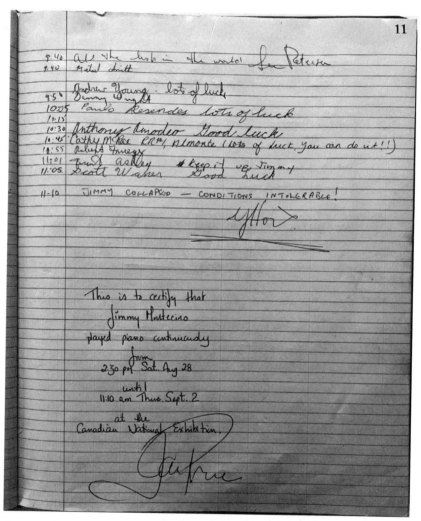

An excerpt from the official log book that documented Jimmy's playing. I made the first entry at 2:30 p.m., August 28, 1976. Kit made this last entry when Jimmy collapsed after 116 hours and forty minutes of continuous playing.

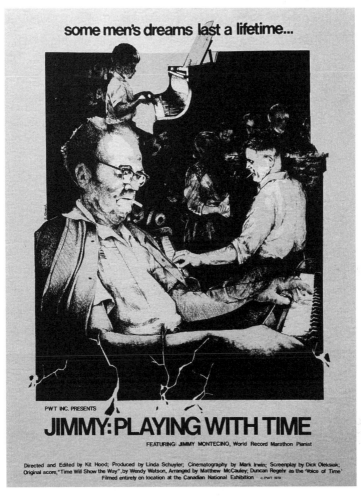

some men's dreams last a lifetime...

PWT INC. PRESENTS

JIMMY: PLAYING WITH TIME

FEATURING: JIMMY MONTECINO, World Record Marathon Pianist

Directed and Edited by Kit Hood; Produced by Linda Schuyler; Cinematography by Mark Irwin; Screenplay by Dick Oleksiak; Original score, "Time Will Show the Way", by Wendy Watson, Arranged by Matthew McCauley; Duncan Regehr as the 'Voice of Time' Filmed entirely on location at the Canadian National Exhibition © PWT 1979

Our poster to accompany the film *Jimmy: Playing With Time* at the Directors'
Fortnight in Cannes.

What had we just done?!

The good news? The ever-resilient Jimmy survived with surprisingly no aftereffects. In fact, even though he hadn't broken the record, he was back at the CNE two days later to receive his $5,000 appearance fee that we had negotiated up front. In other news, Kit became obsessed. For months, he was fixated on the footage. To his credit, during the day, he kept his regular clients serviced thanks to our new Steenbeck. But, at night, he could not let the footage go. He played it forwards and backwards — over and over. He smoked some dope. He experimented with structure. Smoked more dope. Wendy had written a beautiful song for the show, "Time Will Show the Way." I would drift off to sleep with the smell of dope in the air and with Wendy's haunting melody repeatedly playing through the flimsy bedroom wall.

In the end, what started as a novelty piece became a surreal feature-length movie called *Jimmy: Playing With Time*. We submitted it to Telefilm Canada. They liked it and put it forward for Directors' Fortnight in Cannes. We made a sale to CBC. Kit and I now had our first film credit for which we owned our own copyright. We smiled and hugged and said to each other, "This is just the beginning!"

And then Kit and I formally registered our new company as Playing With Time Inc. (PWT).

*

While Kit and I were balancing several film projects at once, I continued teaching at Earl Grey. I had developed and written a media studies course for the Grade 8 level, which had been approved as a pilot program. My students were eager participants in my new curriculum. We watched early Norman McLaren works and made our own experimental films by scratching on old 16mm prints. We played with stop-frame animation, wrote scripts, and eventually divided into groups to make Super 8 documentaries on various local neighbourhood attractions. Periodically, I would show a film to them that could lead to discussions both about the subject matter and the craft.

One Friday afternoon, I screened a relatively new National Film Board film, *The Summer We Moved to Elm Street*. It was one of the few scripted dramas available at the time from the point of view of a young protagonist. I was a bit nervous to screen it, as the protagonist, Doreen, was nine years old, a few years younger than my students. However, the subject matter was mature, dealing with parental alcoholism, so I thought it was worth a try. I wasn't prepared for how strongly my students would react to this material. Despite the age difference between them and young Doreen, they were moved by how an alcoholic parent could affect all family members. We had a great discussion about family values, about responsibilities, about when to speak up and who to tell. Towards the end of the class, I noticed that Angie, a shy girl at the back who rarely volunteered a comment, had her hand up. She started talking about Doreen and how bad it was for her dad to leave her in a car while he got drunk with his friends, but before she had finished talking, I noticed that she had moved from the third-person narrative to the first. She was saying, "I feel really bad when my dad wants to be with his drinking friends and forgets about me waiting outside."

I thanked her for her comments without acknowledging the change in grammar. As the class broke up for the afternoon, I asked her if she would stay behind. It didn't take more than a couple of minutes for her to break down in tears and tell me how hard it was at home with her dad drinking all the time. I promised, if she agreed, I would make her an appointment with the guidance counsellor.

When I first began teaching I started a practice that I used throughout my teaching career, and later as an entrepreneur. I would take a look at my students (or my employees), and envision them wearing invisible backpacks. In each pack would be their own personal and unique stories, and I needed to respect those. Sometimes my students would open their packs up a little and give me a glimpse of what was inside, as Angie did that day after viewing *The Summer We Moved to Elm Street*.

A few weeks later, Angie appeared at my desk before classes started and offered me some rather gooey Rice Krispie squares. "I made these myself," she said quietly. "Thank you for getting me to see the guidance counsellor. Mr. Parkins is helping me, and he got someone to talk to my mom as well."

I was very moved to witness how the story of fictional Doreen had such a positive effect on Angie's life. I knew, of course, that we didn't fix her dad's alcoholism, but Angie now had someone to talk to about it and knew she was not alone. I had no way to know it at the time, but reassuring young people that they are not alone would become a fundamental building block for *Degrassi* storytelling. I wanted more shows like *The Summer We Moved to Elm Street* to engage my students. Search as I would, there was precious little available at the school board at that time.

Over this same period, I was also enjoying my work with the Association for Media Literacy (AML), an organization I was helping to establish for teachers who wanted to include media studies in the general curriculum. However, the excitement of teaching a new course and starting a new association paled in comparison to the fly-by-the-seat-of-your-pants world that Kit and I were creating together. It was clear that with Kit's unstoppable energy and my determined and logical mind, we could make the impossible possible.

I conducted an internal review. I had growing confidence in myself as a filmmaker and as a potential businessperson. I knew from my students that there were unlimited stories to be told for and about young people, and that very little existed on television for them. I knew from firsthand experience that young audiences could connect positively when they saw themselves authentically depicted in a story. I also had a giddy, school-girl sense of excitement about my growing relationship with the erratic, enigmatic, and charming Kit Hood. Yes, I believed the time had come to leave formal teaching.

Bruce, Barb, and Mack, reluctant to see me leave Earl Grey, reassured me that I didn't have to quit, that I could take a leave of absence for a year to "see how it goes." I couldn't do that. I was filled with a sense of anticipation, a wild and reckless need to throw caution to the wind.

Effective December 31, 1977, I resigned from the Toronto Board of Education.

I was twenty-nine and ready for my next adventure.

CHAPTER FOUR

THE EARLY KIDS

"No more chicken shit." That was Bruce on the answering machine. He was letting Kit and me know that he'd finally got the nerve to buy his first house, number 98 De Grassi Street. We bought a bottle of Baby Duck sparkling wine, and Bruce came over to celebrate his new purchase. Fellow producers, Deepak Sahasrabudhe and his wife Sue Miller, dropped by. They too were thinking about buying their first home. The night was festive. When the evening wound down and we walked towards the kitchen, we realized something was amiss. Sue's and my purses were upside down and the contents spilled on the floor. Both of our wallets were missing. While celebrating, we had been robbed.

As the police officer methodically wrote down the details of our robbery on his clipboard, I stifled a yawn. Then, to my horror, I watched as a cockroach crawled lazily across his police report. I knew then what I'd been thinking for a while — we couldn't live above a restaurant any longer. If Bruce could buy a house, we could too.

The next day, Kit and I walked across the street to the local real estate office at 935 Queen Street East. It was an eccentric old Victorian building — part house, part office. Two giant ferns sat in the large office window. Beyond the ferns, hunched over an oversized roll-top desk, we met the diminutive, grey-haired Glen Ferron, in wool pants and a Perry Como sweater. We explained to him that we were looking for a building similar to his, one that we could use both as our home and as an office to accommodate our growing business. Could he find something for us?

Glen looked at us, sizing us up. "Well," he said, "I'm eighty-four years old. Don't do much in the way of new properties. I mostly look after my mortgages, but I was thinking I might just retire. Maybe I should . . . would you like to buy this?"

935 Queen Street East, Toronto.

Kit and I quietly shared a look. We had admired this building ever since we moved into the neighbourhood over a year ago. We asked if we might have a tour.

In the house section, it was clear that someone had once lived here for a long time. All the furniture — blue-velvet overstuffed horsehair sofa and chairs; wooden floor lamps with fringe on the shades; heavy, dark wood end tables — was covered in thick layers of dust. Somewhat embarrassed, Glenn explained his business was once a family affair and his mother had lived in the back portion, while he ran the real estate and mortgage business from the front office. His mother had died in the house a few years back, and, since he now lived in Scarborough, he used only the front office during the week. He apologized that the family had yet to clean up the living area.

While teaching, I'd been very strict with myself regarding money. Each month, I stashed away about $500. It added up over time. With that, plus the cash settlement from my teacher's retirement plan, I had more than enough for a good down payment. We could make this work. Despite his laid-back manner, Glen Ferron was surprisingly quick when it came to negotiating a deal. In the end, we were all happy. He accepted a discount if we accepted the property "as is." He would hold the mortgage. And with that — no more chicken shit for Kit and Linda!

Our mega garage sale. The week before, I used white liquid shoe polish to write (backwards) the announcement of the sale in our front window.

Cleanup was massive. Not only was the house overrun with ancient, oversized furniture, but Glen's mother's clothing was still in the closets. Dresses, size 22, and shoes, size 9, were stuffed on racks, in shelves, and in drawers, along with shawls, stockings, and hefty granny-style undergarments. We held a giant garage sale. Wendy and her new boyfriend, the jovial and big-hearted Lewis Manne, came by to help. As our property was on the Queen streetcar line, word quickly spread along Queen Street to Kensington Market in the west end. Italian and Portuguese women flocked to pick through the racks of amply-sized housedresses. Young couples, gay and straight, came from across the city for bargains on our vintage furniture, and local curiosity seekers found copious oddities to enjoy. The sale was a huge success. At the end of the day, everything was cleared out. We had a new home and a new office.

On the business front, Kit and I were hustling. We picked up more documentary contracts from the Canadian Council of Christians and Jews, TVO, and the Association for Bright Children. But we were both anxious to produce our own films.

★

When I was teaching, Bruce, as the school librarian, had his own budget and the freedom to order all sorts of books. Knowing my fascination with the media, Bruce ordered anything with the word *film, movie,* or *media* in the title. One day, he walked into my class and said, "Guess we'll put this on the library babysitting shelf." He was holding an illustrated book called *Ida Makes a Movie,* meant for much younger children. It featured a large furry cat as a single mom with a feisty young kitten daughter who wanted to make a movie. "Hold on a sec," I said to Bruce. "I might like this story." And I did.

It wasn't the cats that intrigued me, but the story of a young girl who wanted to make a movie and persevered despite interference from her brother and her next-door neighbour. Ida had a story she wanted to tell and was determined to make it happen. I thought

The officers of Playing With Time Inc.: the president (me), secretary (Kit), and chair of the board (Spencer the cat).

this could make a cute short children's film but didn't know the legalities to obtain the rights. Through our friends, Deepak and Sue, I'd heard about a young entertainment lawyer, Stephen Stohn, who had recently been called to the bar. I booked a meeting at Miller and Charlton with Mr. J. Stephen Stohn, Barrister. Mr. Stohn's office was small, and his desk was covered with a mad array of legal documents and books. He looked up from my copy of *Ida Makes a Movie* and handed it back to me. His soft grey eyes met my intense stare. "You don't need me," he asserted.

"Er, okay. Thank you, I guess?"

"You can do this on your own. I can suggest a purchase price and give you a boiler plate pro forma. You can negotiate your own deal. It will be cheaper than hiring me."

"And what do I owe you for this advice?" I cautiously asked.

"Nothing." He playfully smiled. "But I hope you'll remember me!"

Following Stephen Stohn's advice, I took a trip to New York in my summer holidays to negotiate the book rights. I flew in and out on the same day to meet the charming Kay Chorao at the Four Seasons Hotel. Kay was both the writer and illustrator of the book, as well as her own deal maker. I was excited when I boarded the plane home, knowing I had successfully acquired my first rights deal, and for exactly the purchase price that Stephen had suggested.

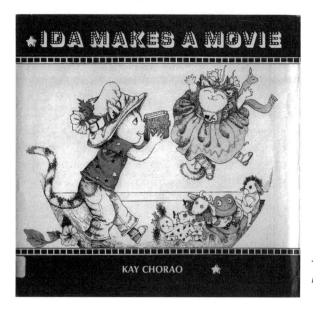

The book cover for *Ida Makes a Movie.*

★

As the characters in *Ida Makes a Movie* were cats, I thought we could make a lovely animated children's film. We had a meeting with our potential distributor, Bob Vale at Magic Lantern, who advised us not to go the animated route, explaining that the market was flooded with animation. What the market needed, he told us, was good live-action, scripted material for young people. "Okay. We can try that," we said.

To help with our growing business, we placed an ad looking for a receptionist/assistant. Amy Jo Cooper applied for the position and in the interview basically said, "Look, I'm a writer, but honestly, I need the money. I can type. I'll be good for this job." Amy had a sardonic wit that appealed to Kit and me. We hired her.

Not surprisingly, Amy did not turn out to be the best assistant, but she could certainly write. Together we talked through the characters and story for *Ida Makes a Movie*. I had initially been attracted to the book for many of its core elements. Ida is a feisty young girl being raised by a single mom in a lower-middle-class neighbourhood. When she enters a movie contest, she wins first prize but for the wrong reasons: the judges have misunderstood her film. I loved the fact that this left Ida in a moral predicament — should she accept the award or not?

Despite the fact that we had great basic material, both Amy and I felt the story needed some higher stakes. Then we realized that it was hard to sympathize with Ida's dilemma as we didn't know enough about the intentions of her movie. In the book, Ida's original film is rather slapdash and is mostly about her dolls. We decided to make the movie a passion piece for Ida: she's upset about garbage in the streets and wants to make a movie about the importance of looking after your neighbourhood and keeping your streets clean. She enlists her neighbour Cookie (who in turn brings many dolls with her) and her older brother Fred (who won't take off his army helmet). Her "actors" are a little difficult to manage, but when all is said and done, Ida is pleased with her movie and happy to enter the contest. She is then confused when the judges misunderstand her message and congratulate her movie about "the devastating effects war has on children." With Ida's motivation clear, and the cats gone, Amy got to work on the script.

Switching from animated to live action meant one big new thing: casting.

I made a handmade sign that we put on a sandwich board in front of our office — "KIDS WANTED" (something you most definitely could not do today!) — and various neighbourhood kids wandered in. Amy told a friend of hers who had a super cute nine-year-old. Bruce recommended some students. Before we knew it, we had a beautiful selection of age-appropriate kids handing in applications.

During my work developing my media studies course, I often met with colleagues at the local teacher's college. I also had meetings there when we were laying the groundwork for the

If you are between ages 6 and 14 and interested in auditioning for a part in a children's film, then Playing With Time would like to meet you.

Requirements:

You must be able to read.
You must be willing to attend workshops and rehearsals.
You must be willing to work on some weekends and
              in your holidays.
Your parents must approve of your participation.

But, who is Playing With Time?

Playing With Time Inc. is a young film production company specializing in films for and about children. Some of our credits include:

KIDS OF DEGRASSI STREET (aired on CBC)
PEARLS IN THE ALPHABET SOUP (for TV Ontario)
BETWEEN TWO WORLD'S (for Toronto Board of Ed.)
GROWING-UP: WITH SANDY OFFENHEIM (aired on CBC)

To apply for an audition please complete the following form, have it signed by your parents, and bring it in (or mail it) to our office at 935 Queen Street E.
              Toronto, Ontario
              M4M 1J6
For further information please call us at 466-6170.
Please attach a recent photograph if you have one.

* ✄

I am interested in auditioning for Playing With Time Inc. I understand that an audition does not necessarily mean that I get a part but I'd like to try anyway.

NAME:_____

ADDRESS:_____

PHONE NO.:_____ AGE:_____

SCHOOL:_____GRADE:_____

My parent(s) approve of me trying out and they understand that if I should get a part the details will be discussed with them.

PARENT'S SIGNATURE:_____

PLAYING WITH TIME INC.
935 Queen Street East, Toronto, Ontario M4M 1J6 Tel: (416) 466-6170

In addition to the sandwich board, we circulated flyers to local schools and community centres. It's easy to see, reading this, that I used to be a school teacher!

new Association for Media Literacy. I took advantage of these connections and asked if I could conduct auditions in that space. Although we had no way of knowing it at the time, this teacher's college building, steeped in academia and pedagogy, would later become the home of *Degrassi High*.

The role of Ida was won easily by Amy's friend's daughter. Zoe Newman was everything we wanted in our lead character: bright, cute, and spunky. The same with Dawn Harrison for Cookie — she was innocent, somewhat petulant, and oh-so-vulnerable. Bruce's student Alan Meiusi won the role of Fred, with his commanding older-brother ways and beautiful eyes. A few other locals were cast as bit players. To help our gang get ready for the camera, I conducted a series of acting workshops in the basement of our local Presbyterian church. We were taking untried talent to camera and needed to support them as much as possible.

We supplemented the young cast with Edna Sternbach as Mom and my brother Michael as both garbage collector and mail carrier. Michael, twelve years younger than me, is my only sibling born in Canada. A sailing enthusiast, he had begun his career in the Royal Canadian Navy, only to be honourably discharged (when he experienced chronic seasickness). Disappointed and unsure where life should take him, he came to Toronto to live with Kit and me. Not only did he have a bit part in our first drama, he was our grip as well. This started him on a whole new career in our industry, and he would eventually grow into one of Canada's top production managers.

Lewis (Wendy's boyfriend) played the part of our exuberant camera salesperson, and the wonderful Elwy Yost, creator and host of *Saturday Night at the Movies* for TVO, agreed to play himself as our avuncular and gracious judge of the movie contest.

We had a cast. We needed a location.

Over a beer one Friday night, I gave Bruce a progress report on *Ida*. Bruce summed up the situation and basically said, "You know I love you, Shooler. Not so sure about your guy, but I love you and this project. I'm teaching during the day, my house is empty. Look after it and my dog, and it's yours."

Deal.

And that wasn't the only support that Bruce would give me. As production was quickly approaching, I needed cash on hand. Even in the days when we had very little money, I was always conscious of payroll. I wanted our cast and crew to know that once they had a deal with Playing With Time Inc., they could count on their paycheque. To keep my promise, I needed cash flow, and for that, I needed the bank. Wearing a black skirt, white faux-silk blouse, and fake pearls, I headed to the bank with a carefully constructed business plan. I met with two middle-aged white men from the small business department who greeted me warmly and asked, "What can we help you with today, dear?"

Dear? I stayed calm as I laid out my business plan, showing what I needed, the receivables that would back it up, and a cash-flow schedule. They studied the plan, then asked, "Do you have a husband who would be willing to co-sign the loan?"

What the fuck did you just say?! No, I didn't say that out loud, but I certainly thought it. Even though Kit and I were living together, I didn't consider him my husband, and I wasn't about to bring him into the finances. I had put all my teacher's savings into our house and new company, which is why I was the president and CEO. Kit's personal finances were a mess as he was in the middle of a lengthy battle over support payments for his ex-wife and two school-aged daughters.

"I would prefer to leave my husband out of this," I told the bankers. I left their office without a deal.

"Fuck," I said to Kit, Amy, and our Siamese cat, Spencer. "I'm not credible without a husband."

"Oh, they're all wankers anyway," chimed in a stoned Kit with a crooked smile. (I hated it when Kit smoked up during business hours.) "You'll figure out something, you always do."

Thanks for the vote of confidence, I thought to myself, but I had no idea how we were going to cash flow our payroll. Later that day, Bruce dropped by on his way home from teaching. I was still seething from my morning's ordeal and angrily replayed it for him. "I'll be your husband," he offered cheerfully.

Two days later I returned to the bank with a letter from Bruce declaring that he was my common-law husband, and a copy of his tax return, confirming his salary as a schoolteacher. "Please let your husband, Bruce, know that we appreciate this measure of comfort. We are happy to do business with you both." And that was that. I had my first small business bank loan. So much has changed in the world of banking over time. Today, we deal with a team of very bright people, many of them women, who are our account executives and various advisors. Oh, they still need their measures of comfort, but at least they don't insist I have a husband, even though now I have a very fine one.

★

I was very excited, yet somewhat anxious, when day one of production on *Ida Makes a Movie* arrived in the summer of 1979. The crew, including DOP Phil Earnshaw, gathered on the porch at our office for crew call. I'd been calling the weather number every half hour since 5 a.m. It didn't look good. We were scheduled to start in the park. Rain was about to fall, at least for the morning. Instinctively, I had previously planned a contingency schedule and had our camera salesperson and the camera store on standby.

Five minutes after the crew assembled, I called it. "We're not starting in the park. We will start at the camera store this morning and do the park in the afternoon."

Kit threw down his script. "I can't do this," he loudly and petulantly spat out. "I'm not ready for the camera store."

"Yes, you are," I quietly affirmed with a tight smile. "We discussed this, it's our contingency. The weather is not good right now."

I asked Amy to make the necessary phone calls to switch our schedule. I left to pick up the talent and said to Kit cheerfully, "See you at the camera store," having no idea if he would show or not.

Kit did arrive (whew), as did Lewis, who was wonderful with the young Zoe. Kit worked quickly and happily, as though the petulant episode on the porch had never happened. The rain stopped and we moved to the park. We got our day. The next day was smoother. I made sandwiches in our back kitchen for cast lunch, drove to pick up the kids as planned, ensured they had the right wardrobe with them, and arrived on set on time for us all to start work. We were off for another day. At the end of that day, the crew assembled in our living room. Kit pulled out the 16mm projector and we watched the rushes from the day before. Despite Kit's initial tantrum, the rushes were charming. Phil's close-ups of our young actors' faces, the back-lighting, the innocence of Amy Jo's words, and the natural direction from Kit all complemented each other. Kit and I caught each other's eyes and smiled — we knew this was magic.

Kit had been strongly influenced by the British "kitchen sink" dramas of the 1960s, films like *Alfie* and *The L-Shaped Room*. These films, highlighting social realism, were set in cramped, mundane settings. This sensibility served Kit well as he navigated the tight location of Bruce's narrow Victorian townhouse, the set for Ida T. Lucas's family home. Where Kit differed from the harsh, realistic British style was in tone. He infused his footage with whimsy and lighthearted charm. The result was captivating.

The rest of the production had challenges: nobody on De Grassi Street liked to be quiet while our cameras rolled. Real garbage day disrupted our morning — we all helped heave garbage into the trucks to speed up the operation. A carpenter next door relent-lessly used his electric drill as he renovated the front porch. We bought his silence for a couple of hours with a box of beer.

Throughout all this, our young cast was exceptional. They rolled with all the interruptions and proved to be quick learners as they adapted to various production protocols. Before shooting began, I had told myself I wanted our set to be professional, expecting our young cast members to be prepared with their lines learned, but I also wanted to create a feeling of summer camp, where the atmosphere was kid-centric. We achieved a good balance, and, in seven days, we got 'er done!

In editing, Kit was, of course, in his element. He loved the footage. We reviewed his cuts every night. Wendy and Lew came

Shooting *Ida Makes a Movie* on De Grassi Street. At the right is Amy Jo Cooper (production assistant and writer), Kit the director, Phil on camera, and me, with pigtails.

by. They offered music suggestions and an original song, co-written by Lewis and his dad. We all knew we had something special. I called CBC, Canada's national broadcaster, and arranged to meet with them.

"This is a very charming film," the execs said. "We would like to buy this, and wonder if you might consider doing more?"

Hmm, let me think . . . Hell, yes!

A few days later, our distributor dropped by the office to take a print of the film. The very next day, he came back with a contract in his briefcase. "Brilliant, you guys. Take a look at the contract. I've guaranteed you $25,000 over the next four years for *Ida Makes a Movie*. And I want more episodes."

Once he left, Kit, Amy, and I collapsed incredulously on the living room sofa. *Did that really happen?* That amount was over three times what the original production budget had been!

And then, in January 1980, when we watched *Ida Makes a Movie* broadcast on air by the CBC, it all became real to us. It was real, and it was magic — we were anxious to do more.

When I look back now at that first drama, I'm amazed at how many elements of the ongoing *Degrassi* series were established: casting age-appropriate actors, taking chances on fresh talent in front of and behind the camera, naturalistic settings and dialogue, setting the stories in a lower-middle-class environment. None of us could have predicted that the little book that Bruce had found by accident would become the first-ever episode of the *Degrassi* franchise.

★

Flushed with excitement from the reception to our first drama, Kit, Amy, and I began blue-skying possibilities for follow-up episodes. We wanted stories that were relevant to young people and reflected their own lives. We settled on an episode about a young girl going to the hospital for an operation and another about a new immigrant family moving into the neighbourhood. We called these episodes "Ida Goes to Hospital" and "Ida Gets a New Neighbour." Kit and I liked the subject matter but were uncertain about building a potential series around a nine-year-old girl who was not necessarily planning to be an actor. We decided instead to build an ensemble cast of characters, where title roles could be shared. These episodes became "Cookie Goes to Hospital" and "Irene Moves In." We also invented an umbrella title for these shows. What better name than *The Kids of Degrassi Street*. The real De Grassi Street had been named after Filippo De Grassi, an Italian soldier who fought for the British and in 1833 was rewarded with a one-hundred-acre tract of land in the Don Valley. When planning a name for our new series, our publicist, Kathryn Ellis, and I decided that for a television title it looked cleaner and more modern to simplify De Grassi to the one word: Degrassi.

Although the enthusiasm in the industry for our project was high, and the money sounded exciting, it wasn't enough to meet

THE KIDS OF DEGRASSI STREET

Local, neighbourhood kids posed alongside our cast for this shot, which would open every episode of *The Kids of Degrassi Street*.

production needs, pay our bills, and keep the bank happy. We continued to juggle documentary and industrial work. Kit kept as many editing gigs as possible, and I took a job teaching film production on Saturday mornings for the Toronto Board of Education's outreach program. I'll never forget one of my serious and somewhat shy students. Saša was very intent on getting this business of Super 8 production just right. His project was thoughtful and the execution precise. Now, when I see Saša Petricic reporting on CBC from tsunami-ravaged Southeast Asia or from the front lines of civil war in Syria, I fondly remember my shy little student.

With our various supplementary income sources, and with CBC, Magic Lantern, and our new international distributor, Isme Bennie, on side, we produced the next two episodes of *The Kids of Degrassi Street*. As we planned new episodes for the following year: "Lisa Makes the Headlines," "Noel Buys a Suit," and "Sophie Minds the Store," we got a request from our broadcaster and our distributors asking if they could see the scripts before we shot these next episodes. *Hmm, this is novel,* I thought at the time. I would later come to learn that this was standard industry protocol.

I headed to CBC for a meeting, feeling like a real professional producer. It was good news — they loved all three scripts. However, they did have one small comment, "We do not want you to cast Peter Duckworth-Pilkington II as the lead in 'Noel buys a Suit.'" This was unexpected. Peter was an established character from the previous episode. To be fair, he was not your traditional TV child star, but we'd loved his pudgy face, unconventional speech patterns, and overall charm. CBC presented alternatives. They had seen a cute blond boy on a cereal commercial and thought he would be ideal. "Cute blond boy selling cereal" represented everything I wanted to avoid in our casting. He was slick, coy, and contrived. Our *Degrassi* kids needed to be "the kid next door." I wanted kids of all varying body types and ethnicities. I wanted them with glasses, bad hair, and clumsy feet. And, most importantly, they needed to possess vulnerability.

It was clear CBC would not budge. They would not support Peter Duckworth-Pilkington II.

I walked out of the meeting without a deal. I headed down Yonge, angry with myself. How could I be such an idiot, walking away from a deal? We had a mortgage. We had bills. I stopped at a pay telephone booth to call Kit and told him I'd blown the deal. "Well done," he cheerfully said. "We don't need those fuckers; we'll make it somehow. Remember Wendy's song from *Jimmy: Playing With Time?* Time will show the way."

As it turned out, Kit was right.

In the early 1980s, something new was happening at the federal government tax department. In 1974, they had provided a capital cost allowance to allow benefits for investors in domestic feature film productions. Now they were expanding this production incentive to include investment in that sassy little sister of the cinema: television. As luck would have it, I had recently met two young lawyers who had several friends and partners looking to shelter their income. Together, we prepared an investment memorandum. I drew up the creative side of the proposal; they did the financials. By the end of the year, we had fully sold all our units and were 100 percent financed for our next three episodes.

★

During this time, Yan Moore entered our lives. Yan (coincidentally married to our publicist Kathryn Ellis) also got his start as an editor in the basement of Hobel-Leiterman and worked for us on one of our industrial documentaries. Until this point, Kit had been very protective of our editing room. But with three episodes to produce and direct, Kit felt he needed support with editing. He turned to Yan. Yan was somewhat shy and nervous when he came to our PWT offices for an interview. The more nervous Yan was, the more he stammered. But, lucky for Yan, Kit already knew that he was a great editor. We would soon discover that Yan also had a delightful sense of humour and a wicked work ethic. We contracted him to edit "Noel Buys a Suit." Every night, Yan left the editing room smiling. "This is going to be a great episode," he would tell us confidently.

Peter's performance as Noel was particularly touching as the troubled young man who wants to support his dad's new marriage but is having difficulty accepting his new stepmom. Independent of his father, and wanting to celebrate his dad's big event, twelve-year-old Noel buys a colourful checked suit for his father's wedding. Meanwhile, his soon-to-be stepmom, unaware of his suit choice, gifts him a striped, multicoloured shirt. Noel is offended by the shirt. To his eye, "stripes and checks don't go" and he refuses to wear the shirt, which of course upsets his stepmom and causes a scene. In the end, Noel extends an olive branch and wears the suit he bought with the offensive shirt. When Kit and I screened the cut with Yan, and we got to the part of Noel's compromise and his arrival at the wedding, we all teared up. "CBC will love this," we had to believe.

I held my breath, and my pride, and called the CBC executives. I asked if they would consider having a look at our completed episode

We walked away from a CBC deal rather than re-cast Noel (Peter Duckworth-Pilkington II). Luckily, both stories — the fictional one and our own professional drama — had happy endings.

and they agreed. When we got to the wedding scene, they cried. We made a deal and got twice the money from CBC we had originally been offered. We were happy, the investors were happy, and we were back in business with our broadcaster and our amazing cast!

We settled into a lovely rhythm with investors, CBC, and our distributors. We expanded production from three episodes a year to four. This seems laughable now, when in 2010, we did forty-four episodes of *Degrassi: The Next Generation* and even more episodes the following years when both *Degrassi* and *The L.A. Complex* were shooting simultaneously. But, back then, we found four quite enough.

Yan was working on the cut of "Casey Draws the Line," loosely based on Norman McLaren's *Neighbours*. Two of our characters, Lisa (Stacie Mistysyn) and Casey (Sarah Charlesworth), have been friends for years and share many things, including a rabbit called Rabbit. When the property gets reassessed, Rabbit's cage is on the property line. The girls have a disagreement that eventually escalates to war. The innocent victim is Rabbit.

Yan was struggling with this episode in the editing room. He called me in one morning. *Uh-oh*, I thought. He was obviously nervous about something. *Does he want to quit?* Actually, the opposite was true. Yan was struggling to say, "The script has, er, emotional problems. I think I have a solution."

"Casey Draws the Line" was the first experience we had working with both children and animals. We had two identical lop-eared rabbits to play the role of Rabbit. One was very docile. She'd allow herself to be cuddled by our young cast and was perfect for close-up shots. The other was somewhat ferocious. He was great for the action shots when he escaped from his cage but was also quick to bite whoever was nearby. The practicalities of shooting with animals, compounded by unexpected rains causing numerous shooting delays, took its toll on our footage. Although we got the script shot in the allotted time, there had not been time to properly work on the emotions of the performances. The story felt flat and didn't build to the poignant payoff we had thought it deserved.

Yan suggested we could set the film in the past and make it about the two girls on their first day back at school when the teacher assigns them to write about their summer holidays. Each would tell their version of the truth as the film cuts back to footage from the summer. It was a brilliant solution. With one day of additional shooting, we saved the show and Yan's writing career was launched. Yan would go on to win top honours as a writer in multiple awards events including the Geminis, International Emmys, and the Prix Jeunesse. I was so grateful that 43 Britain Street had connected the two of us.

At this point, Amy Jo Cooper had moved on to pursue her freelance writing career, and we had a revolving door of various assistants. One day, our distributor told us he had someone he'd like us to meet. We set up a meeting with Sari Friedland. Sari was tall, beautiful, and somewhat intimidating, had incredible attention to detail and extraordinarily long nails. We had an extensive interview with her as our Siamese cat, Spencer, slept in her lap.

When Sari left, Kit and I agreed that she was unique, and just what we needed. We offered her the job and were a bit surprised when she asked for twenty-four hours to consider. Sari had been born and raised in the tony Jewish section of town, Forest Hill. She loved our job description and liked us. She told us her hesitation was whether or not she could report to work on a daily basis in Toronto's east end. We later found out that Sari had a couple of other reasons for her hesitancy — unbeknownst to us, she was a chain smoker and was not fond of cats. It had evidently been very hard for her during the two-hour interview to not only be without a cigarette, but also have a cat on her lap. Twenty-five hours after our initial job offer, Sari called to say she would really like to accept the job, but wondered if we could make some accommodation for her smoking and the cat. We told her the cat was non-negotiable, but we could talk about the smoking. We came to a compromise. She could not smoke inside (this was long before there were bylaws about interior smoking in places of business) but, as we had a large covered porch at the side of the building, we would be happy to designate that as her smoking area. We had a deal.

When Yan met Sari on the first day, he quietly confided to me, "She will never last." As it turned out, Sari and I would work together for the next sixteen years. She was an incredible addition to our company, and her chain smoking on the veranda became legendary. She was notorious for smoking often, but only smoking half a cigarette at a time. The remaining half she would cavalierly toss into our bushes or onto the public pathway. We asked her to make sure to tidy this up and, although we never saw her do it, we were pleased that it was regularly cleaned. Only years later did I hear the true story of how the butts disappeared.

In the early 2000s, a friend introduced me to celebrity hairdresser Robert Gage. Although Robert claimed he was not taking new clients, when he heard I was the co-creator and executive producer of *Degrassi*, he said, "Darling, it would be a divine pleasure of mine to do your hair!" Robert and I started a great friendship. On one of my early trips to his salon, I had my hair washed by his latest assistant, Danette. Robert introduced me as "the fabulous Ms. Degrassi Everything." Danette's eyes widened.

"I know where your office used to be," she said. "In grade school, I attended Morse Street Public School down the street from your Queen Street office and we would hang out behind your bushes to see if we could meet some of the actors. We also hoped that someday we might get a chance to be on the show."

She went on to explain that in the bushes they discovered a whole bunch of half smoked cigarettes. "It was awesome," she told me. "We'd come after school, pick up the butts, and head to Jimmie Simpson Park to smoke them."

Mystery solved, but not without a sense of irony on my part. As I did the math backwards to the time Danette and friends were smoking Sari's discarded butts, it coincided with work our company was doing with the federal Ministry of Health to discourage young people from smoking. *Oh my.*

★

Sari, like so many others in our company, would quickly go on to assume greater responsibilities. In time she would become our

Sari, me, and Yan on set, seven years after Yan predicted our relationship would never last.

production manager. She proved to be especially adept in handling the often-erratic behaviour and scheduling demands of Kit.

With Sari, Yan, and Phil part of our regular creative team and good relationships with financiers, broadcasters, and distributors, Kit and I felt warmly about each other and the company. Playing With Time Inc. had grown to occupy the whole of our Queen Street building, necessitating the purchase of a new home around the corner on Pape Avenue. We paid for a professional design of our logo and etched it, along with our company name, in gold leaf on our storefront window. We bought Sari a new typewriter with some rudimentary word processing ability, invested in an early Macintosh 128K, and purchased a second Steenbeck.

In December 1985, Jim Bawden, who had faithfully been reviewing our shows, wrote in the *Toronto Star*: "There's an emerging bittersweet character to *The Kids of Degrassi Street*, arguably the finest children's series ever to run on Canadian TV. By describing the sharp vignettes as kid's TV, I am aware, I'm already limiting it. As an adult, I have watched from the beginning without any feeling of condescension."

★

Kit and I congratulated each other. We liked the size of our company and the shows we were producing. Kit found time to practice tae kwon do and to sail. I played tennis three times a week and swam at the local club. On alternate weekends, we enjoyed family time with Kit's two young daughters. We had a good work-life balance and would be happy for it to stay that way.

It did not.

One suppertime, in our new home, we took an international call that would eventually have a profound impact on our "perfect" life.

CHAPTER FIVE

THE LATER KIDS

The long-distance phone connection between Munich and Toronto crackled. We strained to make out the singing that was set to a somewhat familiar John Philip Sousa march and went something like this:

You won the Prix Jeunesse,
You won the Prix Jeunesse,
You won the Prix Jeunesse,
Ta dah. Ta dah. TA DAH!

Multiple female giggles followed. Then the recognizable and distinguished British voice of Angela Bruce, head of the CBC's children's department, tried to bring some order to the conversation. "It's true, folks, you are the overall winner of the Prix Jeunesse in Munich. I'm here with Kate Taylor from PBS, WGBH Boston, and she has more great news for you."

"Congratulations, you guys," said a giddy Kate. "My bosses are so impressed with your work, they want to partner with you on your new project!" More giggles. It was six hours later in Germany, and it was obvious that some champagne had been enjoyed. Then we lost the phone connection.

The Prix Jeunesse, affectionately known as the "Oscars" of children's television, is an international event held every other year in Munich. Over a number of days, broadcasters and producers from all corners of the world participate. A few months earlier, CBC had asked if they could submit a *Kids of Degrassi Street* episode "Griff Makes a Date" to the awards. We'd since forgotten about that.

"Well, this is lovely," Kit and I agreed, and got on with our dinner.

★

"Griff Makes a Date" felt special when we were producing it. It was the first lead role for Neil Hope as the troubled Griff. We originally introduced Griff as a member of the "Pirate" gang, who terrorizes our regular *Degrassi* kids over the summer. Now, school is back, and Griff finds himself in the same class as some of our regular kids. Despite their differences, young Lisa Canard and Griff are attracted to each other. Things go well until, when walking together from school, Griff flippantly calls the intellectually

Griff (Neil Hope) on the left with the Pirate Gang.

disabled crossing guard a "retard." Lisa runs off in tears. Griff later finds out that Lisa's new baby brother has an intellectual disability.

Neil himself was a complicated young man. Our "KIDS WANTED" sandwich board had caught his eye, and nervously, he and his father had stopped by to arrange an audition. Neil was dressed in blue jeans and a freshly pressed white shirt. His father was considerably older, polite, and well mannered, but showed definite physical signs of a life lived hard. Neil won the audition for Griff. No one in the audition room could resist the huge vulnerability emanating from Neil's gentle grey eyes, his distinct gravelly voice, and his overall physical appeal. He was to become a cast and fan favourite.

When filming, I'd pick Neil up and drop him off at a walk-up apartment on Danforth Avenue above a music store. I learned this was his dad's home. His mom lived in Etobicoke, a suburb of Toronto. His parents were separated and both heavy drinkers. Some nights, particularly Fridays, Neil would linger in my car, not wanting to go home. He knew he would find his father in a "state."

Neil and me outside our office. We had just returned from a publicity trip in New York, the first time that Neil had been on a plane or away from Canada.

As he and I got to know and trust one another, he confided in me how hard it was to go home some nights. We worked out a plan. When he was nervous to go home, he could call his dad and spend the night with us. He did this with increasing frequency.

These were confusing times for Neil. He definitely loved his mom and dad but didn't know how to deal with the habitual drinking and bouts of anger. Three years or so into our relationship, Neil went home to his dad's apartment to find the seventy-two-year-old dead on the kitchen floor. He had been taken by a combination of neglect of his insulin for diabetes, heavy drinking, and a failed liver. Neil was devastated. He spent more and more time living with us.

Neil's antidote to his troubles was work. He would stay with our company as Griff through *The Kids of Degrassi Street* episodes, and then graduated to *Degrassi Junior High, Degrassi High,* and *School's Out* as fan favourite Derek "Wheels" Wheeler. Once those projects were done, further work as an actor eluded Neil. We would get together periodically for lunch. He had a job in a warehouse and a girlfriend who he hoped to marry. Life wasn't glamorous, but it was fine.

When we rebooted *Degrassi* in 2001 with *Degrassi: The Next Generation,* we had a few story lines for characters from the earlier "classic" series. Neil's character came back for an episode where Joey, Snake, and Wheels go bowling. Neil and I had a tearful reunion in my office. He didn't look good. "Hate to say it," he said, his eyes on the floor, "I have diabetes."

I asked if he was drinking and he said, "Yes, but I'm going to stop."

We talked about his dad and the importance of looking after his health. He confided that his wedding had been mutually called off. We promised to keep in touch and have dinner soon. I gave him my cell number, saying to call if he needed support. He assured me he would. We shared a big hug and Neil was off to Money Mart to get quick cash for his cheque from one day of acting. It was the last time I would see Neil.

Reports of Neil's death were not made public till February 2012. The details were heartbreaking. He had died years earlier, in 2007, alone and anonymous, in a Hamilton rooming house amid unused vials of insulin and empty liquor bottles. He was thirty-five. Stephen and I were on holiday in Saint Martin when we heard the news. I was gut-wrenched. I couldn't move from the bed for the better part of a week. On the sixth day, Stephen had a local doctor make a house call, but no medicine could cure my pain. My main goal for the *Degrassi* franchise was to reassure young people that they are not alone, yet, despite my professional intentions and the long-standing friendship that Neil and I shared, he'd died alone. I felt that I had failed him.

Neil — an introspective moment on set.

★

Back in 1985, times were happier. Angela had ordered a final six-pack of *The Kids of Degrassi Street* and our crew and cast couldn't wait to get back to work — particularly Neil. Angela also promised to arrange a set visit for Kate Taylor from WGBH. At this point, we had already begun development on our next series, *Degrassi Junior High*. We had hired a young writer, Avrum Jacobson, to help with this development. I was excited about the opportunity of aging up stories to the junior high level, something I had wanted to do since leaving teaching eight years earlier.

In 1981, when Steven Bochco's *Hill Street Blues* first came on air, I was captivated by it. I loved the intertwined storylines, some of which were resolved at the end of an episode and others which carried on to the next. I loved the moral dilemmas characters faced, often pitting "what's right" against "what works." I explained to Avrum that I was looking for *Hill Street Blues* in school.

While Avrum developed *Degrassi Junior High*, Kit, Yan, and I prepared a plan for the final six episodes of *The Kids of Degrassi Street*. We wanted to convince our broadcaster, distributors, and investors that we would be creatively ready for the challenge of the new series, *Degrassi Junior High*. To that end, we decided to adopt Bochco's storytelling paradigm and construct the final six episodes of *The Kids of Degrassi Street* as a miniseries with vertical as well as horizontal storylines. We gave this six-pack a subtitle: *The Kids of Degrassi Street: Yearbook*.

As promised, Angela proudly brought Kate Taylor to our set for a visit. They presented us with the beautiful Prix Jeunesse award, a silver and glass orb, with moving parts on the inside, and a person-alized inscription. Our cast and crew were excited to receive the award and to meet an executive from WGBH. WGBH Boston was one of the flagship PBS stations, known for its commitment to children's and youth programming and related outreach support.

When Angela and Kate arrived on set, we were shooting at the local school, Dundas Street Junior Public School, steps from

Bruce's house on De Grassi Street. I was in deep discussion with Yan about script revisions. Kit and Phil were discussing the upcoming shot, a dolly through the corridors to reveal Griff and Lisa in a heated discussion at her locker. Sari was checking that the hair and wardrobe were consistent with our previous scene while the grips laid dolly track. Our kids were in the library catching some tutoring time while the next scene was being set up. I was proud of how our team worked — ever professional, always respectful of our young cast, and welcoming to visitors.

Kate, Angela, and I stayed on set to watch the conclusion of the scene. We then drove to the office to look at some footage with newly promoted editor Robert de Lint, our once-intern and assistant editor. He charmed the executives. Then, we talked development with Avrum. The day couldn't have unfolded better. At the end, Kate said, "You guys are just what we need. I want to bring your new show to the executives at WGBH. And to be clear, if we pull this off, we'll need a minimum of thirteen episodes next year."

Angela was beaming. She enjoyed being a matchmaker and understood the benefits to CBC if we could bring PBS as a partner to the table. When Kit got home, I explained to him excitedly what had just unfolded. He was cautious. "I've been there in advertising," he said. "More broadcasters, more executives, we'll lose creative control."

My spirits were dampened, but not broken. I recognized that our company had the potential to grow quicker than what Kit and I might have originally envisioned. I found myself split in many directions. My first loyalties were always to the script, casting, production, and editing. By default, I was also responsible for hiring, firing, finance, and for all our legal and business affairs. With WGBH potentially on the scene, our world was about to get bigger. I needed help. Then, I remembered that soft-spoken lawyer who had guided me, free of charge, through the contractual requirements of acquiring the rights to *Ida Makes a Movie*. "Kit," I said, "we need a lawyer."

"Why?"

"Because we potentially have a situation and an opportunity on our hands, and I'm not sure how to deal."

A puff of smoke came up. "Fine, do what you will — you always do."

Okay then. I searched for Stephen Stohn, who was no longer at the storefront legal firm on Colborne Street. He was now a partner with the posh firm of McCarthy & McCarthy in the TD Centre, in the heart of Toronto's financial district. As I took the elevator up to the forty-ninth floor, I imagined that the higher I went, the larger the invoices would become. Kit had made it clear he didn't think this was a good idea, and I was starting to agree. As the elevator doors opened, I was about to take the return elevator down, when I was greeted by the calm face of Stephen Stohn. "Welcome to the program," he warmly smiled.

Oh, well, maybe I could stay for a short meeting.

Stephen wore a navy suit of exquisite Italian wool, but the cut was wrong. The shoulders were too big and the jacket sloppy. I later found out that this was by design. Stephen wanted his jackets to carry his cell phone (which was very large in those days), his calculator, and whatever other techie devices he might need, maybe even a slide rule? Yes, Stephen was a geek. And it turned out, a Zen solicitor geek was just what our company needed. Despite Kit's protests, we engaged Stephen as our lawyer.

★

To help build our relationship, Kate and I planned to meet in Chicago for a children's film festival. While there, we shared meals and stories and realized we were both ex-schoolteachers wanting to make a difference in the world of children's television. Kate had been the successful WGBH producer of *Zoom* a few years earlier and was highly regarded at PBS. I respected her credentials as she did mine. After a full day, happy with our new friendship, we prepared to part for the night outside the elevator. Kate said, "Linda, one more question. If you were to make your Prix Jeunesse winner 'Griff Makes a Date' again, what would you do differently?"

I wasn't ready for this. I laughed and said, "I love our show. I'm proud of it and our award." I wasn't quite sure what else to say, or what was expected.

She continued, "When watching it, I noticed that that some parts were stronger than others and thought, if you had the opportunity to revisit it, what changes would you make?"

"I honestly haven't thought about this" was my mystified response.

As I took the elevator to my room, I was unsettled by the questions. I played various scenarios. Did she think my show was flawed and wanted me to admit it? Did she have fixes she would have made and wanted to tell me what they were? Did she like it as is and was just checking? Any way I looked at it, I was unnerved. I was reminded of Kit's caution — too many executives.

I flew back to Toronto, thinking we might want to back away from this deal. Kit happily agreed. Newly hired Stephen said, "Let's take a second look. This could be a breakthrough moment for your company." Stephen's reassurance made me realize I was probably being petty about my awkward incident in Chicago. On his advice, I continued to develop the new *Degrassi Junior High* material with Kate. I was comforted that we did have a lot in common, particularly our commitment to young people and our shared teaching roots. Stephen connected with Kate's WGBH lawyer, and negotiations began.

Then, two interesting things happened. One, we got nominated for an International Emmy for "Griff Gets a Hand," and two, I got kicked in the gut by Kate.

The gut kick came way down the creative development chain. With Avrum, and now Yan, we had developed a thick and rich document for *Degrassi Junior High*. Kate had approved each draft and we were getting excited about presenting it to our respective broadcasters. On the eve of the presentation, Kate asked a simple — but explosive — question. She began gently, "I think it is wonderful that we are developing stories where teenagers deal with tough issues: abuse, pregnancy, bullying, et cetera."

"Yes — that's why we want to make this series. It's relevant. It's real. Thank you for being part of it," I confirmed enthusiastically.

"But," said Kate, "we need to have better resolutions."

What did she just say?

Kate clarified her point. "Kids need guidance," she espoused. "I suggest that we create a character, probably female, with lots of cats — kids love cats — who would live at the end of Degrassi Street. At the conclusion of each episode, the kids could come to her, talk about the issue of the week, and she would impart a thoughtful and meaningful commentary."

Gag me with a spoon.

Degrassi Junior High was not intended to be an "issue-of-the-week show" where things tie up neatly at the end. I wanted to capture the messiness and awkwardness of everyday life, where kids face the consequences of their actions over a number of episodes. They didn't need an eccentric adult weighing in. And neither did I.

Kate and I were at a creative stalemate.

In a saner moment, I considered how the show might be able to work with this extra element. I even wondered if we could produce two versions of the show — our version for CBC and one with the cat lady for PBS. But, regardless of how level-headed I tried to be, I couldn't reconcile this ending with my passion for youth empowerment. We were resigned to the fact that despite Stephen's determined efforts, the WGBH deal was dead.

Simultaneously, our office was bananas over our first International Emmy nomination. A group of us headed to to New York for a glamorous night in the ballroom at Sheraton Center on Seventh Avenue. We were welcomed with champagne — the real stuff, not Baby Duck. There were musicians, celebs, magicians, and, oh yes, a whole contingent from WGBH.

Dinner was good, I think. We knew it was a long shot, but should we win, I was the designated recipient. I silently rehearsed my speech, knowing I'd have thirty seconds. Who should I thank? Who do I leave out? What's politically appropriate, what's not? Finally, our category came up, nominations were announced and . . . we'd won!! Kit and I ran to the stage. I made a speech.

I've completely forgotten what I said. Kit made a humorous comment and we left with the trophy.

We had an EMMY!

Kit and me, giddy with our first International Emmy Award.

The afterparty was awesome. We danced. We drank. We laughed. In the midst of this, I was approached by a smartly dressed redhead who introduced himself as the president of WGBH. "So happy to meet you," he said. I stopped dancing. "Congratulations, this is a big award! And, I understand we will be working together soon on the new *Degrassi* project."

"I don't think so," I flippantly replied, fuelled by award-winning adrenaline and champagne. "We have creative differences."

This was not the response he expected or wanted.

★

The next day we were back in Toronto. That night I had a dream. An excessively large hand pushed its way through our living room window, swiftly lifted the Emmy, and took it away. I sat in a chair, passively watching this happen, making no effort to resist. I was relieved to see the shiny lady disappear. I didn't deserve her. After all, I was just a schoolteacher playing in a sandbox where I didn't belong. I was a fake.

In the morning, I was still nursing a residual hangover from not only the champagne and my disturbing dream, but also the rude and dismissive way I had spoken to the WGBH president. I felt I needed to make amends. This project was so important, we must be able to find a way to sort out our creative differences. But given my rash and flip behaviour, I was convinced we'd never hear from WGBH again.

At my desk, as I popped an Advil and Midol (my period cramps were killer, again), our newly acquired fax machine started to hum. One page, then another, and another. They kept coming, multiple pages of a legal document, spilling onto the floor. I started to assemble the flimsy papers and realized it was — a contract? Yes, it was a contract from WGBH to Playing With Time Inc., to acquire the broadcast rights to *Degrassi Junior High*. I carefully read each page.

I ran to the edit room where Kit and Yan were working. Speechless, I dropped the sheets onto the Steenbeck. Realizing what this was, Yan's eyes lit up. Kit's face went grim. "Throw it out," he muttered. "We don't need those fuckers."

Oh, but we did need them. *Degrassi Junior High* was a far more ambitious and complex work than we'd ever tackled before. We needed a larger cast and crew, and a larger budget. We couldn't manage this with the financing model we currently had. "We're not compromising our creativity," Kit asserted adamantly.

"As far as I can tell, I don't see any clauses about cat ladies or neat resolutions," I offered.

"Drop it, Linda. You know what happened before — Kate waited till the last minute to make a huge creative change. We can't trust those people."

I headed back to my office and popped another extra-strength Advil. I took a breath, then called Stephen. At his request, I faxed the draft contract to his office. Within minutes, Stephen called and confirmed, "Linda, you are right. There is no creative stipulation about a cat lady. I think the basics are here for a good deal. Let's fly to Boston and make this happen." A business trip to Boston with my lawyer! This all sounded very professional. Well, maybe to me, but not to Kit. He stood his ground about not trusting Kate and her fellow broadcast executives. "I've seen it in advertising," he said. "Executives talk a good line, then pull stunts at the last minute." I agreed with Kit that we couldn't compromise the creative, but I also thought we should explore a way to work with this prestigious broadcaster. WGBH Boston, a part of the PBS family, aired many high-quality shows, including the flagship dramatic *Masterpiece Theatre* and the public affairs show *Frontline*. They could potentially be great partners. In the end, Kit and I came to an agreement. If he could be assured that the "cat lady" would never again surface, he would support the deal.

At the offices of WGBH, Stephen and I were treated grandly. We were given the tour, shown various awards they had won over the years, and told that they hoped to add our show to their awards wall. We entered a large boardroom, and the negotiations began. Throughout the course of the afternoon, Stephen gently engaged with the WGBH execs and legal team. His style was positive. He laughed easily yet gave little away. He gave a brief reference to the cat lady and was reassured she was not necessary. Without any grandstanding, he effectively protected the creative. This was the same style that had made him a trusted lawyer to so many in the Canadian entertainment industry, including the Cowboy Junkies, Alannah Myles, Randy Bachman, k.d. lang, and many others. Over the years, I have coined a name for Stephen's style. He presents gently but has a determination that suits his zodiac sign, Taurus. He is a Zen bull.

Although we didn't conclude negotiations that day, Stephen reassured me that we had all the groundwork for a solid WGBH deal. It would take another few months to iron out the fine print, but in the end, our deal was saved. And, most importantly, the "cat lady" was dead.

Simultaneous with our WGBH negotiations, we began our contractual discussions with CBC. We secured a Canadian distribution deal with Magic Lantern, a U.S. distribution deal with the Learning Corporation of America, and an international deal with Paragon Entertainment (the new home for Isme Bennie). For the final piece of the financing matrix, we worked with a young investment broker, Ashley Stanley, who had a number of dentists on his roster looking to shelter their income. He sold all our units before the year-end.

We had our first multi-million-dollar deal and a serious delivery schedule. Now, all we had to do was make it happen.

CHAPTER SIX

ENROLLING IN JUNIOR HIGH

"We're building our own school!" I announced to our office triumphantly. "We need bricks and mortar, rules and regulations, a code of conduct, a faculty, a student body, and a curriculum. And we need them pronto." Our team set out simultaneously on multiple fronts.

Sari was in charge of the location hunt. During production of *The Kids of Degrassi Street*, we had been able to access real school locations during the weekends with a permit. But, with thirteen episodes to produce in a condensed period of time, we needed a more permanent home. Sari found a couple of empty schools in the Toronto area. Even though they offered great space, the exteriors were far from filmic and, most importantly, they were too expensive. Not easily defeated, Sari broadened our search area. She returned to the office one afternoon and announced gleefully, "I've found it!"

The next morning Yan, Kit, Sari, and I set out to 68 Daisy Avenue in the Long Branch area of Etobicoke, a western suburb of Toronto. Here, a twenty-five-minute drive from our east end office, we were introduced to Vincent Massey Junior School. "She's a beauty, eh?" Sari proudly stated.

68 Daisy Avenue, Etobicoke. The perfect location for shooting *Degrassi Junior High*.

Yan, Kit, and I looked at the facade of the 1929 brick building. It was a classic red-brown brick with white window trim, symmetrical in design with wide steps leading up to central front doors. The school size was modest — four classrooms on the main floor and another four on the second floor. The classic design gave her gravitas, and the modest size meant a minimum number of extras required to fill the space. The spacious front lawn, with a beautiful spreading oak tree, grounded the building. This backdrop would provide a perfect setting for scenes of juicy lunchtime gossip, note cramming and cribbing, as well as, oh yes, a tentative first kiss. We were in love before we even stepped inside.

The interior was a little more challenging. Although visually still very appropriate, the logistics needed consideration. Only the top floor was available for rent, as the ground floor was home to an operating school. However, the monthly rent was well within our budget. Knowing we could work out logistics, we signed a lease.

Yan, Kit, and I now turned our thoughts to our student body. We examined our casting process from *The Kids of Degrassi Street*. We liked our commitment to work with local kids, but we needed many more actors for this new show. We widened our search from the local neighbourhood and schools to a citywide scout including talent agents and art schools in the Greater Toronto Area.

Applications poured in.

From preliminary auditions, we selected a short list of about fifty kids, most with no acting experience. We decided to run a series of workshops that would offer some rudimentary acting classes, scene study, and character work. Kit, originally skeptical of our new production, was now all in. He looked at our workshop process as forming the new Playing With Time Repertory Company. This suited his British roots and solidified his ownership in the new production. We hired the multitalented Judy Shiner, who prepared a curriculum for a three-week intensive workshop. Judy was an indefatigable talent and had a great rapport with the kids. She would stay with us through production and would head the art and wardrobe department.

There was a feeling of buoyancy throughout our office.

And then we got a visit from ACTRA, the actors union. "Will you consider becoming a union shop?" I was asked.

"With all due respect," I answered, "I'm not sure how we can do that." I explained that we needed a large number of kids who currently didn't exist in the system. We had been to all the agencies and their only kids were ones trained in commercials — cute but not authentic. Or they were too old. It was important for us to continue our tradition of casting age-appropriate talent. We needed real kids, a lot of them, and we were willing to train them ourselves.

The ACTRA rep, an ex-teacher himself, listened and was somewhat complimentary. However, he did issue a caution. "You will also be needing adults in your show, and the good ones are members of our union. If you remain non-union, you cannot access our talent bank."

I acknowledged this position and we parted company on good terms. This would not be the last we'd hear from the union — the next encounter would not be quite as friendly. But that was still a year or so away.

★

I recognized the responsibilities we were about to undertake as we hired close to fifty underage performers in a non-union shop. I wanted to make sure we created a work environment that would be as safe as a real school. To this end, we mapped out our working conditions, including pay scale, transportation requirements, retirement plan, educational needs, etc. Once confident we had these in order, we called a meeting of all the parents. We shared the overall philosophy of our show. "We want to talk to our adolescent audience in an open and direct way," I explained. "Your child will be bringing home scripts with frank and honest stories about the teenage experience, including and not limited to sexual awakening, child abuse, teen pregnancy, and peer pressure."

Sari talked through the contracting process. She explained that performers would be contracted in one of three tiers at the beginning of each episode. They would also be eligible for our Registered Retirement Savings Plan (RRSP). These financial contributions would remain locked until the actor left our company, at which time they could make their own financial decisions. Over the years, we've heard great stories of how certain performers kept their money in the plan until they were ready to put a down payment on a house; by that time, their investments had grown substantively. Others, of course, cashed them in the moment they were no longer with the company, which, interestingly, was what I'd done with my RRSP the moment I left teaching.

Sari continued to explain that we had also created the PWT Foundation. All our rep company members could apply to the foundation for scholarships for educational pursuits, grants for individual projects, and counselling support. We confirmed to the parents that a tutor would be on set at all times to allow our performers to keep up with their regular schoolwork.

Kit and Judy explained the acting workshop process and how the final character selections would unfold. "We're asking you and your child to make a big commitment to this project," I summed up. "We encourage you to discuss everything with your family, and if you don't feel comfortable, now is the time to opt out, and we will understand. However, if your child does commit, we need to know that they will stay with us throughout the season."

We provided information sheets and parental consent forms for signature, necessary for the workshops to begin. As the meeting wrapped up, a few parents had some private questions, but it was hard to read the room. "Do you think I scared them off?" I asked the team as we later shared a private drink. "Was I too blunt?"

"We'll find out soon enough," replied Kit with one of his enigmatic smiles. "But you did sound a bit like an old school marm."

We had a tense couple of days as we waited for the consent forms and wondered who, if any, might drop out. In the end, no one did. In fact, we got calls from some of the parents expressing their excitement and support for the project. *Whew!* We collected a full set of signed parental consent forms and the acting workshops began.

In hindsight, this all sounds rather extraordinary, and I acknowledge readily that this business model would be impossible today. But in the 1980s, with Canadian independent production in its infancy and a scarcity of child performers, it seemed like the only way to proceed. This was also the era of Gen X, the generation of teenagers who were fiercely independent. They were the children of the boomers, often from divorced homes and/or homes where both parents worked, causing some to refer to the cohort as the latchkey generation. (Our *Degrassi* character Lucy, played by Anais Granofsky, was the embodiment of a latchkey kid.) So, all considered, it's not that surprising that we got buy-in from our underage performers' parents on our unique business model.

*

As we headed towards finalizing our rep company, several cast members from *The Kids of Degrassi Street* were close to making the last cut. Yan, Kit, and I had been wondering what to do about their character names. "Should we keep the same ones from the

ABOVE: At a PWT workshop. Judy Shiner, top left, and I (with half a head) watch, along with cast members, as one of our actors presents a scene study.

LEFT: Our latchkey character Lucy (Anais Granofsky) comes home to an empty house and checks for messages. This was shot in Kit's and my kitchen, and her mother's voice is played by me.

previous series, or allow them to play new characters?" Yan was in favour of new names. He felt old names came with old character baggage and he would like a clean slate. Kit was easy either way, as was Angela Bruce at CBC. Kate had no opinion as the original series had not been broadcast on PBS, so there was no conflict there. I was concerned for viewers of *The Kids of Degrassi Street* that changing character names could be confusing.

"Let's call a meeting," I said democratically.

We invited all of the kids involved — siblings Sarah Charlesworth (Casey) and Chris Charlesworth (Benjamin), Neil Hope (Griff), Stacie Mistysyn (Lisa), John Ioannou (Pete), Arlene Lott (Rachel), Danah-Jean Brown (Connie), and Anais Granofsky (Karen) and asked for their preference. "Should your characters keep their names from *The Kids of Degrassi Street*, or should they play new personalities?" We had a lively discussion, but ultimately, they came down on Yan's side, and for the same reason. They were excited about the idea of starting fresh with new fictional identities. Yan and the writers began to create new character profiles for these actors.

Next up, we needed a crew.

We wanted to work with folks who were professional but also had a good rapport with young people. A key role was that of director of photography (DOP). Following our successful relationship with Phil Earnshaw throughout *The Kids of Degrassi Street*, we assumed he would be part of the new team. But Phil wasn't sure. He'd been doing a number of commercials and making good money. He was considering joining the American-based union IATSE (International Alliance of Theatrical Stage Employees) but did acknowledge it would be fun to work on our new production. Phil asked for a little more time to consider this. Phil's ambivalence pissed Kit off. "Forget it," he asserted. "If Phil's too good for us, I have an even better idea."

From his time in commercials, Kit knew a DOP he particularly admired. We interviewed him and found he was ready for a change of pace and happily accepted our job offer.

Then there was a problem.

After day three of production, as we watched rushes for the second night in a row, Yan, Kit, and I turned sombrely to one another. We didn't like the look. Our shots were beautifully framed and executed, but the tone was dark, shadowy, and moody. This was not the feel we wanted for our school. Complicating matters was the fact that our DOP was slow and, more importantly, was intimidated by our young cast. We had no choice but to fire him and reluctantly put a stop to production.

Over the years, I've been surprised to encounter many crew members who were uncomfortable around young people. They would either dismiss them as though their youthful opinions were not valid, or, as in the case of our cinematographer, they were afraid of them. Over time, I've learned to try to vet these attitudes at the early interview stage.

To minimize the interruption of production and to keep up the energy of our rep company, Wendy and Lew got the gang together and taught them, very enthusiastically, to sing the new school song and our theme song, both of which Wendy and Lew had brilliantly written.

Wake up in the morning.
Feeling shy and lonely.
Gee, I gotta go to school.

I don't think I can make it.
Don't think I can take it.
I wonder what I'm gonna do.

But when I look around and see,
That someone's smiling right at me.
Wait!
That someone's talkin' to me.
Hey, I've got a new friend.

Everybody can succeed.
All you need is to believe,
Be honest with yourself.
Forget your fears and doubts.

Come on!
Give us a try,
At Degrassi Junior High!

Degrassi Junior High theme song
Lyrics by Wendy Watson, music by Lewis Manne

Meanwhile, Sari and I were in crisis mode. Sari got hold of Phil and found him in Kingston shooting a milk commercial. I'm not sure what exactly Sari said to him, but he drove back to Toronto at the end of the day.

I nervously waited. "We made a mistake," I said honestly to Phil when he finally arrived. "We should have hired you for this show."

Phil took a breath. "I made a mistake too," he admitted. "Much as I love the money and some of the creative of commercials, I miss you and the kids."

"All right," we said in unison. "Let's get back to working together."

We gathered the crew for our "second" start of production. I reminded the crew that our young cast needed to be treated with respect and professionalism. I told them to consider our cast as our student body and themselves as the faculty. Kit reminded me that I continued to sound like a school marm.

Production began, again, and Phil was awesome. Sari and Yan loved him. Kit, a little bit stung by his earlier hiring suggestion, quickly joined the "we-love-Phil" club. And, most importantly, the kids adored him.

It felt great to get back to our storytelling. Our serious subjects for the first season were underage drinking, parental abuse, adoption, bullying, and teen pregnancy. On the lighter side, we were having fun with vitamin pills being sold as drugs, bad date advice, a thwarted pornographic viewing, and the formation of our one-song-wonder rock group — The Zit Remedy. We wanted our stories to be frank but not sensational, accessible but not sanitized. We had much involvement from both of our broadcasters, who were supportive about our bold new take on teenage storytelling but understandably cautious.

As we approached our tenth episode, our broadcasters started to show genuine nervousness. Even though they had approved all script drafts, they had concerns about our choice to make a recurring character pregnant. They were starting to doubt if they could stand behind "It's Late," which by necessity acknowledged that a fourteen-year-old had had sex. They knew that we had done a lot of research to make the story as true as possible, but they were not sure their bosses and advertisers would be on side. They wondered if we should push this storyline off for a while.

Nooooo — not my favourite storyline!

To my knowledge there had been no TV show to date with an authentic portrayal of teen pregnancy. This story was not only important for our first season, but it would also be an ongoing story arc throughout season two and subsequent seasons. And, something we could never have foreseen in 1986, this storyline would provide the link between *Degrassi Junior High* and the 2001 reboot, *Degrassi: The Next Generation.*

Teen pregnancy was a subject very close to my heart. My younger sister, Barb, got pregnant at fifteen, and I saw firsthand how this changed her life. As Donald Hoppie had opened my eyes to stories of racial intolerance, and as Bruce had introduced me to the need for LGBTQ+ stories, my sister inspired me to talk openly about teen sexuality and pregnancy.

When Barb became pregnant, my parents' reaction was simply, "Good girls don't get pregnant. This has to go away." And what they meant was "Barb has to leave town — immediately." It was the early 1970s. Dad was involved with local politics and had aspirations to run for mayor. A convenient narrative was constructed. "Our daughter, Barb, will be staying with an aunt for a few months."

"This is not right," I said to my sister when we both realized she was being sent to a home for unwed mothers a few hundred kilometres away.

"I know," she agreed. "It sucks. Mum and Dad think I'm going to come home and pick up my life as though nothing ever happened. Well — I've got news for them. I won't."

Barb was determined to keep the baby. My parents were equally resolved that she would give it up. They believed it was in the best interest of all that the baby be adopted. Barb did not agree, and refused to sign the necessary papers. This stalemate lasted for months.

The day Barb returned home with her baby was a true testament to her strong resolve, and we welcomed a lovely, healthy baby boy, Patrick, into our family. When Mum and Dad met their first grandchild it was love at first sight. To this day, my parents are haunted by how they initially treated Barb's pregnancy based on the social stigma that surrounded it. They have since confided that, could they do it over again, they would have handled it differently.

My sister has also grown a lot since that time. She lives closer to our parents than the rest of us and is tireless in her support of them — driving them to appointments, helping with groceries and meals, and running errands. She's also an amazing mom to her three boys, and an exceptional grandmother to seven. Everyone knows when Grandma Barb is coming, as they hear the roar of her Harley-Davidson motorcycle before they see her. She's a biker gran with a big heart.

My heartache for Barb, back when she was a teenager, made me determined to tell our *Degrassi* teen pregnancy story, a story where Spike would keep her baby, and we could follow the consequences throughout junior high and high school. I needed to find a solution to the broadcaster's concerns.

★

When I was eleven, a travelling salesman stopped at our front door. He was not selling the usual vacuum cleaners, household multi-purpose brushes, or frozen meats. He was selling the future. With the offer of free lessons and a three-month loan of a 12 bass piano accordion, he reckoned I could be the next greatest thing in the world of professional accordion playing. I convinced my parents that this was an opportunity I shouldn't miss. When the trial three-month period ended, the salesman came back and declared that I showed extraordinary ability. He brought with him an expensive, new 120 bass accordion, and a contract to pay for it over time. I was thrilled — and then shocked and embarrassed when my parents asked if they might have a little time to consider this. A few days later, my parents sat me down for a family meeting. They had done some investigation and, for less money than an accordion, I could spend the summer in England, one month at each of my grandparents' houses. They asked me to choose between the accordion and the trip. "You're only eleven," Dad explained, "so the boat fare is half-price."

"Plus," Mum added, "a friend of ours is taking her two children to England for the summer, and she's happy to be your guardian for the crossings."

Only in hindsight have I come to understand that, in that moment, I learned a lot from my parents about producing. They had stopped me from making what they could see was a mistake. They did not say, "No — you obviously don't have the talent to be an internationally famous accordion player, you deluded

As an eleven-year-old, I spent my summer in England with various relatives and dogs.

young girl." Rather, they encouraged and empowered me to make my own choice. In the end, I made the choice they wanted, but I didn't do it to please them; I made the decision that I knew was the best one.

Now I wanted to adopt this strategy with my broadcasters: I would offer a choice to our executives that might settle their nerves about the pregnancy storyline — hoping, of course, that they would eventually come to the right conclusion.

★

The final scene of "It's Late" was written as Spike left the clinic with the results from her pregnancy test. (Yes, back in the 1980s, you could not get immediate, reliable pregnancy test results.) In the original script, she told her mom she was pregnant. To buy us time before making a final decision in the editing room, we offered to shoot two endings.

Shane looks on as Spike tells her mother two bits of news: 1. She is pregnant. 2. She is not pregnant.

Meanwhile, our editor, Eric Wrait, Kit's old friend and mentor, had a thought unrelated to the broadcaster concerns. Even though the script called for the pregnancy reveal (or non-reveal) to happen at the very end of the show, Eric suggested we move the reveal scene earlier and put the conversation in the school stairwell as the last scene. In the stairwell scene, Spike confides to Shane — the father of her child — that she doesn't want to be pregnant, that she's too young. This repositioning was brilliant, but only worked if we knew she was pregnant. It made for a thought-provoking ending. "Let's try it," I said to Eric.

Even though this did not play perfectly into my new plan, I explained to the broadcasters what we had done and reminded them we still had the old order and safety if necessary. They agreed to look at the current cut. CBC called the next day. They liked the new order and pregnancy choice. They approved the cut. We now waited for PBS's comments. Kate had convened a number of WGBH executives to watch the show with her. According to Kate, "There was much animated discussion." In the end, they approved the pregnancy choice and the new order of scenes, conditional on the show being accompanied by a teacher's guide for which they would pay.

The gamble with this bold storyline paid off — big time. In 1987, "It's Late" won our second International Emmy. Both broadcasters were ecstatic. They would each get their own statuette to add to their awards shelves. In our acceptance speech, Kit happily ad-libbed at the end, "We will call Spike's baby Emma, after the Emmys!" And we did, little knowing how long a screen life this new, tiny character would have.

We finished production of the rest of our thirteen-part season with relatively little internal drama. Now it was time to party.

We'd already held a celebratory boat bash a few weeks earlier. The parents and families of our young cast had been so supportive throughout production that we wanted to thank them. We rented one of the Lake Ontario party boats for the last evening of summer, just before real school started. All our kids, their parents, and their siblings were invited to attend, along with the crew. The event was

The controversial episode "It's Late" became a winner in many ways. Here Yan, Kit, and I celebrate our second International Emmy along with broadcasters Angela Bruce (CBC) and Kate Taylor (PBS).

so successful it became an annual event for the next six years. But now, with production officially wrapped, it was time for a crew-only party, no minors.

Kit and I invited the gang to our house. Of all the crew, Kit and I were definitely the oldest. Most of our team was in their early twenties and this was a first-time production job for many of them. They had worked hard, played the responsible role of "faculty," and were now ready to cut loose. Wine was abundant, served in large cardboard boxes with plastic spouts. Cheap beer was everywhere. Joints were rolled. Music blared as our home became a blowout, anything-goes party for all who had worked so hard throughout the season. I lost count as to how many folks might be in our hot tub, but I didn't care. I wasn't really sure what people were cooking in my kitchen, and I didn't even mind that water pistols had magically appeared and a chaotic soggy chase was underway throughout the main floor. We had wrapped on season one of *Degrassi Junior High*, and we all knew it was *great*.

As the party raged, I had a quiet moment to myself.

We did it, I thought. *We made our show. We're giving a voice to youth. And we have made very little compromise.*

With this happy thought, I flashed back to a lively breakfast meeting with Kit and Yan a few months earlier when writing the "It's Late" script. Over eggs and bacon, we pondered who we should get pregnant. We had narrowed it down to three options, Stephanie Kaye (Nicole Stoffman), Caitlin (Stacie Mistysyn), or Spike (Amanda Stepto).

"Stephanie is too obvious," Kit asserted.

"I'm not ready for Caitlin to have sex yet," I jumped in — then quickly apologized. "Sorry, I'm starting to sound like a broadcaster!" I smiled, but secretly knew my defence was a lie. My quick reaction was actually one of maternal protection. Stacie Mistysyn had been with me since the early days of *The Kids of Degrassi Street*, and my gut response was to protect her as though she were my daughter.

"Well," said Yan, "Spike it is, then. And she's the best choice. Up to this point, we know little about her character. I say we go with her."

So, as simply as that, Spike became pregnant.

Oh, if only it were that easy in real life.

CHAPTER SEVEN

FRIDA AND ME

I heard the back door close as Kit came home. It was Sunday evening in early autumn 1985. A few days earlier, as the fall chill filled the air, I had traded in my open-toed sandals and halter tops for soft leather boots and comfy sweaters. A warm glow filled the living room from the fire I had lit, and Kit joined me for a glass of wine. He had just returned his two daughters to their mother's house after we had shared a delightful weekend with the girls, including a visit to Buffalo to visit the Albright-Knox Art Gallery. There we enjoyed the Picassos, the Impressionists, and the Rauschenbergs. The highlight, of course, was the mirrored room. I loved hanging out with Kit's girls, but it didn't stop me from a feeling of emptiness. "Kit," I began hesitantly as we both watched the fire, "I've always imagined that someday I would be someone's mom. I'm not getting any younger and am just thinking . . ." I trailed off as I saw that Kit had gone somewhere else.

I knew this would be a difficult conversation. When Kit and I first got together, he revealed that he'd had a vasectomy. After the birth of his second daughter, he and his former wife had made the decision that two children were enough. As I started to pour another glass of wine, trying to fill the silence, Kit looked at me. "I've been doing some research," he offered. "And I've seen a specialist; I think that my vasectomy might be reversible."

I stopped pouring.

"I know this is something you've wanted for a while, and I have an appointment for next month."

"Kit! You'd do that for me? For us? That's incredible!" With that, I abandoned my wine and threw my arms around him. I had not expected this. Our friends Wendy and Lew were the next to know the news. Over a joint, Lewis reassured Kit that all would work out well.

"It's clear, man, you're going to Toronto East General Hospital — it's on Coxwell Avenue. Get it? Cocks-Well! You're going to be just fine."

And Lew's predictions were correct. Kit had a somewhat painful but successful operation. His sperm count was optimal. And then — we waited. Month after month. Painful period after painful period. My cramps were almost as unbearable as the monthly disappointment of no conception. Now it was my turn to see my doctor who referred me to a fertility specialist. After a number of tests, he gave me a tentative diagnosis. "You might have endometriosis," he said. "This will explain your painful periods and why you are having trouble conceiving."

"But why, how would I get this?"

"We're not sure. Endometriosis is a painful disorder where tissue that normally lines your uterus grows outside the uterus. It can be caused, among other things, by retrograde menstruation as well as the attachment of endometrial cells to latent scar tissue."

"Now we know what this is, we can cure it, right?"

"There is no easy cure. They do say that exercise can help."

"Exercise? I attend aerobics classes three times a week. I play tennis three to four times a week. I ride my bike regularly and I swim wherever possible. I *do* exercise!"

"Okay, I hear you. First, I'd like to confirm my diagnosis with a laparoscopy — go in with a camera and assess the extent of the damage. Sometimes, the very act of doing this can be therapeutic and clean up some of the lesions."

My first laparoscopy was scheduled for the day after we wrapped production on "It's Late." (I couldn't get away from the irony of how easy it was to make a TV character pregnant while I struggled.) Despite story concerns from the broadcaster, actual production of "It's Late" had gone well. We'd wrapped on time and on budget. The next day I packed my bag and headed for the hospital. The laparoscopy involved a general anaesthetic and an overnight stay. The end result? Yup, I had a good case of endometriosis. With the diagnosis came a number of plans of attack designed to clear up the chronic condition. I was prescribed numerous drugs; when one wasn't effective, another was tried. Some were anti-inflammatories, some a special combination of oral birth control, some male hormones. I remember various miserable side effects. Sprouting facial hair was something I was not thrilled about.

Meanwhile pre-production and production of season two of *Degrassi* began. When my schedule permitted, I made time to see a counsellor. "It's just not fair," I told her. "I always assumed that someday I would be a mom, but what with endometriosis and infertility, I feel empty — my life seems meaningless."

After a few sessions, where she tried various ways to bolster my sense of self-worth, she thought for a bit and said, "Linda, I feel like you are holding onto something deep in your subconscious, and together we have not been able to unlock it. I'd like you to see a colleague of mine. He works out of Oakville and is a therapist who works through hypnosis."

I smiled at the notion. "I'm really strong-willed and can't imagine allowing myself to go under."

"Just give it a try. It won't hurt."

A few weeks later, I parked my car in front of a bland three-storey walk-up in a nondescript part of town. Like the exterior of the building, the therapist's office was without character. It was scantily furnished. "You're going to have trouble with me," I warned him playfully.

He gave me a good-natured smile. "We'll see about that. Now lean back and get yourself comfortable."

I sank back into the well-worn wingback chair. *Hmm, he's got a lovely voice*, I thought.

Slowly, he moved a crystal on a chain and asked me to focus on it. I lightly drifted off. Then as I heard a light clap, I snapped back. "Wow," I said. "So that didn't work."

"Excuse me. You've been out for a while."

"Seriously? How long?"

"About twenty minutes."

"Wow, I thought you'd never get me under your spell."

"Oh, you weren't under my spell. You were under your own, your subconscious was talking." I looked at him somewhat skeptically. "I want you to think about scar tissue. You mentioned it — a lot."

I drove back along the highway trying to figure out if I'd just spent time with a genius or a quack.

As I arrived at the office, there was no time to continue that internal debate. Kit had his knickers in a twist about the latest schedule Sari had prepared for the upcoming episode. "I told you, I don't want to shoot the bowling alley in the morning — I won't be ready."

"But it's the only time we can access the location," Sari repeated patiently.

Yan was staying far away from this argument. He'd heard too many of them before. Plus, he had to have a new script ready in two days' time. Our receptionist handed me a bunch of yellow message slips. She giggled and acted like a schoolgirl as she dramatically pointed to the one on top. *Sex Delights called, and they want to discuss "lighting."* "Someone going to light up your life?" she whispered and gave me a cheeky wink.

"Sex Delights?" I queried.

"Shhh," she signalled. She didn't want the rest of the office to hear; she wanted my dirty secret kept between the two of us. Then it dawned on me: no, it wasn't Sex Delights, it was Sescolite, the lighting company I was dealing with for the renovation of our new house. My new fixtures were in. "Whoops, sorry!" she said with an embarrassed grin.

The next message was from PBS. They wanted to talk to me; they didn't like the twins' wardrobe. "Okay, I can deal with that in the morning." The next one had *URGENT* written in bold letters. *Please call Angela Bruce at CBC as soon as you get back.* I doffed my coat, grabbed a coffee, and dialled our broadcaster.

"We have a bit of a sticky situation," began Angela. "Seems one of the union reps is good friends with one of the parents of your cast. They both want you to make your production union. Our legal department is feeling the pressure. What can you do?"

Now, normally, with a CBC agreement, you'd think that a union requirement would be a foregone conclusion. But this was the early days of independent production — broadcasters and producers were all learning on the fly. Historically, on *The Kids of Degrassi Street*, we had been contracted as an acquisition, not a co-production with union requirements. For *Junior High*, we continued with the same form of contract. Technically, we were good. But here was the rub. My initial argument about not enough kids in the system wasn't as strong now. There were a number of young actors in the system — many we had trained — and now the union wanted to sign them. Later that afternoon, I got a call directly from the union. "Your company needs to sign on with us. You have unhappy parents. We don't want to have to shut you down. But you might leave us no choice."

With Sari's help, we hastily called a parents' meeting. Our parents had already bought into our unique infrastructure. They liked the idea of the PWT rep company with its workshops and contracts. They appreciated the PWT Foundation offering support for extra needs, and the RRSP for future financial stability. However, might the union now be a more attractive option?

We laid out to the parents that we were at a crossroads. A debate ensued. Overwhelmingly, the sentiment was similar.

"I did not sign up my child with PWT to join a union, I signed her up for the experience and the subject matter," said one parent.

"I believe in you guys. You treat my boy well, we don't want a third-party interfering," said another.

There was one dissenting voice — the original agitator — who wanted their child protected by a union. It was put to a parents' vote. With the exception of one, it was unanimous to retain the status quo. Out of respect for the one dissenting voice, we offered to write that character out at the end of the season so they could pursue union opportunities. The parent agreed with our option.

I then had to call the union rep back and to explain where we were at. "This is not a good situation," he stated firmly. "We are not happy with you or the CBC. But right now, as you remain a non-union shop, our hands are tied. You hire one person from our membership, even for a day, and we will shut you down immediately. We are watching you."

Next, I needed to call CBC. Even though they were not totally happy with the answer, they too recognized the validity of the current contract and, in less harsh terms, repeated the union warning. We'd dodged a bullet, for the short-term at least.

As I settled into bed that night, I tried to tell Kit what had transpired in my most unusual hypnosis appointment, three days earlier — everything at work had been so harried I hadn't been able to talk to him about it before now — but it was too late. Kit was already stoned and in another head space.

I had a dream, one that had been recurring: A cat. Lying on her side. Her malnourished kittens are gathered around her teats, but they can't feed. The whole inner section of her body is hollowed out. Where the nurturing organs should be is an open wound. Raw, open nerve endings are exposed to the air. She raises a slow paw, signalling the young ones to approach, but she can offer them nothing. Their hungry squeaks send chills through my body.

I sat upright in bed, suddenly awake. My head was full of thoughts of internal damage, of a reproductive void. *Scar tissue? Is my infertility due to scar tissue?* The fertility doctor had said endometriosis could be caused by "retrograde menstrual material and/ or scar tissue." I remembered the British doctors being worried about scar tissue after the crash. Could the accident be responsible for my infertility?

I was engulfed by memories that I'd spent years trying to bury.

*

Having dropped out of university, I began my hippie travels in the British Isles in the spring of 1968 with the intention of finding a short-term job to make enough money to head to France. There, I would bolster my high school French, then keep travelling east — Morroco, Turkey, the whole hippie trail, then Thailand, Japan, or however the spirit might move me. I was a few days away from heading to the continent as I worked my final shifts at a pub in the bucolic Yorkshire Dales in the north of England. A couple of nights earlier, I'd met Simon as he sat at my bar nursing a pint of bitter. In his mid-twenties, Simon already owned and operated two thriving clubs close to my pub, and had plans to expand to London. He was young, ambitious, and good-looking. I was wearing a particularly hot outfit that night: short white go-go boots and a colourful Mary Quant knock-off minidress.

"So, luv," he flirted. "What is it you miss most about Canada?"

The answer was easy: "Being at the cottage, swimming in the cool northern lakes — oh, and even more, waterskiing."

Our family did not have a cottage, but I had been invited many times to friends' summer places. With a sparkle in his eye, Simon said, "My club is closed Sundays. You get the day off. We'll go waterskiing at my family's place in the Lake District."

The night before our adventure, I had the closing shift at the pub, which meant I was done by 11 p.m. I went upstairs to my room and carefully selected outfits and swimwear for a day at the lake. We hit the road in the wee hours of Sunday morning. There were three of us in the car: me, Simon, and his friend Elliot, also in his mid-twenties, who was an investor in the clubs (Elliot's girlfriend couldn't get the time cleared from work on such short notice). We had our swimsuits, a picnic courtesy of my pub, a few beers from

Simon's club, and, as early morning turned into day, we had the sun on our side. All the ingredients collided for a perfect day off.

Simon's family getaway spot was well appointed, and the boat was fast. We took turns between driving and skiing. We swam, played cricket on the shore, then we swam, skied, and boated some more. We had a couple of beers at lunch and that was it. If we were drunk at all, it was from the feeling of the sun caressing our young bodies, the joyous sense of freedom from work, and the exhilaration of living loose. As the sun started to lower, Simon made us face the sobering reality — we needed to hit the road. We climbed into the car with our red faces and sunburned noses, our muscles aching from the pull of the water-ski rope. We had that blissful feeling of three new friends, physically exhausted, having shared the joy of a very special day off.

The drive home seemed much longer than the trip up. There was a lot of traffic, which made sense considering it was a Sunday and the weather had been unseasonably exceptional. We were all starting to feel the effects of the day's strenuous activities, coupled with the fact that none of us had slept the night before.

"Let's grab a cuppa," Simon said as we approached a pit stop.

As we got back into the car, I watched as Elliot awkwardly folded his long legs into the small back seat. I suddenly realized how uncomfortable he must have been scrunched up in the back and felt badly that I hadn't noticed this earlier. I offered him the passenger seat. He politely refused, saying, "You are the guest of honour, you sit in the front."

But Elliot had met his match in me. I felt terrible that I'd been so selfish and would not get back into the car unless he took the passenger seat.

"Bloody hell, mate. Do as she says!" barked Simon. And we were off for the final leg of the journey.

What happened next is not that clear. I remember thinking that we all needed to stay awake and alert. I positioned myself in the middle of the back seat, an arm resting on each of the driver and passenger seats, both legs to one side. (There were no such things as seat belts in those days.) This kept me close to the two boys and allowed me to keep a conversation going and keep them, particularly Simon, who was driving, alert.

At one point, I dozed off, then snapped awake and opened my eyes to see — for a split second — our car heading right into the path of a double-decker bus.

Was it five seconds, five minutes, or five hours later? I had no idea. As I fuzzily regained a level of consciousness, it hit me.

The smell. Putrid burning rubber.

The sound. A hysterical hissing like water being released from an overzealous pressure cooker.

The sight. Nothing: complete darkness.

In the back seat, the smells and sounds grew stronger and more nauseating. I was trapped. Relying on blind instinct, I pushed the front seat forward. Motivated by survival adrenaline, I pulled myself out of the wreckage.

"Oh God, someone's alive," said a voice.

I collapsed on the pavement.

And then the taste. Something metallic, in the back of my throat. My throat was being flooded. Please go away. Go Away. *GO AWAY!*

I was screaming.

I started to register a voice. A reassuring voice that was actually very close. *Is my head in someone's lap?* Yes, I was lying on my back, my head in an unknown lap. "You are going to be okay. You are going to be okay," the voice reassured me over and over.

I hung onto every repeated phrase. My screaming subsided. Only much later, when I got my soiled clothes back from the hospital, did I realize what a bloody mess that total stranger had cradled in his lap. I often think of him and his kind words. I think of my blood spilling onto his clothes and his hands. He was my lifeline. I wish I could have thanked him.

Those vivid images that I'd tried so hard to keep safely stored in the far recesses of my mind for so long, now overflowed in my head.

★

The next day I made an appointment with my new GP to discuss my growing thought that the accident and my infertility might be related. It had been over fifteen years since the crash, and I had no hospital records of the event that I could provide. She asked me to describe exactly what had happened to me during the accident. I shared what I remembered the British doctor said — it appeared that when the crash happened, my head flew forward and was cracked open on the gear shift and my legs were torqued ninety degrees from the upper part of my body. I shuddered.

"That sounds horrific," she sympathized. "It could well be that the crash caused your endometriosis, particularly if it happened close to the beginning of your period, when the full lining of the uterus could have been pushed backwards causing retrograde menstruation. Also, from what you describe, you would have had numerous internal tears and bleeding. The resulting latent scar tissue could provide a welcoming home for wayward endometrial cells."

Turning forty in the British Virgin Islands. My healthy exterior belies my inner turmoil.

So, it was a distinct possibility.

For the next couple of years, I continued various fertility workups. I became obsessed with my temperature, taking it daily and plotting the results on graphs. But with each failed attempt, my enthusiasm faded. As did Kit's.

Kit and I had a vacation planned to Tortola in the British Virgin Islands to celebrate my fortieth birthday. The day before we left for our trip, I flushed all my various infertility drugs down the toilet. On the day of my birthday, February 12, 1988, I awoke with one goal — I would swim forty lengths of the resort's Olympic-sized pool. With each length, I would allow my body and soul to be cleansed — to be released from the rigours of daily drug routines and obsessive thoughts. On every lap, I repeated the mantra, "I will never be a mother. I will accept my infertility." Kit watched from the sidelines. He later told me he felt helpless, like an audience of one watching a Greek tragedy unfold.

★

A couple of years ago, good friends of ours, Hunter and Valerie Thompson, wonderful art collectors and art patrons, invited us to a private viewing of selected works by Frida Kahlo. Hunter and Valerie, who have homes in both Toronto and Mexico, were instrumental in getting the works of this extraordinary Mexican artist to the Art Gallery of Ontario. I was familiar with some of Kahlo's works and knew to expect surrealistic elements in bright bold colour, depictions of her tumultuous life as wife (twice) of Diego Rivera, and many self-portraits. I did not expect that this exhibition would touch me so profoundly.

I found myself transfixed in front of a painting called *Henry Ford Hospital*. Frida depicted herself in hospital lying naked on a bed as she hemorrhaged. Her body was twisted. From the waist up, she was turned to the viewer, from the waist down she turned away by ninety degrees, twisted the way I had been in the crash. Six objects flew around her. The largest was a medical illustration of a male fetus. All six objects symbolized her pain and intense desire to understand why her body could not carry a baby. All objects were connected to her stomach by red, ribbon-like umbilical cords. Technically, this work depicted her anguish following a miscarriage. Although I never experienced a miscarriage, the emotions transmitted from this painting hit me at my core. I was moved by the heartbreaking sense of loss, pain, and confusion.

Frida Kahlo, *Henry Ford Hospital*, 1932. Oil on metal, 31 x 38.5 cm. Collection Dolores Olmedo Museum.

I knew that Kahlo had been in an horrific streetcar accident when she was eighteen. Her body was pierced by a metal handrail. It impaled her through her pelvis and punctured her abdomen and uterus. She created numerous intense and often macabre self-portraits capturing the anguish of her infertility. Her work confirmed for me what my doctor suspected. I was now convinced, at a deep, cellular level, that the car accident had caused my infertility.

In a strange way, this revelation was comforting. It didn't mean that my heart would no longer ache for the baby I would never hold. But it did give me a level of peace that had eluded me for years.

In a silent ceremony, in the privacy of my own mind, I crowned myself with a new title: "Linda Schuyler, Degrassi's Childless Matriarch."

CHAPTER EIGHT

PRIME TIME FOR THE KIDS

January 17, 1987.

Kit bustled about the house, putting a TV set in every room. I ran the vacuum throughout and generally tidied up as Sari made a shopping list for snacks and drinks. Tomorrow we'd be holding a screening party. *Degrassi Junior High* would have its national debut at 5 p.m. on the CBC. Our mood was buoyant. That morning, we had discovered our new show was the cover story for three of the national television guide books.

"Hilarity and heartbreak part of the curriculum for kids growing up in new series *Degrassi Junior High*," said *Star Week*.

"*Degrassi Junior High* picks up where the *Street* left off, teaching life's lessons and training young actors," reported *TV Guide*.

"No Glib One-Liners in Degrassi Junior High" was the headline for the cover story in *Broadcast Week Magazine*.

Not satisfied with three covers, early the next morning, Kit and I rushed to the corner store to buy copies of all the daily newspapers. We were particularly interested in what Jim Bawden of the *Toronto Star* would have to say. He had been such a fan of *The Kids of Degrassi Street* we couldn't wait to read his review.

We opened the paper to the Entertainment section and read:

DEGRASSI KIDS' SEQUEL TOO CUTE

How time flies is the first thought you'll have about *Degrassi Junior High*, the 13-part sequel to *The Kids of Degrassi Street*. It debuts tonight at 5 on Channel 5.

The sequel boasts 54 young cast members, many new faces to the series. Of the original kids, 12 auditioned for the second show and were accepted but some have come back with new names and characters. Confused? That's how I felt when I spied Susi who is now called Casey [sic] (played by Sarah Charlesworth.) . . .

The stated goal of *Degrassi Junior High* is to deal with such "meaty" issues as drugs and homosexuality. Growing up is hard to do, says the series. But I can never quite forgive these teenagers for growing up in the first place. They were such great, believable kids.

In addition to his nostalgia for our previous show, Jim criticized the "cutesy sitcom lines" and referred to our storylines as "forced and unreal." And I thought, *I should have seen this coming.* I was worried about the confusion factor of character names. Yet, it was me who recommended due process by allowing the kids to have input into the selection of their character names. At the party later, I tried not to let Jim's disappointing critical review spoil my spirits. After all, we believed in our show and were anxious to share it with homes across the country. And, as our publicist Kathryn kept reminding me, "Linda, we did get three covers!"

And then Monday morning, and the ratings. Not great.

Fortunately, as each week went by, our ratings inched up, both north and south of the border. And then, the day my beloved episode ten, "It's Late," was scheduled to air, we got a turnaround from the *Toronto Star*.

In a glowing review, Bawden said, "Sometimes a series starts slowly and gets better every week. That's the case with *Degrassi Junior High* . . . I've changed my original opinion, I like *Degrassi Junior High*."

Yes! Thank you, Jim.

★

With forward momentum building, we were able to secure development and then production deals for season two of *Degrassi Junior High*. As part of our second season deal, I tried to convince the CBC that our ratings could improve if we had a better time slot. My request was not considered.

And then something brilliant happened. Wunderkind Ivan Fecan came to town. Prior to returning to Canada, Ivan had spent two years as the VP of creative development for NBC. He was now the new director of English programming for CBC at the ridiculously young age of thirty-three. Back home in Canada, Ivan wanted to make his mark. Early into his tenure, I got a call. "Ivan Fecan would like to meet you."

I found my best business attire and headed downtown. Ivan's office had been freshly painted. I seem to remember off-white walls and some touches of pink and grey, an air of freshness and newness to the whole room. After the initial introductions, Ivan wasted no time getting to the point. "I've been watching your show. I like it. It's been badly programmed."

"Yes," I agreed enthusiastically.

Ivan continued. "I want to move you to Monday nights at eight-thirty, right after *Kate & Allie*."

"Oh," I muttered, less enthusiastically. "That's later than I thought. I was thinking maybe seven?"

Ivan looked at me like I might have two heads. "Seven p.m. is fringe time. Not all affiliates are on board. You want national prime time."

Prior to my coming to the meeting, Kit, Yan, Sari, and I had discussed the possibility of a prime-time offer. Yan put it poetically: "Our show has not been written for prime time. It's a good show, but we will disappoint the audience. They are looking for a steak dinner and we'll be offering hamburgers — very good ones, but hamburgers nonetheless."

Now I had to explain this to Ivan — without the food analogy. "But we haven't written and produced our show for prime time. We might disappoint that audience," I scrambled to say.

Ivan's expression now suggested I might have three heads. He slowly and patiently continued, "Trust me, a popular American sitcom will be a strong lead-in for you."

Now, you'd think that a smart producer would stop here and realize that a very wise executive has given a lot of thought as to how to best schedule her show. But I didn't stop.

"I'm afraid that you are putting unrealistic expectations on our little show," I blurted out.

Even more pointedly, Ivan patiently continued, "Linda, I am the scheduler, you are the producer. Can we each do our own jobs?"

"Well, could we make a deal? If we are not successful at eight-thirty, rather than cancel us, will you try us at seven?"

I'm not sure if Ivan's expression was one of complete exasperation or slight amusement. Either way, we had a deal. *Degrassi Junior High* would move to 8:30 p.m., with a fall-back plan of 7 p.m.

It would turn out, of course, that Ivan's instincts were correct, as so many of his programming choices would be over the years. And over those years he was a great supporter of me, my companies, and my shows. It would be Ivan and Susanne Boyce, both originally from CBC, who would later bring *Degrassi: The Next Generation* to CTV in 2001.

Ivan's arrival at CBC in the late 1980s marked the beginning of a glorious upswing for *Degrassi*. Once we'd moved to prime time,

Monday nights at 8:30 p.m., our audience grew stronger each week. In 1990, *The Fresh Prince of Bel-Air* became the lead-in to *Degrassi High*, and weekly we drew an average of 1.4 million viewers. At that time, a show in Canada (population of 27 million) was considered very successful if it broke through the one million mark.

To solidify the educational component of our show, PBS created teacher guides for each of our episodes. This expanded distribution to school boards, and libraries made *Degrassi* an integral part of the health and sex education curriculum in Canada and the U.S., providing young people with information that was otherwise unavailable. This was light years ahead of the sex education that I had received in high school.

*

When I had attended high school in Paris, Ontario, it was evident when the sex talk would happen. The small windows at the top of the wooden door to our classroom would be covered with black construction paper. When we entered the classroom — girls only! — we saw dusty pictures on the chalkboard of a penis and a vagina, although they were never identified as such. Our coach, Mildred McMillan, presided over this class. "Millie," of indeterminate age, was a legend at PDHS and a strong, no-nonsense fighter for girls. However, it was clear that she was much happier on the volleyball courts than in the sex-ed classroom. Her lecture was all about biology. The male member would arise, the female would open, the male member would enter. Egg and sperm needed to connect for a new life form to begin, much like it was with the flowers.

Fortunately, back in university for the second time in the early 1970s, I became aware of a new feminist publication, *Our Bodies, Ourselves*. This groundbreaking book called our biological parts by their correct names and gave the straight facts about sex and sexuality. It gave women permission to have thoughts about orgasms, masturbation, and sexual fantasies. It taught us how to hold a mirror between our legs and view our own vulva, clitoris, and the entrance to our vaginas.

In the late 1980s, as we developed and produced *Degrassi*, it was clear that sex education in the elementary and high school systems had not caught up with the forward feminist thinking of *Our Bodies, Ourselves*. The syllabus had progressed a little since my Millie days, but the focus was still on biology, at least with the body parts now properly named. There was no talk of how emotions fluctuated with the physical changes, no discussion on the impact of LGBTQ+ realities, and no guidance for protocols for sexual hookups and activities. *Degrassi* stepped in to fill that void. Over the years, I've been told by people, both young and old, how important that part of our show was to them. I would often get calls from old friends, thanking me for a particular episode and how it opened up lines of communication between them and their daughters or sons about subject matter otherwise difficult to broach. Sometimes I would receive this feedback from unexpected sources, as happened on a trip to L.A.

In the spring of 2015, after an extraordinary run of fourteen years, *Degrassi: The Next Generation* was cancelled on both CTV and TeenNick. Within a few days of this, I found myself with my writers on a plane headed to L.A. Almost thirty-five years since the launch of the first *Degrassi* episode, I would never have envisioned that once again I'd be pitching *Degrassi*. Yet there I was, preparing to pitch *Degrassi: Next Class* to Netflix.

We arrived promptly at 4 p.m. at the laid-back Netflix office, located in a three-storey walk-up building in the heart of Hollywood. Multiple awards adorned the walls. Two young executives ushered us into a modest boardroom as we waited for the third. We filled the time making small talk. I tried to read the room, but the young execs gave nothing away.

Finally, Brian Wright, who was an executive on the soon-to-be highly successful *Stranger Things*, rushed into the room out of breath and apologized for his lateness. Brian looked at me, extended his hand, and smiled. "So glad to meet you Linda, and full disclosure . . . I'm a Canadian and confess that I got all my sex education from *Degrassi*!"

The meeting was successful and we secured a forty-episode order for *Degrassi: Next Class*. We were about to become part of the amazing world of streaming, and simultaneously be released to over 180 countries in seventeen languages.

★

Back in the days of *Degrassi: Junior High*, we took our commitment to sex education very seriously. To help validate our agenda, we enlisted the services of legendary sex guru Sue Johanson. During the 1980s, Sue, a therapist and sex educator, became popular with audiences young and old for her long-running, straight-talking, phone-in show, *The Sunday Night Sex Show*. Sue joined our show as a consultant behind the scenes and as on-camera personality Dr. Sally. Dr. Sally makes her first appearance in "Great Expectations," when Yick (Siluck Saysanasy) and Arthur (Duncan Waugh) call her show to tell her that Arthur had a "leak" during the night, and he doesn't understand why. "Oh," chuckles the amiable Dr. Sally, "it's perfectly normal — you were having a wet dream!"

Arthur and Yick call Dr. Sally. Both actors found this scene hilarious and had trouble getting through their takes without cracking up. Duncan had a very different response when the scene aired.

This scene caused unintended consequences for us. The day after the show aired, Duncan's mother called me. "Duncan came home in tears today," she said, holding back her own tears. "The kids at school laughed at him and teased him because he didn't know what a wet dream was. They think that Duncan, the actor, is the same as his character, Arthur."

Kit, Judy, and I immediately put our heads together. We developed a theory called the X Factor. The X Factor was the invisible, protective space our actors needed to build around themselves to separate themselves from their character. Judy put the cast through a variety of exercises and role-playing. She had the actors engage in conversations with their imaginary characters. In the follow-up discussion, it turned out other cast members had dealt with similar blurred lines. Nicole Stoffman (Stephanie Kaye/Kobalewscuy) said she would often get annoyingly random strangers chanting at her, "All the way with Stephanie Kaye!" Amanda Stepto (Spike) shared that some kids made fun of her pregnancy storyline and had called her a slut. She found this frustrating and hurtful, as she herself hadn't even had sex yet. On the flip side, Pat Mastroianni (Joey Jeremiah) told us how his fictional character actually helped his social standing in school. In a 1989 CBC interview, Pat said, "Back in Grade 9, I was a total wimp, loner, loser, nerd . . . when I started *Degrassi* my confidence [built] up . . . I'm more confident, you know . . . I'm more studly!" These incidents were all touchstone reminders of the responsibilities we had undertaken by casting age-appropriate actors.

★

In our office, fan mail was rolling in. It was the days of snail mail and our mail carrier daily arrived with sacks of it. As well as letters, we received teddy bears, baby clothes, and blankets for Spike's baby. Part of me found all this attention exhilarating and celebratory. On the other hand, as I gently held one of the little stuffed animals, a gift for a fake baby, I couldn't help but think of my own unborn child.

Our cast loved receiving their fan mail, and we had to come up with protocols for how to respond. Requests were also arriving for our cast to participate in various community activities, fundraisers and industry events. Through WGBH Boston, our cast made many appearances in schools, libraries, and malls in multiple states throughout the U.S. In Canada, we were invited to special events in most provinces and the Yukon. And, thanks to the stellar distribution efforts of Isme Bennie, we were now broadcast in over forty countries around the world and receiving international requests for appearances.

When Amanda Stepto, accompanied by Kathryn Ellis, took a publicity trip to England, they visited Covent Garden. Amanda, dressed in her usual punk style and signature spiked hair (her own hairdo that we co-opted for the show), was asked by an American tourist if he could get a picture of a "real British punk." Amanda laughed and said she was from Canada. Then the young man suddenly recognized her. "Oh my God, you're Spike! That's even better. I watch your show every week!"

Similarly, when Kit and I, along with Stacie Mistysyn and Pat Mastroianni, were invited to Sweden and Denmark, we had a very hectic schedule of publicity appearances. When we had a small window of free time, we took the opportunity to go

Me, Pat, and Amanda at the airport after a successful publicity trip. The scariest part of these adventures was keeping track of everyone's tickets and passports.

for a swim in Copenhagen's large, sun-drenched public pool. As we climbed out of the pool, a small shriek was heard a few feet away. The shriek became a kerfuffle, and before we knew it, we were surrounded by a soggy gang of Danish teenagers, desperately calling for pens to get autographs. We were all impressed that Stacie and Pat, in bathing suits and with wet stringy hair, were recognized so far from home.

★

Back in Canada, as the year was drawing to a close, we were getting excited to attend the third annual Gemini Awards, honouring achievements in Canadian television. Earlier, when the call for entries came out, we made the bold decision to enter the category Best Dramatic Series. The previous year, we had won as Best Children's Series, but now that we were airing in prime time, we thought we would take a chance in the top overall category. On the awards night, we held a "champagne and Shirley Temple cocktail reception" at Kit's and my home, then headed to the Metro Toronto Convention Centre for the gala event. It was a spectacular night. We swept the ceremony with a directing award for Kit, an acting award for Pat Mastroianni, the inaugural Multicultural Award, and we won for . . . Best Dramatic Series. As we made our jubilant way into the afterparty, Dayo Ade (B.L.T.) scooped me up in his arms and carried me into the dining hall.

There, our youthful energy and giddy excitement was met with disdain. There were many disgruntled nominees that night who were extremely unhappy to have been eclipsed by not only a youth show, but a non-union one as well. The pushback continued long after the night — and gained momentum when we again won Best Dramatic Series the following year. A couple of years later, the Academy created a new category for youth programming.

Our heady night of wins coincided with the wrap of season three of *Degrassi Junior High*. As our audience and reach had grown, so had the needs of production. The size of our cast was

Pat Mastroianni, Dayo Ade, and I celebrate our incredible night of Gemini wins, 1988.

In 1989 we won again for best dramatic series, and Stacie Mistysyn (Caitlin) took home the Gemini for best performance by an actress in a leading role.

expanding, and our stories were requiring more varied locations. Our four classrooms at Vincent Massey Junior School were bursting at the seams. We need a new location. In a bold creative move, on what would become the last episode of *Degrassi Junior High*, we created a dramatic finale. "Bye-Bye Junior High" had all our characters, dressed in their prom finest, hurriedly ushered out of their year-end dance. They stood in front of the school and watched in awe as the school burned down. I call this a bold decision, because it was not savvy. We had no idea where we might find a new location, and we were going to need one in a few short months. Then, serendipity intervened.

Each year, we were fortunate to have a co-op student from one of the local colleges work with us in production. In late spring, David Yonson, our intern at the time, invited me to attend his graduation. Once the formal part of the graduation ceremony was concluded, the chair of the department, Don Gray, told us he had some exciting news that he wanted to share in the form of a film that he had made.

The film started out very slowly as it outlined, in great detail, the history of Centennial College. I wondered if I might be able to quietly slip out of the auditorium unnoticed, until I spotted the shots of a building that I knew well: the old teacher's college at Carlaw and Mortimer. It was in this building where I'd worked with other like-minded teachers a few years back to start the Association for Media Literacy. This was also where I'd conducted the first auditions for *The Kids of Degrassi Street*. Don's film explained that Centennial had just bought this building and it would be the new home for their growing media studies department.

"Will students start classes there this fall?" asked one of the grads as the film ended.

"Ah, there's a bit of a glitch," Don said. "Before we can be ready for students, we need to undertake rather extensive renovations. At this point we don't have the budget for that. But . . . we are working on an aggressive fundraising campaign."

As the festivities wrapped up, I waited patiently till Don was free. "Don," I started, "I think I have a proposition for you that could work well for both of us."

CHAPTER NINE

A Fresh New Start

K it, Yan, Sari, Judy, Laura Vickers (our outreach coordinator), and I couldn't believe our luck. We were standing near the top of Carlaw Avenue, a quiet, tree-lined street in east-end Toronto, staring at the old home of Toronto's Teachers' College. Built in 1955, the large two-storey rectangular building, with multiple windows, was a stark contrast to the classic red brick architecture of the 1920s that had provided the home for *Degrassi Junior High*. Using our own keys, recently given to us by our landlord, Centennial College, we let ourselves in the front door to find an imposing foyer with a grand ramp connecting the first and second floor. Kit spied an old wheelchair beside the abandoned principal's office. "Hop in!" he offered mischievously. "Let's explore our new home."

Kit started to push me slowly up the ramp. In the upstairs hallway, he picked up the pace till we were running through the seemingly endless corridor. I lifted my arms upward, wind rushing through my hair. All this space was ours! Kit screeched to a halt at the end of the hall and turned right. He picked up speed down a new corridor. Another screech, another corridor. And another . . . and another. Recklessly, as I held on tightly, he pushed me down the ramp. At the bottom of the incline, we found Yan deep

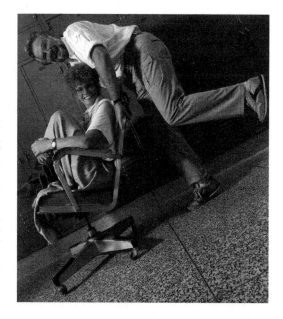

When Kit and I won a Toronto Arts Award, the photographer recreated a fanciful version of our fun "ride" through the halls of Degrassi High.

in thought. "I predict a lot of story is going to happen on this ramp," he mused. "In fact, right now I envision a scene during initiation where Joey Jeremiah will push a penny up the ramp with his nose, supervised by seniors."

We left Yan with his contemplations and began our exploration of the main floor. We discovered a full-scale auditorium, a large cafeteria with a working kitchen (*Our craft services and caterers will love this*, I thought), and multiple bathrooms. Perhaps the biggest discovery was the fact that the school, built in a rectangular shape, housed an interior courtyard in the centre with windows on all sides. This place was perfect for *Degrassi High*.

With our new space confirmed, we had renewed energy and a growing confidence from our broadcasters. Our cast shared our enthusiasm and couldn't wait to be called for the first read-through for *Degrassi High*. As they all assembled, we marvelled at what a bonus we got from our philosophy of "casting age-appropriate talent." Each year when our actors reconvened for the kickoff of the new season, it was like attending a family reunion. "Oh my, how much you have grown!" "Your voice has changed!" "When did you become blond?" "Whoa, what's that tattoo on your back!" Now, technically, our cast wasn't supposed to make hair and body-marking changes without checking with us first, but somehow that seemed to get forgotten, and only added to our authenticity.

The cast settle into their new home at Centennial College.

Our characters were still "our characters," but we got to watch them grow and evolve over time just as our real-life actors were doing. This was particularly evident as we started production on season one of *Degrassi High* with our older actors and bolder storylines.

Season one started with a two-parter, the aptly named, "A New Start." The story begins when Erica (Angela Deiseach) comes home from summer camp to find that she is pregnant. Erica's twin sister, Heather (Maureen Deiseach), is determined that her sister must keep her baby; after all, Spike had made it work. Erica does not feel ready. Through the device of identical twins, we were able, in a balanced way, to hear the voices of both pro-life and pro-choice. Having considered all the options, Erica makes the choice that is right for her. She chooses abortion.

This story, written by Yan in the late 1980s, would not have been possible without the tireless work done by second-wave feminists, from the early 1960s (when I was starting high school) to the 1980s.

Early in life, I apprenticed for a career as a homemaker . . .

. . . that ambition didn't last!

Kit and me on set with Christopher Charlesworth (Benjamin).

The original *Degrassi* gang in front of the iconic De Grassi Grocery (a real store). When the sign fell down in a storm we paid for repairs.

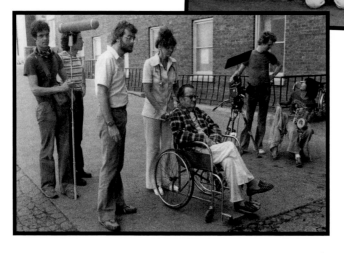

Working as extras, marathon pianist Jimmy Montecino and I play elderly patient and nurse in *The Kids of Degrassi Street* episode "Cookie Goes to Hospital."

Camping at Wasaga Beach with Kit, Bruce, and his dogs in our company VW van. I had hand-painted the Playing With Time logo and name on the side.

With writers Yan Moore and Susin Nielsen unloading supplies from our new VW van. (The red one died.) This time our logo was professionally designed and painted, but that couldn't disguise the multiple bangs and scratches.

The *Degrassi* kids are off the street and attending junior high.

Ever the versatile extra, here I play a teacher — not really a stretch!

ABOVE: On stage at the 1988 Geminis with the whole cast of *Degrassi Junior High* the night we won the inaugural Multicultural Award (now the Canada Award). Back in 1974, it was a multicultural grant that allowed me to make my first documentary, *Between Two Worlds*.

Celebrating our second International Emmy, NYC 1987, Phil and I find a new use for the table centrepieces.

In Munich, 1992, accepting our second Prix Jeunesse for "Bad Blood," *Degrassi High*.

Fan mail poured in from countries all over the world — Belgium, Israel, Ivory Coast, Jamaica, France, Australia, and Algeria to name a few. *Degrassi* fans are the best! Multiple boxes of fan mail are kept in the Media Commons Archives, at the University of Toronto.

ABOVE: On the set of *Degrassi High* with Dayo Ade (B.L.T.).

LEFT: Pastor Gene Hall is not a *Degrassi* fan.

CHRISTIAN-PATRIOTS

RACE MIXING IS WRONG

PASTOR E.S. (GENE) HALL
BOX 258, SNELLVILLE, GA 30278

MOST PREACHERS FAIL TO PREACH THIS
TRUTH. BUY RESEARCH BOOK $2.00
RACIAL LOYALTY KEEPS ANGLO-SAXONS FREE OF BREEDS

Bible Studies, Instructions
Publications, Information.
*Member of: The American
Colonization Society, Inc.

King James Version, Published in 1611 *
To Our Identity Kindred Around The World.
"...congress shall make no law respecting an establishment
of religion, or prohibiting the free exercise thereof;.." .* PROTECT UNTO DEATH *

"RACIAL LOYALTY KEEPS IDENTITY PURE AMONG OUR NATION"
CHRISTIANS ARE MORAL RACISTS OR IMMORAL RACE-MIXERS

29Jan.1990

Degrassi High
P.O. Box 2222-D6
South Easton, Ma.02375

"Quality Program"????????

OF THE MOST IMMORAL KIND OF BRAINWASHING OF IMMORALITY, IS MY OPINION
OF YOUR TV FILM.

Shame be upon you. Did you have your daughter play the part of kissing
the ███ boy? Or was it your son, the ████? The Bible calls them,
the ████, look in ACTS 13:1 for this truth, so it is only natural to use
this name.

The Bible teaches and commands RACE SEPARATION. Why do you advocate,
and promote mixing? If you do not know this truth, send a donation for
the Bible research book and learn truth.

Race-mixing is a sin, and creates mix-breeds, which the Bible calls
BASTARDS:"DEUTERONOMY 23:2. Shame be heaped upon you, the weight of
this problem will be heavy on your Soul, if you still have one. Maybe,
the buzzards laid you on a log and the Sun hatched you to cause such
terrible sins, the young must be taught truth, not lies.

Please stop such, change your ways, improve your life and help improve
the life of others. TEACH:"VIRGINITY".

In Jesus name and teachings.

Pastor Gene Hall
Pastor Gene Hall

RECEIVED 3/27/90
RESPONDED ____
LOGGED ____
DATABASED ____

*BREEDS ARE BASTARDS/OUTCASTS, NOT ACCEPTED BY CHRISTIANS:*DEUTERONOMY 23:2*

MIXING UP THE DEGRASSI GENERATIONS

LEFT: Spike and baby Emma. Emma (named after our Emmy award) becomes the link from classic *Degrassi* to *The Next Generation*.

LOWER RIGHT: Siluck Saysanasy (Yick Yu), with Cassie Steele (Manny) and Miriam McDonald (Emma), takes on a new role as talent coordinator on *Degrassi: TNG*.

Two generations of *Degrassi*.

Erica (Angela Deiseach) makes her way to her abortion appointment. This story in the late 1980s would not have been authentic without the presence of protesters.

In fact, most of our early *Degrassi* storytelling owed its legacy to the fearless crusaders who championed women's control of their own reproductive rights, abortion, and issues of domestic violence and gender inequality.

★

Shooting in our new location was a dream, but not without its challenges. As our cast were aging up, their school studies did as well. Our tutors were busy keeping up with the cast's real school curriculum, including tests and exams that needed to be administered on set. Sometimes, cast members could not be excused from their regular school for an exam, so our production schedule would need to shift to allow them to attend their real school.

Our bold storylines required much research and debate, both internally and with our broadcasters, which put additional strain on our writing department. Yan got stellar support from Susin Nielsen and various freelancers, but he continued to work around the clock.

Kit set the directing bar high when he rolled camera on "A New Start." He was proud of his work but struggled to keep up the quality with the relentless demands of ongoing production. We augmented the directing department with John Bertram and Eleanore Lindo. Both directors were hardworking and had tremendous respect for our show and young cast. But it was a no-win situation for Kit. He couldn't do all the episodes himself, but when he handed over the reins to others, he was highly critical of everything they did.

I thrived on all the activity. I likened series production to the diagram of the pig in the python. The season would begin quite calmly with the exciting period of development when storylines were arced out for all the episodes. Then scripts would start to be written. As these scripts ramped up into pre-production, other script writing started. Then production began. At this point, writing, pre-production, and production were all in play. Then post-production would be added, followed by mixes and packaging. For a period in the middle of the production season, all departments would be working at full capacity. At this apex of the python diagram, I would be in full air traffic controller mode, working to ensure a safe take-off and landing for all episodes. As production approached the end, the early activities would start to drop off — first writing, then pre-production. By the end, only post was working. While I marvelled at how efficiently the pig-in-the-python production model operated, I couldn't deny the fact that it was exhausting. Exhilarating, but exhausting.

By the time we'd completed post-production on the final episode of the season, Kit, Yan, and I felt like the title of our finale episode: "Stressed Out"! We continued to be proud of our show, but the three of us were drained — tempers flared and meaningless arguments sprang up. Kit headed to our country place in Grafton, Ontario; Yan retreated to the sanctity of his own home; and I took refuge at our east-end Toronto bungalow. Kit and I had been together for almost fourteen years, and the strain of being partners in life and business was wearing on us both. I wondered how much longer we could juggle the two.

I appreciated the opportunity to have some "me" time. I signed up for an intermediate tennis clinic at my club, enrolled in a Japanese cooking class with Sari, and started a new knitting project — a fisherman's rib-stitched afghan. As I sat alone at night, with the sound of my clacking knitting needles, my mind wandered. *How is it that even with our shared interests and common goals, Kit and I end up fighting and snapping at each other?* I knew Kit harboured a lot of resentment for the fact that his family had been abandoned by his dad when Kit was only a toddler. His mother had been a war bride; she had left her native England with her Canadian lover and quickly had two boys close in age, Kit being the younger. Her married relationship was abusive. She made her way back to England to live with her authoritarian parents. Kit's grandfather was particularly demanding of the two young boys. Kit's brother dealt with the strict environment by challenging rules and channelling James Dean. Kit became the "good boy" and resented his role. He was further deeply hurt when his idol, his teenage brother, died in a motorcycling accident.

Even though I understood the root of Kit's resentment for authority and his fear of abandonment, I couldn't understand why I was so often on the receiving end of his anger. Did he see me as an authority figure? He often referred to me as a "school marm." Was he afraid I was going to leave him, and he wanted to strike first? I also didn't know how I could continue to cope with Kit's frequent mood swings and contradictory behaviours.

I could only assume that during this same period, with his "alone" time, Kit was asking similar questions about me and our relationship. I also knew that he was stoned on a daily basis, as was confirmed by his many rambling, and often incoherent, telephone calls to me.

After a few weeks, Kit and I regrouped for Christmas and the premiere of *Degrassi High* on television. Time had been a good healer and as the show started, our differences began to fade away. We let the show wash over us and enjoyed our press.

Lynne Heffley of the *L.A. Times* wrote, "Degrassi — still proving itself one of the gutsiest series on television . . . a classroom discussion of abortion, talks with unwed mother Spike and with a clinic counselor, give both sides of the issue passion and weight. . . . That's the strength of this funny/serious series. What happens to each character will be referred to in the future — there's no sitcom amnesia at work . . ."

In the *Toronto Star*, Antonia Zerbisias called us "a gutsy show, particularly in light of the current political and emotional climate."

The exhaustion, the anger, and the lashing out had all been worth it. Both CBC and WGBH renewed *Degrassi High* for a second season. In short order, I was able to get our investors, both public and private, to commit to a new season. Our cast and crew were eager. Yan was excited about developing more stories. I was just so happy with our show, our stories, and our process, I couldn't wait to do more. But — Kit had doubts.

I knew that Yan, Kit, and I were a great creative team. And I also knew that despite Kit's tantrums and venomous thoughts about broadcasters, investors, executives, and anyone in authority, he really, deep down, enjoyed his job as director. But ever since the first production day of "Ida Makes a Movie," I'd had to walk a fine line between what Kit said and what he would do. His outbursts, usually kept private, were becoming more frequent — and more public.

I decided the three of us needed a weekend getaway — a chance to walk in the country and discuss, in an easy and open manner, our futures; an opportunity to listen to each other's concerns and explore common ground. Kit and I headed to the country on Friday night, and Yan planned to join us on Saturday morning.

On the Friday evening, Kit and I had one of our best talks ever. He shared with me that he thought I got to do all the "fancy" stuff. I'd fly to Boston for WGBH meetings, spend time at the CBC head office, fly to Ottawa to talk to funders and politicians, attend conferences in Florida, L.A., Munich, and New York. He was feeling left out. He felt marginalized. This was a revelation to me. I knew how much he hated those kinds of meetings and thought he was happy that I took them on.

Kit also made an interesting observation about me. He said he found it very hard to be on the sidelines of my life as I struggled to come to terms with my infertility. Kit called it my "obsession" and said that I was burying myself in work to hide from my true feelings.

There was truth in both these observations.

When Yan arrived the following morning, he was pleasantly surprised at how well Kit and I were getting along. Yan had always been sympathetic to my fertility struggles. However, he did venture to share that Kit might have a point about my zealous work ethic.

Yan was surprised to hear that Kit resented me doing all the "fancy" stuff. Yan told me he was grateful I took it on, as he would most definitely not want that end of the business. He acknowledged that Kit might feel marginalized, but at the same time, couldn't imagine Kit doing that part of the job.

Yan shared how much he loved to write and how much he enjoyed our process of the "daily draft." He said he appreciated Kit's and my input into the scripts, even though at times he would get fed up with Kit constantly asking "why."

Kit, me, and Yan at a daily draft script meeting. I often found myself caught in the middle.

All in all, it was an open and positive quasi love-in.

Then came Sunday. It started well enough. After breakfast, we asked ourselves the blunt question: "Are the three of us committed to a second season of *Degrassi High*?" Before directly answering it, I promised to involve Kit in more of the "fancy" stuff. In fact, I offered, "You know, I'm having dinner with Angela Bruce tonight in the Beach. She's anxious to hear the results of our retreat. Why don't you join us?"

Kit agreed it would be good for him to get more involved on the broadcaster side and tonight would be the perfect way to start. He also promised Yan that, though he would still ask the whys, he would try for a "nicer" manner. Yan said he was just happy to keep writing. By lunchtime, we had a consensus that the three of us would commit to one more season. This would most likely be the last one, but we would go forward. We hugged it out.

As we each had our own car, we drove separately back to the city. We had done a lot of talking, and more importantly, a lot of listening. I was touched by Kit's honest assessment of feeling marginalized and promised myself I'd work at including him more. He was my partner and I needed to work harder at the relationship.

Kit took an extraordinarily long time coming home. He walked through the door just as I was getting ready to leave for dinner with Angela. "Hurry and get changed," I encouraged him. "I don't want to be late."

"No need for that. I've had time to think in the car. I think you are good at this broadcaster stuff. I don't want to spoil a good meal by trying to play nice. You go."

"Oh." I was a little surprised. "Maybe you could come and just join us for dessert once all the business stuff is out of the way?"

"Yes, that might work. I'll probably see you later then."

Angela was already seated by the time I got to the restaurant. "I've ordered some wine," she said. "I'm hoping to celebrate?"

"Then let's change that wine to champagne — my treat!"

Angela gave me a broad smile. "Ivan will be thrilled. He wants to keep your show in that same great prime-time slot. It works so well with *Fresh Prince* as a lead-in. And WGBH will be happy too. They've been calling to see if we had any news. This is splendid."

"Cheers!" We simultaneously said, while clinking our glasses. We enjoyed a pleasant meal together, catching up on each other's news. We talked about the implications of the demonstrations in Tiananmen Square, about the mess of the oil spill from the Exxon Valdez and, of course, we chatted about our cats.

As we looked through the dessert menu, my attention was drawn to the front door. Even from a distance, as Kit approached, I could tell he was stoned.

"Kit!" Angela exclaimed. "I'm so happy to see you and so glad for your good news."

Angela, a fellow Brit, had a soft spot for Kit even though she found him challenging. She knew he was a great director and was happy to indulge him as an artiste. Kit grumpily sat down and judgmentally eyed the almost-empty champagne bottle. "Been celebrating something?"

"Of course," chirped Angela. "We're getting a new season of *Degrassi*!"

"Well, if that's what Linda told you, then I guess that's what we'll do. Linda always does what she wants."

The sarcasm was not lost on Angela. She looked at her watch and decided to forgo dessert, something about needing an early start in the morning. She promised to call me the next day to sort out production contract details.

"What was that all about?" I spat out through gritted teeth.

Kit gave me a big, stoned smile. "It's true. You got what you wanted. You wanted this weekend to get the go-ahead for production and you . . . GOT . . . WHAT . . . YOU . . . WANTED. Like you always do. You manipulated me and Yan, and now we have to do a year's work that we don't want to do."

My face burned as people looked our way.

"Well then, don't work. We'll manage without you. Probably be better that way anyway."

"Oh, you can't do that, you know I'm a key man on the contract."

I walked out of the restaurant and headed home. We slept in separate rooms — again. The next morning, I got a somewhat lame apology. Too little, too late. The Angela dinner incident was a turning point for me. I felt undermined, disrespected, angry. I vowed I would get myself out of this relationship once we finished our new production season. I also pledged that our next season would be the best ever.

CHAPTER TEN

School's Out — For Good?

I was walking on eggshells. I had gone forward and signed the contracts with CBC and WGBH for *Degrassi High*'s second season but had no idea where Kit's head was at. I was reminded of the first day of production of *The Kids of Degrassi Street*, ten years earlier, when Kit had thrown down his script and said he couldn't do the contingency plan. Yet he did. He showed up and got the job done — well done, in fact. "Will the same be true this time?" I wondered.

We had a lot of *Degrassi* episodes under our belt since "Ida Makes a Movie" had aired in 1980. In six years, we'd done twenty-six episodes of *The Kids of Degrassi Street*. *Degrassi Junior High* began production in 1986 and in three years we had completed forty-two episodes. The first season of *Degrassi High* saw fifteen new episodes produced, giving us a total of eighty-three. Would Kit find a way to participate in the new thirteen episodes that our broadcasters were asking for in *Degrassi High* season two?

Without waiting for an answer to my unspoken questions, Yan and I began work on the script for our season opener, another groundbreaking storyline. In the backdrop of "A New Start" in the previous season, we had introduced the school bullies, Dwayne (Darrin Brown), Tabi (Michele Johnson-Murray), and Nick (George Chaker). These characters drifted through

Dwayne (Darin Brown), one of *Degrassi's* bullies, flexes his muscles in front of an intimidated Scooter (Christopher Charlesworth).

storylines of that season creating misery for many of our regular characters, especially Joey Jeremiah. For the opening of the new season, we created a twist with one of our bullies.

In the early 1980s, a virtual tsunami had swept through gay communities in Canada and the U.S. Young, healthy, gay men were suddenly and inexplicably dying. The AIDS epidemic had hit. I was personally affected on two fronts. A wonderful friend of mine, the gentle and empathetic guidance counsellor whom I had met during my teaching time at Earl Grey, was diagnosed with AIDS. This was particularly difficult for him, for like Bruce, he was not "out" at school. With failing health and a growing unease about the board discovering his sexuality, he resigned from the job he loved. A few months later he would succumb to the deadly disease.

At the same time, I had a tearful conversation with my friend Nancy Sinclair. Nancy had taken a leave of absence from Earl Grey to become our on-set tutor. She was a powerful mix of patience and firmness and wouldn't let our cast fall behind in their studies.

Nancy was also a single mom who adored her teenage son, Aaron, who was charismatic, artistic, and charming, as well as "out and proud." Nancy was devastated when she shared with me that Aaron had AIDS. It was 1989. *Degrassi* needed to tell an AIDS story.

A coalition called People With AIDS (PWA) had recently been formed in Toronto to help provide practical and direct support services for people living with AIDS and HIV. I contacted PWA, wondering if I could call on them for some story advice. I wasn't prepared for their enthusiastic response. "You want to do a story on AIDS, on *Degrassi*, on TV, in prime time? For real?"

"Yes," I confirmed, and proceeded cautiously. I was expecting some pushback on my next point. "We are also considering making our main protagonist straight."

A small hesitation, then even more enthusiasm. "We'll help you however we can." PWA had been trying to build awareness that HIV and AIDS were not strictly limited to the gay community. Showing a straight character with HIV would help further their educational agenda.

Part of the outreach offered by PWA included workshops in the schools. A couple of PWA members living with AIDS and/or HIV would sit down with a class and talk openly about the realities of the disease. The workshop included building awareness that the disease was not limited to the gay community and could be transmitted within the heterosexual community. Our story approach dovetailed perfectly with their agenda. PWA admitted that they had a problem and not many schools had taken them up on their workshop offer. Too many parents and teachers didn't want a PWA member near their kids; they harboured the belief that if their child or student came in contact with an HIV-positive person, they would be at risk to contract it themselves. This was, of course, a myth, but a widely held one at the time. Yan and I decided to include a PWA workshop in our script. We wanted to explore the myths and dispel them.

I was excited when I read Yan's first draft. Even though he and Kit hadn't spoken for months, I let Yan know that I would like to share it with Kit.

"We all know that, at the end of the day, Kit is driven by a good story," I said to a dubious Yan.

"Fine," he agreed reluctantly. "But I'm not taking any of Kit's comments."

"Okay," I negotiated. "If Kit has comments, and they are good, I will relay them to you directly — deal?"

"Deal."

I felt like I was back in my parent's home at suppertime and my brother and I were not talking. "Mum, will you please ask Tony to pass me the rolls?"

"Dad, would you please tell Linda I'll pass the rolls to Mum, once I have helped myself." Yes, the executive conversations at our office had sunk to that type of juvenile level. This was in stark contrast to the sophisticated stories we were creating.

Later that afternoon, Kit walked into my office and unceremoniously threw the script down on my desk and surprised me by saying, "Brilliant — let's do it!"

I was pleased, but at the same time knew what the realities of this season would be. I would need to be the intermediary between Kit and Yan. I didn't like this, but I knew it was the only way to get the job done.

Our opening storyline, "Bad Blood," was sensitive and topical. One of our bullies, Dwayne, who enjoyed a rather active sex life over the summer, has tested positive for HIV. He keeps this a secret until he is challenged to a fight in the boy's washroom by his nemesis Joey Jeremiah. Normally, Dwayne would handily win the fight, but he already has an open cut and wants to walk away from the altercation. Joey, surprised by this unusual behaviour, goads Dwayne till he breaks down and admits his health issues.

As our PWA consultants would continue to work closely with us during production, I wanted to make sure that our young cast would be comfortable around people with HIV and suggested we run our own workshop for our actors. When our parents heard about this, for the first time since the union incident in season one of *Degrassi Junior High*, I received pushback from a couple of them. They were concerned for the safety of their children. With the folks from PWA, we then planned to offer two workshops — one for our actors and another for their concerned parents. In the end, thanks to the beautiful presentation from Ken Campbell and Robert Hawke, we got total buy-in from both our young cast and their folks. We then hired Ken and Robert to play themselves in the "Bad Blood" dramatic version of the workshop.

During production of "Bad Blood," we all knew we were making an important episode. Despite the continued stony silence between Kit and Yan, everyone came with their A-game. We completed a standout *Degrassi* episode for which we received our second Prix Jeunesse as well as a number of other awards. I particularly liked the SHINE Award, which was presented to "honour *Degrassi*'s accurate and honest portrayal of sexuality."

*

One day, deep into production on *Degrassi High* season two, we got a surprise visit on set from our big boss, Ivan Fecan. Usually when a broadcast executive makes a set visit it is planned days in advance to accommodate busy schedules. But on this grey December day Ivan showed up unannounced and with a grim look on his face. "Have you heard the news?" he asked sombrely.

Having had a long day of dealing with the large and small issues of production, I, like the rest of my team, was unaware of what was happening in the outside world. The year was 1989 and none of us had cellphones with constant news updates. "There's been a terrible massacre at the École Polytechnique in Montreal. Fourteen women have been killed; others injured. It appears to have been the work of one man."

I sat down, feeling sick to my stomach. "But why?"

As we would eventually find out, the gunman was on an anti-feminist mission. The École Polytechnique, a renowned engineering school, had recently opened its registration to women. The gunman, who had applied unsuccessfully to the school, blamed his rejection on the presence of women. He took his revenge by killing fourteen of these women and then taking his own life.

In the late 1980s, mass killings were a rarity. It was ten years before the deadly high school murders at Columbine, which appeared to spark hundreds of school shootings across the U.S. in the coming decades. The horrors of the massacres at École Polytechnique and Columbine would deeply colour development of *Degrassi: The Next Generation* in later years.

"So," Ivan continued, "this is how it affects us. As you know, *Degrassi* is scheduled to air tonight at eight-thirty."

I suddenly got it. Our upcoming episode was "Nobody's Perfect." In this episode, we followed the story of Kathleen (Rebecca Haines) as her boyfriend begins to physically abuse her. It was a powerful story written by Susin Nielsen and directed by Eleanore Lindo and the opening scene was quite graphic.

Ivan concisely laid out the options: "Do we pull the episode from the lineup tonight? Do we delay it for a week or maybe indefinitely? Or, do we just stick to the schedule as is? We only have a short time to decide."

He and I got a cup of tea and found a quiet place to talk. "Nobody's Perfect" was a story where we depict the ugliness of boyfriend abuse, but the final message is one of strength and empowerment, saying to young girls and women, "You don't need to put up with this." Ivan and I both believed in the message. We decided the show would air as scheduled.

The whole incident was jarring and a sobering reminder of the responsibilities we have as storytellers to our young audience. (I would remember this moment later on the set of *Degrassi: The Next Generation* on September 11, 2001.)

As I wrapped up with Ivan, Kit approached, and stared questioningly at me. "What did the fucker want?" he spat. Reeling from the news that Ivan had shared, and Kit's combative attitude, I fought back tears as I tried to pull my thoughts together. *Fourteen young people dead. Their only crime was being female.* Kit took my silence as "attitude."

"Fine," he said, "be like that. Don't tell me what our executive wanted. Keep the 'fancy' boy to yourself." He stormed off.

By this point in the season, Kit had become a walking black hole. I was constantly running interference between him and various crew members. Right now, I wanted nothing more than to go home and try to process what had transpired in the last hour, but the art department was calling me. They wanted me to check out the decorations for the year-end dance that would be shooting tomorrow. As I walked into the gym, I was met with glitter balls, streamers, and balloons offering a festive juxtaposition to the sobering news of the day.

The next morning, there was a magical quality in the air as we shot the final scene of "One Last Dance." Lots of storylines were wrapping up. A small yet impactful moment was captured between Dwayne and Tabi as they slow-danced together. It was a lovely message of hope. Yes, Dwayne had HIV, but he was living with it, as were his friends. It was a great bookend to the season opener.

Production on "One Last Dance" was bittersweet. No one really knew if this would be the final season for *Degrassi* or not. It certainly

The whole crew celebrates wrap on "One Last Dance," while wondering if this is the end of *Degrassi*.

felt like we had more stories to tell, but a lingering question hung in the air: Was "One Last Dance" really the last *Degrassi* dance?

With production wrapped, on a whim Kit flew to Salt Spring Island on the west coast to visit friends. Within days of being there, he made an impromptu purchase of a sheep farm. He said it reminded him of growing up with his grandparents on the Isle of Man. Yan, completely exhausted and resolutely still not talking to Kit, decided the only way to cope was to move, with Kathryn, to Arizona for a few months. Kate and the team at WGBH had come to the difficult decision that season two of *Degrassi High* would be the last for WGBH Boston. As the show had been aging up each year, they were finding it increasingly challenging to raise money from the children's department at PBS. Kate and the team at WGBH had been wonderfully supportive and innovative partners for five years.

I was left alone in Toronto, and CBC was asking for more *Degrassi*.

Ivan and I had a heart-to-heart. I explained that I didn't think I could wrestle another season out of the team. I also admitted that we'd have further financial challenges now that WGBH was out of the mix. "Would you consider a feature-length show as a finale?" I asked. "I think I might be able pull the team together for that, and I have some thoughts on financing that could fill the gap left by PBS."

"If you can make that happen, Linda, CBC would be proud to continue partnering with you."

"I'm on it!" I enthusiastically offered, secretly having no idea how I could pull any of this off.

I had separate phone conversations with both Yan and Kit to try to nail a feature storyline. Somehow, with Yan in Arizona and Kit flitting back and forth across the country, dictated by the rhythm of sheep, we came up with an outline. We planned to capture that tumultuous summer after high school graduation and before the start of new adventures, a time when old friends find themselves embarking on separate journeys. In true *Degrassi* style, it wouldn't be complete without its issues, and we had many: drinking and driving, boyfriend infidelity, abortion, anxiety, a bad breakup, pot smoking, a car crash, a near drowning, condom demonstrations with a banana, a proposal, a wedding, and more.

The CBC loved it.

In hindsight, I realized that alongside teenage angst, we were also reflecting the tumultuous relationship of Yan, Kit, and me. We had been a very small creative team. We had told a lot of stories together, and we were tired. I would remember this when gearing up for *Degrassi: The Next Generation*. I would consciously build a creative team with more depth and watch for burnout.

But right now, I had priorities. I gave Yan the go-ahead to start script writing in Arizona while I focused on ways to fill the financing hole left by the departure of WGBH Boston.

★

On one of my "fancy" trips, as Kit liked to call them, Kate and I travelled to New York to meet with broadcast executives at WNET. They were big fans of *Degrassi* and looking for ways to grow their audience. At this point, WNET was broadcasting the third season of *Degrassi Junior High*. They had already received some great press coverage in the *New York Times* and other prestigious publications but felt they could increase their audience with a new broadcast schedule. Kate and I were there to do press interviews to promote the new time slot of Sundays at 10:30 a.m. This seemed like a most odd choice to me, but I'd learned my lesson about arguing with broadcasters on their scheduling wisdom, thanks to Ivan. We had a productive press day and, as it ultimately turned out, their time shift was brilliant and their audience more than doubled.

During that trip to New York City, WNET executives had invited me to drop by whenever I was next in town. I liked the guys and promised to keep in touch. As I was now dealing with a financing deficit for the *Degrassi* feature, I thought it might be a good time to drop by. When I called to set up the appointment, they said that my timing was perfect as they had something they would like to run by me. I assumed it was another publicity gig and let them know I was game for whatever they needed. Over sushi lunch, they repeated that *Degrassi* was going from strength to strength — it was really striking a chord with both their urban and suburban audiences. *Okay, Linda*, I thought. *It's time to make your pitch.* But before I could start, they continued, "We know that *Degrassi* has lost its funding partner WGBH. We would love to come and fill that gap for you to continue . . ."

I paused with my chopsticks in mid-air.

". . . but we don't have the resources for a series."

"Yes," I commiserated. "Always challenging."

"However," they continued, "PBS is winding down its long-running anthology series *WonderWorks*. In their final year, they are focusing on *WonderWorks: Family Movies*. At WNET, we have funding to acquire one of these movies, and wondered if you would be interested in developing one with us?"

I lost the grip on my chopsticks and a large piece of barbecued eel splashed into my cup of green tea. I forgot about the eel — in fact, I forgot about all the rest of my lunch — as I enthusiastically launched into the pitch for *School's Out*. They had no idea we were planning a *Degrassi* movie and were as excited as I was. There would be follow-up meetings with Stephen and their legal team, of course, but the three of us ended our lunch with "Let's do it!"

Once I reached LaGuardia, I rushed to the first payphone I could find and called Salt Spring Island. Kit had just come in from sheep-shearing lessons and was somewhat distracted. I told him the great news.

"Well, aren't you clever," he said and hung up.

My next call, to Angela Bruce, was met with greater enthusiasm. She promised to walk straight to Ivan's office and let him know.

Many long-distance script meetings happened in the next few weeks until we could delay no longer. Both Kit and Yan needed to come back to Toronto and start working as a team. We had a script meeting scheduled for 10 a.m. Monday morning; I was trusting that both Yan and Kit would show.

And they did.

It seemed that the sheep had had a mellowing effect on Kit, just as the Arizona air had on Yan. There was an excitement about this feature-length project. Kit had long made it clear that he was done with the series but could commit to a dramatic feature. Yan shared the same feelings from his writer's perspective. No formal truce was declared, or apologies offered, but there was an inherent understanding that we would all pull together for the final *Degrassi*.

The anticipation built as we brought the cast together for the *School's Out* read-through of the script. Throughout the session, there were repeated gasps and yelps from the cast. They couldn't believe some of the storylines that we had developed and were particularly surprised by some of the language. We had left the odd "asshole" and "fuck" in the current draft to indicate that we saw this as a different period of their lives than high school. At first, this language was intended only for tone, but with each subsequent draft of the script, it stayed.

In the end, the language survived right to the production draft. On the day of production on those colourful scenes, we filmed as written, but also filmed a safety. In the editing room, we did the first cut with language. Both broadcasters approved them.

Eventually, WNET understandably backed down and the safety was put in their final show. However, when *School's Out* aired in Canada it included a "fucking," a "fucked," and a couple of "assholes." It was noted that this was the first time such language had been used on the public broadcaster in a scripted show. I had mixed feelings about the attention; I really preferred that the discussion following my shows was about content. But Kit was beaming. He thought he'd finally got one over on the fuckers. *School's Out* aired with language only once in Canada; all later versions used the safety.

The reaction to our grand finale was certainly mixed.

"Far too dark" and "Far too melodramatic," said some.

"The best *Degrassi* EVER," declared others.

★

This publicity shot for *School's Out* was taken by the lake in front of our Toronto beach home.

The day after *School's Out* premiered, I was driving home from the office, wondering what "home" really meant these days. I was startled out of my thoughts by the ringing of my car phone. It was one of those early models that was mounted near the gear shift and always snagging my pantyhose. I found it more of a nuisance than useful. It rarely rang.

"Hello," I ventured.

"Linda, it's Ivan. You won your night! *School's Out* got over 2.4 million viewers. You must be very happy. I am!"

I turned my car into the liquor store and bought an expensive bottle of champagne. When I got home, Kit was sitting on the porch. I handed him a glass of bubbly and sat silently beside him. We rocked wordlessly in our twin wicker chairs, looking out over the vast waters of Lake Ontario.

I loved our recently acquired beach house. Living in the Beach, in the far east-end of Toronto, was like having a cottage in the city. The minute I'd walked into this house with the real estate agent, I knew I was sold. I had been living in Toronto for twelve years, and never really felt at home. All my previous houses with Kit were office/homes. Many nights, I would fall asleep to the sounds of Kit editing, and often our home would be used as a filming loca-

tion. Our previous house had been frequently used as Lucy's house, and it was in our guest bedroom that Spike got pregnant at one of Lucy's legendary parties. When I stepped through the front door of 1 Munro

LEFT: Our house in Broadstairs, England, early 1950s.

BELOW: One Munro Park Avenue, Toronto, late 1980s, prior to renovations. (This street view is the side of the house. The front faces the lake.)

Park Avenue, I felt like I was home, and silently vowed we would never use this house as a location. I knew immediately that the Christmas tree would sit in the living room window overlooking the lake. We would have breakfast in the octagonal window area and afternoon tea in the west-facing sunroom. I imagined walking along the beach at morning and at night. I was strongly reminded of my childhood home in Britain.

My formative years in England had been spent in Broadstairs, a picturesque British seaside town, on the white chalk cliffs, just forty minutes north of the famous Dover. Like 1 Munro Park, it was a single detached house. It had balconies at front and back that allowed the sounds of the sea to be heard from any one of the four bedrooms. It also had a lovely garden, private garage, and driveway. This could sound like rather luxurious accommodations for a young family facing the economic restraints of post-war Britain. Well, there were some realities about living there.

Of the four bedrooms, only two were used for sleeping by our family. Mum and Dad had the second largest bedroom, and Tony and I shared the smallest room. The third housed Dad's plastic sign business and was the headquarters for his pirate taxi service. He pursued these entrepreneurial efforts in addition to managing the local bowling alley for the soldiers on the U.S. base still stationed in the south of England.

The largest bedroom in the house was for convalescing children and their mothers. Broadstairs was a seaside town where many folks with ailments sought cures by taking in the "sea air." My mother, trained as a nurse, saw a business opportunity for herself that could augment Dad's endeavours. She provided room, board, and nursing for convalescing children, or the "sickies" as my brother and I unkindly called them. "They're not *sickies*," Mum would correct. "They are convalescing, which means they are getting better." (We still called them sickies.)

Whenever possible, Tony and I would head to the beach. Here we would swim and wade at high tide, and when the tide was out we'd scour tide pools for baby crabs and snails. We'd sometimes climb into the smugglers' coves but knew not to linger or we could get trapped when the tide came in. It was well known that pirate's ghosts haunted these caves and they liked to eat young children and wash them down with rum. Low tide was particularly fun when Dad was home. He would allow us to venture out quite far along the coast, and, if lucky, we'd catch a lobster or two for dinner. It was at this beach on the English Channel that Dad taught me to swim.

My dad teaching me to swim in the chilly waters of the English Channel.

These wonderful, carefree childhood memories came rushing back to me the day I first stood on the porch of 1 Munro Park Avenue overlooking Lake Ontario. Never, in all the homes I'd lived since Broadstairs (and there had been many), had I felt this flood of warmth and security. I felt like I was home. Now Kit had me questioning that. We had been here only a year and he'd spent most of that time out west with the sheep. He'd never really wanted to buy this house in the first place. He called it too pretentious, grumbling something about the "Magnificent Ambersons." At the time of purchase, he said, "Well, if you really want it, Linda, you will make it happen." Secretly, I'd hoped that this house would save our troubled relationship, allowing us more separation between home and business.

★

As the sun started to go down, and the warmth of the champagne set in, the conversation slowly started. Kit and I both knew the end was coming, not just for *Degrassi* but for us as well. We let that thought hang silently in the air as we raised our glasses.

"Here's to two-point-four million." Kit smiled.

"Pretty darn fine," I agreed.

We looked out at the lowering sun as it reflected like a glittering pink blanket across the lake.

"Remember that heady night in the New York ballroom when we won our first Emmy?" I asked Kit.

"Yup." He smiled. "I was so proud of the way you stood up to those WGBH fuckers!"

"Oh, Kit." I shook my head. "That really was not my finest hour." But I couldn't help smiling about how obnoxious I had been to potential new business partners.

"We've come quite a distance since we documented Jimmy Montecino and that wacky piano marathon at the CNE," Kit mused.

We paused to hear distant laughter waft up from the beach.

"I really appreciate how you stood by me through my infertility," I offered up quietly.

"And likewise, you were there for me through my divorce and custody battles."

I don't remember who was the first to say it, but the words were uttered, "It's over, isn't it?" We both nodded.

In the early days, I always knew that Kit had a dark side, something my buddy Bruce had seen early on. But my immediate attraction to Kit was to his "manic imp" side, to the guy who could make me feel like there were no limits, that opportunities were boundless, that an elderly marathon pianist would make a great film subject. As the years went on, I saw less of the high-energy side and more of the darkness. Sometimes I was taken aback by how quickly one replaced the other, as it had that Sunday of our retreat and subsequent dinner with Angela.

I privately wondered if Kit needed a psychiatrist. He probably felt the same about me.

We vaguely talked about splitting personally yet continuing as business partners. He could live on the sheep farm, me in the Beach. Kit could run a feature division and I could head the television side. Neither one of us had any enthusiasm for this compromise.

As we drained our champagne, the moon started to rise over the lake. It was a cloudless sky and light from the moon danced over the lightly rippling water. I was not deceived by this magical moment. For all our fond reminiscences, I knew that in the cold light of day there would be a mood change.

I knew we were heading into an acrimonious separation, but right now, this was a moment to savour.

CHAPTER ELEVEN

MOVING INSIDE THE TENT

People in the industry were talking about me, and it was not good. "Linda Schuyler's company, Playing With Time, should be called Playing With Dimes, she's so cheap."

"How does she manage to get a show on prime time and remain non-union? It's disrespectful."

"Linda Schuyler exploits kids."

I replayed these words over and over as I rattled around my empty house.

Yan had shared these comments with me at lunch earlier in the day. He hadn't wanted to, but I'd pried them out of him. Since Kit and I had split, I knew people were talking about both of us. It was particularly dark that night at the house. No moon. No stars. The lake looked like a black hole, mirroring how my heart felt.

On the Kit front, he and I were involved in a nasty, but predictable, custody battle. Kit didn't want the company. In fact, he swore he was through with production altogether, but he couldn't abide the thought of me buying him out. We were also fighting about the house, the house that Kit had never wanted. The house from which he moved 4,800 kilometres away to live on a sheep farm. Yes, that house had now become an obsession for him. He said his soul was there and that I would be responsible for destroying his soul if I bought him out. "But, Kit, you never liked this house! You said it was too grand."

"No, I never said that. You are remembering that because it is convenient for you."

As the hurtful gossip from lunchtime played on an endless loop in my head, I started to hear the distant rumblings of other voices. *Hey, Brit girl. Yes, you, shit girl. Go back to where you came from.* My childhood bullies were never far away. I set the house alarm and climbed the stairs to bed, dreading another lunch tomorrow.

I tried but couldn't sleep. Past failures insisted on revisiting me. I was transported back to a grey November morning in 1967 as I waded through the mud-soaked campus of the University of Waterloo (U of W), a new post-secondary facility still under construction. For my introductory computing course, I had to get the computer to solve an equation. It was a simple calculation, and I already knew the answer. But I had to speak to the computer using basic binary commands, typed on individual cards. I had already been granted a couple of extensions and was running out of time. I entered the computer building, an imposing cement structure with the middle hollowed out. In the chasm, stretching up multiple floors was "the mainframe," the pride of U of W. I despised that miserable piece of equipment. It was so unforgiving of typing errors. But I was convinced, this time, I'd gotten it right.

I expectantly approached my cubby to pick up my cards. They were neatly stacked with a cheerful red elastic holding them together. I pulled off the rubber band, and — *NOOOO, not again!* — ERROR. ERROR. And ERROR.

I walked out of the building and leaned my back against the cold concrete wall. I allowed myself to slowly slide down until my bum hit wet mud. Close by, bulldozers rumbled as they broke soggy ground. A gust of icy wind shot towards me and grabbed my cards. I offered no resistance as the error-infested bits of paper were tossed, almost playfully, into the bleak November abyss. I was done with the University of Waterloo.

I knew quitting was the right decision, but the hard part would be explaining it to my family — they were used to me being near the top of the class. I didn't want to admit that I was a failure, particularly as there had been much excitement around the fact that I was the first family member, on either side of our family, to attend a post-secondary school.

I tried to turn my failure into a success story. I convinced my parents that I would work and save up money. Then I would embark on a journey of experiential education (a popular phrase at the time) by taking a year or so to work my way around the world. Surprisingly, they bought the whole notion, once I had reminded them that, at my age, they had left home to actively participate in the WWII effort — Mum as a nurse and Dad as a pilot. However, after only seven months of travel, I returned home to recover from my horrific car accident. Not only had I failed at traditional university, but my experiential education was a disaster as well.

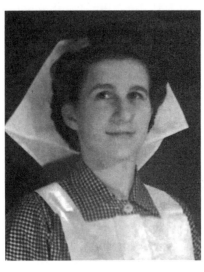

Mum and Dad circa 1943.

Upon my early return, I started my teaching studies at London Teachers' College, the only post-secondary school to which I was able to gain acceptance on short notice. Here, I found myself a few short blocks away from Western University, where Brian Schuyler, my old high school sweetheart (we'd gone steady for four years) was studying for his MBA. I hadn't seen Brian since before I'd left for my hippie trip. I don't remember who called who, but we agreed to meet for coffee one morning. To our delight, and perhaps surprise, we easily reconnected. In some ways, it was as though my travels and the accident had never happened. It had been a few months since the crash. Because my face had healed well and my internal damage was invisible, the only hint that something had happened was my slight limp. To Brian, my parents, and friends, it was as though I had never been in a near fatal collision. And unwittingly, I played right along with that scenario. Rather than dwell on the realities, it was easier to say, "It was a pretty bad crash, all right, but I've been very fortunate to get out of it virtually unscathed." If I'd had the ability to assess my actions at the time, I would say my approach was one of resilience, like immediately getting back on a horse after a bad fall. It would take me many years to realize that what I'd thought was admirable resilience was unhealthy denial.

In no time, Brian and I were dating again, got engaged, and then married. It just seemed like the right thing to do and Brian certainly was a warm and wonderful guy. I had interpreted my crash as a message: I wasn't meant to strike out on my own. I had been a cocky and foolish girl to think I could be independent. I was destined to be a schoolteacher. And . . . wife.

Brian and me, ready for senior prom. Brian was school president and I was the president of the Girls Athletic Association. We were Paris District High School's overachieving "it" couple! Mum made this dress for me.

For five years, I did my best to live a traditional and conservative lifestyle. At school I was an energetic, enthusiastic Grade 7/8 teacher. At home, I was a dedicated housewife. I cooked, cleaned, made my own clothes, and even knitted an Aran sweater for Brian. Feeling pressure from his family, Brian and I did our best to start our own family. Despite our efforts — no luck. It was a bitter disappointment to Brian that we weren't able to conceive. However, each month when my painful period came, I was silently relieved. I was not ready to add mother to my roles as teacher and wife.

In the fifth year of our marriage, things changed. Brian applied successfully for a job in Toronto with Lever Brothers. Ever gracious, he offered that when we moved, I wouldn't need to keep working. He was happy to be the provider (a thought I found mildly distasteful). I also knew Brian hoped that, without the pressures of teaching, I might be able to get pregnant. Despite my apprehension of being a "kept woman," I accepted Brian's offer to not work and used this opportunity to return to university at U of T.

Through my media studies and my women in film courses, and with lively interactions with my fellow classmates, I started to rediscover independent thought. It didn't take long before I realized how my veneer of conventionalism and conservatism, which I had unintentionally presented to Brian after the accident, was false both for me and for him. I had tried to be everything that he and his family wanted. After five years, I couldn't pretend anymore. By 1974, our young marriage was over. Another failure.

★

Now, almost twenty years later, in the dark of night, my epic failures were vividly on display in my crowded head: An aborted university attempt. World travels abruptly ended by a crash. A botched marriage. And now I added more: another collapsed relationship, a failed business partnership, and a sullied reputation.

Ugh. I didn't want to get out of the bed in the morning, let alone go to lunch with Stephen Stohn.

I called Stephen's office first thing to cancel our appointment. Stephen would have none of it. "I'll come to your office," he volunteered cheerfully, "and we can grab a bite nearby."

"It'll be a short lunch," I warned him.

Once Stephen and I were settled at my local diner and had placed our orders for the city's cheapest and best-ever BLTs, Stephen got to the agenda.

"I want to help you plan the next phase of your professional life," he offered.

"Don't waste your energy," I intercepted. "I have no professional future."

"Wait a minute, Linda," he said back quickly. "You should know that people are talking about you."

"Yes . . . I do know. *Child exploiter. Cheap. Disrespectful . . .*" I fought back tears.

Stephen raised a quizzical eyebrow. He started to tell me about a baseball game he'd attended a few nights earlier. He was with Doug Barrett, a fellow entertainment lawyer and board member of the Canadian Film and Television Producers Association (CFTPA — now Canadian Media Producers Association). Doug told Stephen, "Linda's success has been truly amazing. We need to get her more politically involved with the industry. We need to get her inside the tent." Stephen capped the story by saying he and Doug wanted me to consider running for the board of the CFTPA.

Whoa, this was unexpected. I told Stephen that it was too late, that I had decided to return to the classroom. Now he looked shocked. "I thought Ivan had made a connection for you to meet Jeff Sagansky, head of programming at CBS? Like Doug, Ivan believes in you and wants you to succeed."

It was true. A few weeks earlier, Ivan had been entertaining Jeff in Toronto. He'd held a small gathering of independent producers to introduce us to the CBS executive. Jeff and I had gotten on well, and he welcomed me any time to L.A. "Before you dust off your teaching certificate, maybe you'd want to contemplate your other options," Stephen tactfully suggested. "Might even be time for you to consider engaging a U.S. agent."

Well, I thought, *there are a few months before I need to re-commit to teaching, maybe it's worth seeing what else is out there.* And, if truth be told, I did have an idea for a new series percolating in my head — something about Gen Xers living downtown, navigating their world view as they intersected with the boomers — not fully formed yet, but tentatively titled *Liberty Street*.

In short order, Stephen and I booked L.A. meetings with William Morris, International Creative Management (ICM), and Creative Artists Agency (CAA). Our meetings were loaded at the front of the week to allow for follow-ups prior to the prearranged pitch meeting on Friday with Jeff Sagansky. Holy shit, I was heading to Los Angeles to shop for an agent and to meet with a top U.S. broadcast executive to pitch a show! What a welcome relief from the realities that had become my current life.

Mindful of finances and on the recommendation of our U.S. distributor, I booked Stephen and myself into a three-storey walk-up, two-bedroom apartment in Santa Monica. Our apartment was a short walk from Shutters, my current favourite hotel in Santa Monica, but in those days two rooms at Shutters for six nights would be like six months of mortgage payments. (Only later did I find out that Stephen was a huge fan of luxury hotels and had been somewhat shocked by the notion of our budget-conscious apartment — but he never complained about our walk-up for the week.)

Once checked in, we set up the dining room as our office. Stephen pulled out a couple of maps of L.A., some sticky notes, and multicoloured pens. He meticulously located all our meetings and marked them on the map. He then charted various routes and calculated approximately how long it would take to get us to each location. It was a beautiful exercise in Google Maps, years before the technology.

I watched Stephen carefully plan our week's activities and thought, *I've never had anyone take charge this way.*

With logistics established, Stephen pulled out a spreadsheet he had prepared on his computer. "I want you to start listing the qualities that you're looking for in an agent." He showed me a scale beside each blank category ranging from one to ten. "Fill in the blanks with your criteria for an agent. Following each meeting, you will assess the potential agent using your list and my scale."

I dutifully started to fill out boxes and was struck with the enormity of this whole endeavour. This was all about *me*. And in the back of my mind, all I could hear was, *Oh you and your fancy ideas and meetings, you're never going to make it on your own. Go back to where you came from, Slimy Limey.* I left the dining table and headed to the small balcony. I looked across Ocean Avenue to the vastness of the Pacific beyond. It was black. It was infinite. I knew this view from my hometown in Broadstairs, England, and from the front porch of my Toronto home. I knew this vista could offer the potential for everything, or be a bottomless pit of nothingness. I thought about Kit. *He's right,* I reflected. *I'm fooling myself to think I belong here.* But then I looked through the window and saw Stephen toiling on his computer. He offered hope and optimism. Maybe it wouldn't hurt to give this a try — for a few days, at least.

*

The next morning, Stephen and I set out for ICM, located in a somewhat austere building — black, with a lot of glass, multi-levelled, and very functional. Our meeting was like the building: efficient. The agent and his assistant, both well dressed, had obviously done their homework on me and were very complimentary. They said all the right things but, like the building, lacked passion. However, they wanted to represent me and that felt good.

Stephen and I grabbed a burger at a nondescript mom-and-pop shop. He congratulated me on a successful meeting and whipped out his laptop. "Right," he said, "let's fill out the spreadsheet and rate ICM."

As I applied numbers from one to ten in various categories — likeability, sincerity, experience, other clients on their roster — Stephen kept a close eye on the clock. Suddenly he snapped his laptop closed and we were on the move.

William Morris was located in a long, low-rise building. Once inside, we were faced with a rambling rabbit warren of bustling offices, ringing phones, humming faxes, and overworked copying machines. Here we met the casually dressed Jeff Alpern, with his easy smile and confident attitude. Jeff made it clear that he was a *Degrassi* fan and would be delighted to represent me.

Wow, so far two for two!

On our way back to our apartment, Stephen asked me to drive by the CAA building. We were due there in the morning and he wanted to be sure we knew where we'd be going. This was one impressive building. Set back from the road and separate from all other buildings, it had the air of a contemporary temple — big, white, postmodern. I thought this place was just far too grand for me. I contemplated cancelling the meeting. After all, I already had two offers for representation. But Stephen kept me on track.

The next morning, twenty minutes early, we waited in CAA's enormous sunlight-filled atrium. An assistant with extraordinarily long legs rising from four-inch heels offered us water. I couldn't take my eyes off the painting in front of us, an almost thirty-foot-high original Roy Lichtenstein mural, *Bauhaus Stairway*. We later found out that the building's architect, I.M. Pei, had commissioned this work from Lichtenstein. The work was both human and architectural. Later, when I got back to Toronto, everyone wanted to know what stars I had seen walking through the halls of CAA. They were disappointed to know that I had registered no one — I was instead mesmerized by the Lichtenstein.

Precisely at 10 a.m., an impeccably dressed David Tenzer and his assistant met us and ushered us into an oversized boardroom. Nothing about this place was small. On the table were more varieties of flat and sparkling water than I had ever seen before. I was prepared for polite rejection and instead we got a very thoughtful pitch as to why CAA and David would be the best representation I could have. At the conclusion of the meeting, David said, "Before you rush to a decision, I'd like to take both of you to lunch at The Ivy tomorrow if you are available."

Stephen and I laughed as we headed to our rental car. "If we're available? Of course, we're available!"

By mid-week, with the help of Stephen's spreadsheets and an exquisite lunch at the Ivy, the choice became clear: David Tenzer at CAA would become my agent. Now it was time to get ready for Friday's meeting at CBS with Jeff Sagansky.

David invited Stephen and me to his office so we could prep for the meeting. David suggested it would not be prudent for him to attend our CBS appointment as it had been set up by Ivan. Instead, David spent a couple of hours helping me hone my pitch and providing background on CBS's current mandate. "Jeff's been brought in to jack up CBS's lacklustre ratings," David explained. "Jeff believes the baby boomers are a suburban phenomenon and he's going to win them over. He's looking for a younger audience and more women. Look what he's done with Monday nights with *Murphy Brown* and *Designing Women*."

Right, I thought, wondering how my modest project, *Liberty Street*, about a group of twenty-somethings living in a rundown urban apartment building (two years before *Friends*) might fare in Jeff's view of the current TV landscape. I shared my concerns with David.

"Linda," he explained. "This is a first meeting. You are building a relationship. Your job is to make a smart first impression. This might be your first CBS pitch, but trust me, it won't be your last."

★

Stephen and I were both in the kitchen of our walk-up early the morning of our CBS meeting. We sat silently sipping coffee.

Stephen picked up the map and the sticky notes. "Show time," he said. Not surprisingly, we arrived early and the receptionist showed us to seats near the elevators. With four heady days of meetings and prep behind us, we were both somewhat at a loss for things to say. I surprised myself when I broke the silence and said, "This past year has been one of the unhappiest ones of my life."

"Mine too," Stephen volunteered.

I was shocked. "But Stephen, you always appear so happy. You have a beautiful wife, a charming son, a prestigious job, and — you drive an awesome car."

"It's not all it seems," Stephen continued. "Rosemary and I are splitting. I'm moving into an apartment within the next few months. We're still working out separation details, particularly custody."

Gobsmacked, I wanted to ask more, when the receptionist arrived. "Mr. Sagansky will see you now."

Jeff, as with the three agents earlier in the week, was familiar with *Degrassi*. "I've followed your success on PBS and CBC and internationally. It's impressive," Jeff offered. We shared our mutual affection for Ivan. He told us of his mandate at CBS and then, it was my turn to pitch my show.

By the end of the meeting, it was clear that David had known exactly what to expect: "You're building a relationship," he had said, and he was right. It was obvious that Jeff liked me. He encouraged me to come back with my next pitch but, at this moment, I had no CBS development deal.

"Should I be disappointed?" I asked Stephen, as we headed to the parking lot.

"Absolutely not," Stephen asserted. "We've come to L.A. to get you an agent and to introduce you to the L.A. scene. We had an agenda. We have successfully completed it. Well done!" He smiled.

"Yay, mission accomplished!" I laughed, then cautiously added, "Actually, I have one more item on my agenda, but I didn't want to tell you till we'd cleared everything else."

"Yes?"

"I would like to go to South Central."

"Pardon?" said Stephen.

When I knew we were travelling to L.A. I'd thought, *I can't leave without visiting the site of the recent Rodney King riots.* When I'd watched footage of the unrest on TV, I'd been both moved and angered. I didn't know if the media had blown the riots out of proportion, or if racism in L.A. really was that deep. "Sorry I didn't mention it before, but I need to see it firsthand."

Stephen looked at me. I could tell he knew I was serious, then he looked at our rental car. In another of my economically prudent decisions, I had arranged for a car from Rent-A-Wreck. I'd been in L.A. a few times before, filming segments for OWL TV, and found Rent-A-Wreck prices to be the best. I had reserved my favourite car, a Pepto-Bismol pink Mustang convertible.

"I'm not sure it's wise for us to go there, particularly in this car."

"It'll be quick, I promise. Trust me, I need to do this."

As we drove through South Central, both sides of the street were in ruins. Mile upon mile of burned-out buildings lined the road. Bright blue sky poked through open holes that were once windows and roofs. Charred front doors were crudely boarded up. These places had been someone's entrepreneurial dreams. *The media has not overplayed this*, I realized. Abandoned, burned, and looted vehicles were strewn along the roadside. It was all a vicious image of anger, hate, injustice, and disparity — a stark contrast to the world we had inhabited for the last week. I couldn't articulate it, but I had a feeling in the pit of my stomach, the same that had sat there so uncomfortably when Donald Hoppie told me that he wanted to be white. *This is what systemic racism looks like*, I thought.

★

On the flight back to Toronto, I was sobered by the two sides of the City of Angels that I had experienced. I tried to process what I had just seen in South Central with the messaging from my first film *Between Two Worlds*. My early film was praised for raising awareness of racism and initiating meaningful dialogue. Yet, here we were, seventeen years later, and racism was uglier and more pervasive than ever. I then thought about all the social messaging that we had undertaken through *Degrassi*. Did this mean that films like *Between Two Worlds* and television shows like *Degrassi* ultimately had no impact? If that's the case, why am I bothering with social messaging? I knew this thought was somewhat disingenuous, but it was convenient at the time. It gave me permission to leave high school and teenagers behind.

I was pleased that David Tenzer at CAA wanted to represent me. I had no idea how it would all work out or what opportunities might come about, but I was ready for fresh prospects and maybe, eventually, a move to L.A.?

Over time, David and I would discuss various projects and options. He was always willing to give advice on matters large and small and became a friend. In the end, there would neither be a move to the States nor a major U.S. network deal. But what I got from those meetings was something far more valuable — I got validation, many times over, that I was a real producer. Nobody had referred to me as a recycled schoolteacher, as an unwanted immigrant, or as a useless and manipulative partner. I was a producer in my own right.

Once home, I found myself replaying the abbreviated conversation that Stephen and I had started outside the elevator at CBS. I wanted to pick up the phone and ask Stephen if he was really about to become single. I wanted to let him know how great he made me feel when he took control of our agenda. I wanted to share with him that, for the first time in years, I felt as though someone was looking out for me. But, at that moment, he was my lawyer and I was his client.

It would be a few weeks before he and I would be able to pick up that unexpected conversation. In the meantime, we each returned to our own realities. And mine was brutal. I was met with some very terse letters from Kit's lawyers suggesting that I'd been negligent and unresponsive, and worse, was confronted with a multi-page letter from Kit reminding me what a dishonest, deceitful, and lying person I was. It included more accusations of me destroying his life, his soul, and the very essence of his being, and a spiteful suggestion that the world would be a better place if I were not alive.

Yikes.

I needed to build a new life — and fast. I hunkered down and assessed my assets. I didn't get a deal with CBS for *Liberty Street*, but I did have an interesting intellectual property on my hands. I reworked it into a movie of the week and pitched it to CBC as the pilot for a series. They bought it. I formed a new company, Epitome Pictures Inc. (based on the name of the apartment building in *Liberty Street*), of which I was the CEO and sole owner. This company would be a signatory to the Alliance of Canadian Cinema, Television and Radio Artists (ACTRA), the Writers Guild of Canada (WGC), and the Directors Guild of Canada (DGC). And, thanks to Doug Barrett, I put my name forward to run, successfully, for the board of the CFTPA. As Doug and Stephen had hoped, I was moving inside the Canadian production industry tent.

★

Eventually, Stephen and I picked up our personal conversation. After several necessary business phone calls, we agreed it would be great to finally get together for a face-to-face meeting. Stephen suggested the Four Seasons. *Out of my price bracket*, I thought, *but hey, why not?* When we both arrived, for the first few minutes our conversation was surprisingly stiff. One look at the menu and it was clear that the cheapest and best BLTs would not be offered here. I opted for an omelette with salad and have no recollection of Stephen's choice. We updated each other on our progress on various files, including the current development of *Liberty Street* and the negotiations with CAA. Stephen reached into his vast inside jacket pocket and pulled out an envelope. "As you requested," he said, "my invoice for the L.A. trip." He fumbled as he handed me the paper and our fingers touched. Neither of us pulled away. We allowed our hands to fall to the table and rest against each other's. Then our eyes met. For a split second that felt like a lifetime, nobody else was in the room but us.

"Excuse me," the waiter said, "who has the omelette?"

"That'd be me," I said, pulling my hand away.

Once our meals were delivered, Stephen and I had an awkward silence, then both began to talk at the same time.

"You go first," I said.

Stephen said somewhat hesitantly, "We must remember that our relationship is covered by lawyer-client privilege."

"Of course," I replied, somewhat surprised.

"Sorry, what was it you were about to say?" he asked.

"Forget it. Not important."

"No really, what?"

"I was going to ask," I tentatively said, "if . . . you would like to come to dinner at my house this weekend?"

Stephen paused, then slowly allowed a smile to cross his face. "Yes," he said. "And about what I just said — forget it!"

Lawyer-client privilege be damned!

*

After our first dinner, Stephen and I, although then in our mid-forties, were like schoolkids. Both of us were so enthusiastic about our unexpected and surprisingly passionate relationship. For the first time in my adult life, I felt like I was partnering with an equal. Stephen didn't want to play *Father Knows Best* to me, nor did he want to find ways to undercut me. Quite the opposite. He respected my ambition and dedication to storytelling and was enthusiastic to see me grow and do well. And I only wanted the same for him. Now, after more than twenty-five years of marriage, remarkably the spark is still there. We've stayed in love by continuing to support each other unconditionally while embracing and respecting our own independent spaces.

When Stephen and I shared our magical lunch at the Four Seasons, he was living in a small apartment around the corner from his matrimonial home. It was early in his divorce proceedings, but one thing was clear: Stephen would retain joint custody of his son, eight-year-old Max. I had met Max a couple of times when Stephen and his family attended our annual end-of-summer *Degrassi* boat bashes. Over the years, I watched him grow from a cuddly baby to a rambunctious toddler, and now to a bright and funny child. He was, and is, very cute.

Stephen adored his son and was eager for me to get to know him.

Ever proper, Stephen wanted to ease Max into the notion that sometimes he and his dad might have a sleepover at Linda's house. He decided the best way to introduce this thought was to plan a "camp-out" on my front lawn. Stephen outfitted himself with a tent and sleeping bags and engaged Max to help pitch the tent. The two were somewhat awkward in their efforts. Fortunately, I had a roommate in those days, Danah-Jean Brown, one of my *Degrassi* kids (Connie in *The Kids of Degrassi Street*, Trish in *Junior High*). She had experienced the sudden death of her single mom and was struggling. I was happy to share my home with her and help, where I could, to get her life back on track. She was great

Danah helps Max erect the tent in front of the house.

company and a good sport. Danah assessed the Max and Stephen situation, rolled up her sleeves, and dove in. Soon the tent was being capably erected by Danah and Max, while Stephen and I sipped wine on the veranda.

The four of us enjoyed a barbecue dinner, then Danah and I headed in for the night, leaving the boys in "the wild." Somewhere in the wee hours of the morning, I was awoken by the creaking of the front door. I came downstairs to find both Max and Stephen dripping wet and looking for towels. We had all forgotten about my automated irrigation system, which operated at night. Our campers could have withstood the sprinkling of water on the outside of the tent, but they woke up to find water gushing through the tent floor, drenching their sleeping bags. The tent was right on top of one of the main irrigation heads. The commotion downstairs woke Danah. There was only one thing to do in a situation like this: make hot chocolate and laugh.

When Stephen and I realized we were serious enough about our relationship to want to move in together, we knew Max was a critical consideration. Stephen and Max adored each other, and Stephen wanted to give Max and me space so we could forge our own connection. One evening, when Stephen had a late meeting, Max and I had dinner together. After his homework was done, it suddenly became important to both of us to know the weight of the human head. We decided the best way to figure this out would be for us each in turn to lie on the dining room table with our head hanging freely over the end. We would then position the bathroom scales on top of the ottoman, which we had placed on top of the dining room chair to give us approximately the same height as the table and would allow our heads to rest freely on the scales. Simple, right? However, try as we did, we couldn't get the right height for the scales. Eventually, we aborted the mission and decided to go upstairs to the library and consult the encyclopedia.

Later, as we sat reading together, I was able to start the first of various casual yet important chats with Max. I wanted to reassure him that I was not going to replace his mother. He had a great mom who would always be there for him. He and I were breaking new ground and would have to forge our own unique relationship. When he was a little older and studying French in high school, Max introduced me to the French word for step-mother, la belle-mère. We both agreed this was a great word, and adopted it for our relationship. Later in life, when Max was in his mid-thirties and overcome by a terrible illness, it would take all three of his parents — Stephen, Rosemary, and me — working as a team, to bring him back to us. I was so grateful that our early groundwork led to this atmosphere of trust.

*

On the professional front, CBC was pleased with our pilot movie and proceeded to order the series *Liberty Street*. Stephen left the top floor of the TD Centre, home of McCarthy Tétrault, to start his own law firm, Stohn Henderson, with Graham Henderson, a fellow entertainment lawyer and husband of singer Margo Timmins. My company, Epitome Pictures, was a major client of the new law firm.

In *Liberty Street*, we created an urban apartment environment that was home to a group of twenty-somethings living on their own for the first time. It was a show that was less about issues and more about attitude. When Douglas Coupland was interviewed for his seminal novel, *Generation X* (1991), he talked about a generation that was "sick of stupid labels and sick of being marginalized in lousy [McJobs]." We tried to capture these sentiments along with the twenty-something search for the existential meaning of life. While some storylines did touch on social issues, they were more about finding your voice and asserting independence.

When we called wrap on the first season of *Liberty Street*, I realized that I had jumped in with both feet and, despite Kit's predictions to the contrary, I had not drowned. However, to be honest, *Liberty Street* was an uneven series. A bit like my experience with *Blue Mountain Crude*, when I had come off the success of *Between Two Worlds*, it was hard to follow the success we'd been enjoying for over ten years with *Degrassi*. But I was gradually gaining more confidence.

While working to stay afloat in production, I was enjoying my new involvement with fellow producers at the CFTPA. I accepted a committee position as the head of the Ontario producers panel. And then . . . we had a "Common Sense Revolution." Mike Harris was elected as the new Conservative premier of Ontario and immediately froze all funding to the arts. As the chair of the CFTPA Ontario panel, I now had a job — get money back for film and television production in Ontario: no small task.

We formed a coalition with the Ontario Film Development Corporation and various guilds and unions. To help us strategize and plan, we hired a lobbyist. With his help, we prepared solid numbers quantifying economic performance, job creation, and related spinoff benefits. Meetings were set up with bureaucrats, then with deputy ministers, and finally with the ministers of both finance and culture. It was a long, slow process, but we kept steadily at it. I allowed myself a small smile as I thought back to my earlier engagement with bureaucrats when I had "accidentally" blown the fuse during a government official's screening of our film.

Eventually, success. A bill was passed to create a tax credit system for film and television production in Ontario. A beautiful Inuit sculpture was presented to me as thanks by the group. *What an opportunity*, I thought. *I've learned so much about our parliamentary system and lobbying and what it feels like to be inside the tent.*

Throughout this period of political activity and consciousness-raising, I'd had two other important productions on my hands: one, securing contracts for a second season of *Liberty Street* and two, planning our wedding. Stephen and I were making it official.

★

Our wedding was a festive affair: three hundred people at our beach house enjoying a midway, set up in our driveway, complete with shooting games, whack-a-mole, and plush toy prizes. As well, we had a fortune teller, a mini-putt green on the beach, and a roving Dixieland band. Food stations, catered by Mövenpick, were dotted throughout the house and garden, including an oyster bar on the sand. Large towers of helium balloons swayed in the water at the shore of our house. The weather, a mid-September day, was perfect.

When it came time for the speeches, everyone gathered in the large tent on the upper front lawn as my sister, our MC, took centre stage on our veranda. As she started to speak, I could see Max and his buddies running up from the beach. They'd been sucking the air from the helium balloons. Max's face was red from running and helium, his shirttails half out, his shoes covered in sand. As he joined us on the veranda, he said quietly, in a very high-pitched voice, "I'm ready to go!" and then convulsed into giggles. Stephen and I both looked at him somewhat quizzically as if to say, "You're going to give a speech with that voice?" Fortunately, Max, Stephen's best man, wasn't scheduled to speak till the end, after my sister Barb, then Bruce (my maid of honour), Stephen, and me.

Our speeches were short, breezy, and heartfelt. Then it was eleven-year-old Max's turn. Miraculously, the flush-faced imp, with tousled hair fresh from the beach, became an articulate and sincere

speaker. And whew, his voice had settled. Talking to the crowd of family and friends, he ended his speech by saying, "Linda makes my dad very happy, and that makes me happy."

Eleven-year-old Max finishes delivering a beautiful toast to his dad and new "belle-mère."

I'm not really a crier, but at that moment I couldn't hold myself back. I was being welcomed into a new family complete with a husband and a beautiful stepson.

The magic of our day continued throughout our honeymoon. Stephen and I had been offered the apartment of friends of ours in Venice, Italy, right off St. Mark's Square. We ate fish at a local restaurant, sipped bellinis at Harry's Bar, lunched at the Guggenheim, and watched the sunset over the lagoon from the Hotel Danieli. A water taxi took us to the train station where we boarded the romantic Orient Express, bound for Paris. Before our trip, I had researched outfits appropriate for the Orient Express. Many dressed in the flapper style of the 1920s. I was uncomfortable with a costume, but did opt for a low-waisted, knee-length silk dress that I adorned with a long set of pearls. Stephen wore a trimly tailored Etro suit. Together we entered the dining car to the strains of a three-piece string quartet caressing the air and found a bottle of champagne on our private table. We felt as though we were in an ethereal time warp embracing both *The Great Gatsby* and *Doctor Zhivago*.

In the City of Light, we visited Père Lachaise Cemetery, toured Rodin's house and gardens, enjoyed café au lait at Les Deux Magots, and ate fresh baguettes and brie on the bank of the Seine. Despite being immersed in Old World charm, we kept an eye on emails. We knew that *Liberty Street* was selling well internationally and our distributor, Atlantis Films, was pleased. However, we also knew that our ratings on the CBC were not strong. We felt in our hearts that there would likely be no season three of *Liberty Street*. And somehow, I was not fussed. I liked my new series, but I knew there was more opportunity out there. With twenty-six episodes of *Liberty Street* under my belt and a successful win for the industry with the tax credit, my confidence was growing. Kit's words, causing self-doubt and insecurity, were fading. Like my old childhood voices, they would never be far from the surface, but right now, I had them in check.

I said to Stephen, "You know, for a while now, I've had an idea for a show that I think will be just perfect for our company and CBC."

Stephen's response?

"Well, let's get home and make that happen!"

CHAPTER TWELVE

Building a Studio and a Soap

At Thanksgiving in 2019, my ninety-six-year-old mum and I were sitting on the front veranda at our farm, reminiscing about life back in England. I was young when we'd emigrated, but certainly old enough to remember much of our British life. We both recalled fondly our post-teatime ritual. At exactly 6:45 p.m. every weekday, we would stop whatever we were doing and gather around the radio. First would come the familiar jolly theme song — *La-de-da-de-la-de-da, la-de-da-de-la-da* — and then it was . . . *The Archers*! Stories of three farm families living in a fictional town in the Midlands, working hard to make ends meet raising pigs, sheep, and crops, while looking for meaning in their relationships.

"Do you remember when they had that terrible outbreak of hoof and mouth disease?" Mum asked.

"It was tragic," I recalled. Like most of England, we all cried when the farmer's wife, the one with all the young children, died from that awful disease. I was only seven but remembered it clearly.

Mum and I laughed. Oh, the power of storytelling in the media.

"It was a shame," she mused, "that your soap opera got cancelled. I really liked that show."

"So did I, Mum." And it owed its roots to *The Archers*.

The success of BBC's *The Archers* had led to the development of further British soaps on both radio and television, including *Coronation Street* and *EastEnders*. I loved all these shows. And it was that connection with real folks that I wanted to bring to Canadian audiences. This was what I had discussed with Stephen while returning from our honeymoon. Stephen encouraged me to meet with Yan to see if he might share my enthusiasm for the project. Over lunch, I began to tell Yan about my early connection with soaps. "Stop," he said. "I know exactly what you're talking about. My father was a diplomat, and when he was stationed in The Hague for a few years, we always had access to the BBC. We would listen to *The Archers* at 6:45 p.m. every night. I loved that show. It gave me a sense of community, something I was lacking as an itinerant dip kid."

"All right then — we need to start giving Canadian audiences their own community. Let's develop unique characters and storylines for a hometown crowd," I said.

There was nothing else like this in the English-language Canadian television landscape. Even though there was no immediate business plan evident for this domestic production, I knew that the success of the show would depend on loyal audience engagement. We would need the support of a domestic broadcaster as well as an innovative financing plan. As I discussed our challenges with Stephen, I also explained, "I want to develop a show that we can produce quickly and efficiently, keeping the costs low and the melodrama high. I'd like it to become a training ground for first-time writers, actors and others." Stephen nodded in agreement.

"And," I added, "most importantly for our audience, I want to capture the romance of everyday life."

Stephen was completely behind the initiative and together we secured a development deal from the CBC. As part of our development, I contacted the producers of *Coronation Street* and *EastEnders* and arranged for Yan and me to take a trip to their studios in England to study their technique. Their process was efficient. They had all their interior sets lined up in the studio beside one another. A strict amount of time was allotted to each scene and three cameras were used on pedestals for easy moves. Portable change rooms were nearby to allow for efficient wardrobe changes, and hair and makeup were mobile. On the backlot, the exteriors to match the studio interiors were constructed at 80 percent size to save space and cost. When shooting scenes in these exterior locations, no accommodations were made for weather; shooting continued rain, shine, sleet, or snow.

When home, I shared all this with Stephen, and we jointly agreed that if this was going to work, we would need to control our location. We needed our own studio. Our original intent was to rent, but we soon realized that would be a bad idea as industrial leases were usually for ten years. With our past experience on *Liberty Street*, we knew that a show could be cancelled at any time. We didn't want to be encumbered with a lengthy commercial lease, so we decided to look to purchase and hopefully build equity.

Once again, Sari started a location scout while Yan and I began to plan our characters, setting, and story. Using Toronto's east end as a model, we captured the refined elegance of Playter Estates, mixed it with the pride of ownership in modest Cabbagetown, and stirred in the practical realities of the low-income housing in Regent Park. For story efficiency and richness, we designed these all on one street. We created three basic families: the Mackenzies (Playter Estates), the Hayeses/Hernandezes (Cabbagetown), and the Wilkeses (Regent Park). From there, we created extended families, friends, and enemies spanning three generations and built a community hub at a local shopping mall populated by various businesses and services. We called the show *Riverdale*, a nod to one of our local neighbourhoods.

We were already falling in love with our characters and stories the same way we hoped our audience would.

★

Simultaneously, on the industry front, I was continuing my responsibilities with the CFTPA. I had become the national vice-chair working with the incumbent chair, Tom Berry. Tom, my mentor, was an enigmatic raconteur, superb lobbyist, and a magician when it came to turning out a proliferation of low-budget feature films, financed through intricate deals. He had a contagious boyish grin and was a pleasure to work with, as was the energetic and highly resourceful Elizabeth McDonald, our CEO. The three of us were constantly on the lookout for new funding opportunities for our industry.

Folks outside our industry often questioned why independent producers were constantly expecting government support. "Shouldn't the free market system of supply and demand govern your business?" they would ask. We would explain that if we were widget manufacturers, this might be true, but as part of the Canadian cultural industry, we needed protection from the production behemoth south of the border. The cost of large U.S. shows, supported by their big population base, would be fully financed at the time of production. This meant the U.S. shows could be sold into Canada and elsewhere in the world for a fraction of their original cost, severely disadvantaging a Canadian production.

In early 1996, Tom, Elizabeth, and I started to hear about a new government opportunity. We heard whispers at first. Then whispers gave way to rumours, till eventually real conversations were happening, speculating that Sheila Copps, our minister of Canadian heritage for the current Liberal government, had $100 million in her purse for Canadian television producers. "Is this really possible?" we asked ourselves. Then we got a call from Ms. Copps's office. She wanted to meet with Tom and me, as stakeholders, at our earliest convenience.

"Yes," our minister coyly confirmed to us in her Ottawa office. "I do have $100 million for your industry. Our government continues to be committed to strengthening your industry and creating an environment to encourage Canadians to tell their own stories. But the fund comes with caveats." She explained that she wanted everyone in our industry to "play nice" together. Her public money would match private money from the cable companies, and together these funds would be distributed through the

Canadian Television Fund (CTF). She wanted the new board to represent all aspects of our industry. We were asked to be part of her advisory committee.

Tom and I were very circumspect throughout the meeting. Then we called Elizabeth. "Holy shit. It's true," Tom informed our CEO as we shared supper together. We all agreed this was going to create amazing activity in our industry over the next few years. Ms. Copps's plans required eligible projects to roll camera before March 31 of the following year. Our industry was ready to embrace the challenge.

★

Back in Toronto, Stephen and I took a final look at a property that could support the needs of *Riverdale*. It was five-and-a-half acres of land overlooking a ravine — enough space to construct a realistic backlot with a functioning street. The warehouse itself was over one hundred thousand square feet of empty space waiting to be transformed into shooting stages and offices. I've always loved buying and renovating property. To date, I'd bought, renovated, and sold over almost twenty residential properties — but never a warehouse. Our bankers, the Royal Bank of Canada, were supportive. They would provide a mortgage and a small business loan for roof repairs and renovations . . . and they didn't even require that I produce a fake husband.

On Christmas Eve 1996, days after our touching and memorable Christmas dinner with my dear friend Bruce, Stephen and I took possession of our new acquisition and excitedly arrived for a tour. We had been informed that the electricity was off, so we showed up with heavy duty flashlights. However, we were not prepared for the dramatic sight that greeted us. It was a relatively mild December evening, with temperatures warm enough to melt residual snow, and much of that snow was dripping through our porous roof. Multiple garbage cans had been strategically placed to catch the leaks, but they were not sufficient. Water overflowed onto the cement floor. We looked at each other as our flashlights illuminated the streams of water and we heard the unrelenting sound of rain falling — inside. But were we daunted? Maybe for a moment; but, no. We both had a vision for what this could become and were anxious to get moving.

Two weeks earlier, we had received confirmation from the CBC that we had a season one pickup for *Riverdale*. Sheila Copps's new public/private fund was officially announced, and we were approved for financing if we began production before March 31 of the coming year. Construction began immediately and we needed two crews at work, one to design the look of the show and embrace the practicalities of production, the other to design and construct our administrative offices. Different teams, different pots of money.

On the administrative front, John Thompson (JT), whom I had worked with through countless renovations, knew I believed that a good working environment for my team provided for greater creativity. My biggest concern about the new building was the lack of sunlight. We'd already planned to put exterior windows in all the offices, but some of the corporate workspaces, including our boardroom, were interior and got no natural light. One afternoon, I got an excited call from JT. "I know how to solve the daylight issue," he said. "Come and meet me on site."

We stood amid the construction activity. People with jackhammers, table saws, and screw guns were all busy at work. Cables were everywhere and a generous layer of drywall dust covered all surfaces. JT, Stephen, and I cleared a path to the area that would become the boardroom. "Imagine," said John, "this interior wall as a bank of windows. It will open onto an interior courtyard. We will plant a Japanese garden with English influences. We just need to remove a thousand square feet of roof, et voilà, interior garden, interior sunlight. What do you think?"

Stephen and I shared a look. "Brilliant," we both agreed. We loved JT's suggestion but had no idea how we could finance it. And then something serendipitous happened. A few years earlier, I had made a modest investment in Showcase, a newly formed pay channel seeking a licence from the CRTC. Robert Lantos, who'd got his start in the film business with low-budget features, wanted to convince the commission that his new specialty channel would be a class act. He had reserved one of the investment units to be purchased by a consortium of independent producers and I had bought into that group. When it came time for the hearing, I and a couple of other independent producers were invited to be part of the panel. Robert knew I brought value to the panel for my *Degrassi* work, and, oh yeah, I was a woman.

Robert was successful with the licence and, after waiting a respectable amount of time, wanted to buy out the independent producers — we had served our usefulness. Interestingly, a small detail in the offering said that if one of us in the independent unit wanted to sell their portion, the others in that group would have the first opportunity to buy. This option appealed to me and fellow producer Michael Donovan (*This Hour Has 22 Minutes*). Two times in the past, Robert had tried to get producers to sell and each time, Michael and I teamed up and opted to buy the portions of whoever decided to leave. The unit was now owned by only Michael and me. Robert's people were becoming more anxious and more aggressive about getting their unit back. The very day I was mulling over the roof removal project, I got a call from one of Robert's people with a very attractive offer. I knew I had to call Michael.

"Michael," I hesitated. "I'm . . . going to cave."

"No, you can't. Do you know what this unit will be worth in another few years?" He then said he wished he was able to match Robert's offer and strongly suggested I consider staying in. But I had made up my mind. In a few short years, I had seen a $20,000 investment become over $200,000. This was more than enough to open the roof and build an inner garden.

Stephen and I called JT the next day. "We're a go with the roof removal project," I said. "Only one small change. We want to remove not just one thousand square feet, but two!" Over the years, our courtyard was worth every serendipitous penny. It hosted script meetings, job evaluations, research reports, and private coffee sessions. It provided natural beauty and tranquility amid production chaos.

With a portion of our warehouse roof removed, we were able to build a magical Japanese-style garden below.

★

Riverdale's deadline of March 31 was fast approaching. We ran twenty-four-hour shifts to get several kilometres of cable installed throughout the studio, all leading to our editing bay and switching room. Plumbers were everywhere adding toilets, removing old fixtures, and getting us up to code. Gaffers rigged up lights. Grips purpose-built scaffolding and intricate rigs as carpenters erected flats. On the backlot, houses were being constructed, sidewalks poured, trees planted, lawns seeded, streetlamps installed, and the street paved.

On Monday, March 31, 1997, at 8:10 a.m., mere hours before the funding deadline, I held the clapper board and snapped it shut to announce the beginning of principal production of *Riverdale*,

Provincial Minister of Finance Ernie Eaves cuts the ribbon to officially open our *Riverdale* backlot. During Eaves's term, Ontario introduced a tax credit program to support film and television production.

Canada's first prime-time, English-language soap. Everyone applauded and production began. The team had hit its target.

Once cameras were rolling, I retreated from the excitement of the set to what would become my corner office. In the middle of the room sat an old milk crate with a caulking gun resting on the edge of it. I flipped the box over and sat. Even though Stephen and I had been so resolute throughout all our prep, I would be lying if I said I didn't have doubts. I knew this was an ambitious project and I allowed a list of potential problems to fill my head. *What if we have a fire? What if the backlot gets vandalized? What if the story department can't keep up to the script demands? What if we have to stop production because the caterers give the cast and crew food poisoning? What if production money dries up?* On and on. After an indeterminate amount of time, I heard a tentative knock on my door.

"Linda, are you there?" my assistant asked. "We've been looking all over for you. CBC executives are here and anxious to do a first-day tour."

"Of course," I said. I shook the renovation dust off my skirt, pulled a hand-held mirror from my purse, applied a little lipstick, and said cheerfully, "I'll be right there."

Considering everything on my calamity list, surprisingly little of it transpired in that first season. Of course, we had some hiccups along the way, but all told, our fledgling project, with a whole new approach to production, went remarkably well.

On Monday, September 22, 1997, we held a launch party in the CBC atrium to celebrate the first episode on air and simultaneously released an innovative interactive website. The air that night was festive and full of hope. We were also buoyed by the cover story that we had received a few days earlier in *TVtimes*.

The playful cover of *TVtimes* the week of the *Riverdale* launch. The publisher later received some reader pushback saying it was inappropriate to depict a marital affair on a national cover.

The article, by Eric Kohanik, captured the playfulness of our show with the title, *Soap Bubbles. Lies, treachery and laughs . . . it's all just part of a typical day on Riverdale.*

The following morning, we found other reviews and ratings were . . . not great, but okay. We did get a particularly scathing review in *The Globe and Mail* saying, "The only good acting in this show is by Gilmour, the dog." Ouch. But we weren't discouraged. We knew it would take a while for people, critics especially, to adapt to our somewhat melodramatic style. We knew the ultimate key to success rested with our audience and we needed time for them to engage. We'd pulled off an extraordinary feat of hard work, miracles, and magic, and now it was out there — right across the country.

Between seasons, we hired a British director from *EastEnders* as a consultant. We watched the first season with him and he pointed out story arcs that engaged him, and others that needed improvement. Our writers soaked this up and began work on season two with renewed energy.

Our momentum built throughout the second season and so did our ratings. Our stories started to generate much fan speculation as to what would happen next in our soapy antics.

We were settling into a nice rhythm as CBC ordered script development for a third season. "Do we dare believe we are on the way to establishing our own Canadian *Coronation Street*?" Stephen and I quietly asked each other in the privacy of my office. "It will be brilliant if we really pull this off!"

Then some unpredictable events unfolded.

CBC, along with all the other Canadian broadcasters, were taking their time turning development deals into production orders. As we approached production time, we anxiously waited for the phone to ring to formalize our third season pickup. Finally, my assistant popped her head in the door and announced an urgent call for me. "Sorry," she said. "I didn't get her name."

"Must be the CBC," I confidently thought. "This will be our season three production confirmation."

I picked up the line and realized why my assistant hadn't heard the name. There was much hyperventilating from the other end as I struggled to make out the caller. "*Elizabeth!*" she finally shouted. "It's Elizabeth McDonald from the CFTPA. Now that you're the chair you need to be the first to know. The Canadian Television Fund has run out of money."

"That can't be," I said. "None of the 100 percent Canadian shows have been ordered yet!"

"Well, there's been a run on service production — the industrial shows that are part-American but still qualify for the fund. They got their broadcast orders early and have cleaned out the fund for this year."

"Well, that's an unintended consequence," I lamely said. "Can we verify this?"

Elizabeth reassured me that she had several calls out and would get back to me as soon as she knew more. She also reminded me that there was a CTF board meeting at the end of the week, so she hoped there would be a resolution at that point.

"Whoa, you look like you've seen a ghost," Stephen joked as I entered his office.

"No time for jokes," I said, and I soberly relayed the news.

Once we both absorbed the gravity of the situation, Stephen and I split forces. He swung into action for Epitome, while I turned my attention to the larger industry picture. I talked at length with Elizabeth and other CFTPA board members as to how we might find an elegant resolution to this situation. This surely was not the "playing nice" that Sheila Copps had envisioned.

Meanwhile, Stephen, like many other producers, put in an urgent call to the CBC, explained the situation, and asked for verification of our pickup. He got our finance department to rapidly fill out our CTF application and dispatched one of our security guards to the CTF office to stand in line in case more money became available. By the end of the day, over two dozen applicants were queued up outside the CTF head office. That night, Stephen and I took coffee and donuts to all those in line. Everything was odd.

And all 100 percent Canadian producers were scratching their heads wondering, "How did this happen?"

We all anxiously awaited the results of the Friday board meeting. At 5:05 p.m. I got a call from Elizabeth. "You're not going to like this," she said reluctantly. "There has been no resolution. There was a glimmer of hope when the board proposed a plan to 'borrow forward' into next year's government funds, but, once discussed with government bureaucrats, this was shut down."

I could not believe what I'd just heard. A board of fourteen, some of the brightest minds in our industry, could not "fix" the Canadian content issue for 1999, meaning no 100 percent Canadian television production for the year. I refused to accept these results. Then it dawned on me. At Sheila's insistence, the fund had been fashioned as a public/private partnership. *Hmm, if the public side can't "borrow forward," maybe the private side can,* I thought.

Over the weekend, I began a series of phone calls. I called Robert Morrice, in charge of independent production financing at the Royal Bank, and asked him a theoretical question: "Would the bank be willing to loan the fund against the collateral of next year's contribution, from the private side — the cable portion?" When Robert got back to me with a positive response, I tracked down Richard Stursberg, the current chair of the production fund. I ran the notion of a "borrow-forward" past him. "Interesting idea, Linda, but I don't know how this could work."

"Richard, I think you can convince the Royal Bank to cash flow this. Let me give you Robert Morrice's home number."

By early Sunday morning, I got a call from Richard. "Genius," he said. "We are going to do a 'borrow-forward' from the private side with the assistance of the Royal Bank. Thank you for you making this happen. I'd like to invite you to the press conference we will be holding tomorrow morning to announce the new plan."

Yes, it was all about cash flow. That simple lesson was one I learned early in my career when I bought a Steenbeck with a production grant.

★

Sheila Copps, our then Minister of Heritage and mastermind behind the new Canadian Television Fund, pays a visit to the *Riverdale* set.

Canadian productions from coast to coast were in business again. Season three of *Riverdale* was a go. A bullet had been dodged both for the industry and for our company.

Our new season began to air around the same time that the CFTPA hosted its annual conference in Ottawa. As I was now chair of the CFTPA, I had many obligations over the next few days, and I wanted to do a good job, especially knowing I was the first female to hold this position. As I chaired our board meeting, one of our board members formally thanked me for saving domestic production, and I got a round of applause. He requested his thanks be recorded in the minutes. I blushed. "Not necessary," I offered, though I was secretly thrilled by the recognition from my peers.

As our meeting adjourned, two of the senior board members asked if they might have a cocktail with me. I had a speech to prepare, but didn't want to be rude, so I joined them at the bar. As drinks were delivered, it became obvious that the two of them had an agenda.

"Linda," Guy #1 began, "we know that you have been working very hard as our chair and we appreciate all your efforts, but . . ."

Guy #1 looked to Guy #2.

"But," Guy #2 continued, "the board does have some concerns. We think you might be a little too, well, ambitious."

"Oh," I gasped. I hadn't seen this one coming.

"Perhaps you are just a little bit too self-interested." Guy #1 and Guy #2 nodded in unison.

"Are you asking me to resign?" I asked.

"No, sweetie. Nothing of the sort. You're doing a great job. We want you to stay, just maybe tone it down a bit."

I slowly walked back to my hotel room feeling shame and humiliation wash over me. I hadn't felt like this since I was a teenager and my dad had picked me up at the cop shop for drag racing.

★

It was the summer after high school, around 2 a.m., and I was at the wheel of a casual boyfriend's souped-up Chevy. At a stoplight, a big guy, with muscles bulging from his rolled-up T-shirt sleeves, cigarette hanging from his mouth, pulled up beside me and started revving his engine. Rick, too drunk to drive himself, heard the challenge of the roaring engine and said, "You can take him!" My eyes lit up. I sneered at the muscle shirt, depressed the clutch, threw the car into gear, gave her a good rev, and as the light changed — gunned her. And then the sirens started.

Police stations at 3 a.m. are simultaneously busy and bleak. We sat waiting as various other infractions were processed. By the time they were ready for our questioning, Rick was quite coherent. Somehow, because he wasn't driving, and I didn't own the car, we got off with only a warning. But — our parents were called.

"So, this is why I taught you to drive?" Dad asked rhetorically as we drove home in silence. I knew my dad was angry with me, deservedly so. At least in the drag racing incident, I knew I had done something wrong. I had no idea what damning mistakes I had made as CFTPA chair.

★

Back from the conference, feeling chastised, there was little time to dwell on my reprimand — it was full steam ahead on *Riverdale* season three. When our new season hit the air, it garnered its highest ratings to date and kept improving week after week. Folks across Canada were connecting with our stories to enjoy the "romance of everyday life." We had audience engagement.

Jayne Eastwood (Gloria Wilkes), Ken James (Stan Wilkes), Lynne Griffin (Alice Munro), Paul Soles (Costas Stavros), and Marion Gilsenan (Joan MacKenzie) enjoy their soapy roles in *Riverdale*.

As we looked for innovative ways to keep our series alive with high volume and low cost, Stephen secured a new financing source, Procter & Gamble. P&G were willing to back our production and, with our government funds in place, we just needed our broadcaster on side. We were confident CBC would order season four imminently.

And then, we waited. And we waited some more.

A few months prior, as money had been tightening for our national public broadcaster, there was a change to the head of English-language production at CBC. We had enjoyed strong support from the previous head and had trusted that that support, along with our climbing ratings and inventive financing model, would transition positively to the new executive. Then, in early spring, our assistant excitedly got off the phone to tell us that our new CBC broadcast executive was in the area and wanted to make a visit. "Must be good news!" she smiled confidently.

Stephen and I shared a look. We knew this was not a good-news scenario. Broadcast executives don't just "happen to be in the hood." The meeting was short. There's not much to say when the series that you believe could become a mainstay of Canadian television is cancelled.

I fought back tears as I made the short drive from our office to the house. As the news of the cancellation spread, one by one, various cast and crew members dropped by the house. So many had bought into the vision. They had fought against odds to make an impossible timeline happen. They'd joined forces to find cost savings at every turn. They'd celebrated the lives and joys of our characters and stories. The evening became an impromptu wake, complete with shared stories, condolences, profanities, pizza, beer, wine, and tears. By midnight, the last folks left, and Stephen headed to bed.

Alone, I watched the embers die in the fireplace. I had shed a lot of tears in the last few hours and had consumed a fair amount of red wine. I heard Kit tell me, "You're going to fail without me." I thought about Guy #1 and Guy #2. I could see them shaking their heads in unison, like the grumpy old men on *The Muppet Show*, saying, "The cancellation is a real shame. But really, Linda, hubris, you know. You should have seen it coming."

With my confidence shattered and my sense of my self-worth cancelled along with my show, I swore it was just not worth it. I was done with the television business — for good.

CHAPTER THIRTEEN

THE KIDS COME BACK

It was a perfect early summer day in 2000. I had the top down on my BMW, cruising nicely in the fast lane. Stephen was in the passenger seat, baseball cap pulled low over his head to protect his face from the sun. Max and his best friend Adam chuckled in the back as they enjoyed the speed and the wind in their hair. We'd had an adventurous day at Presqu'ile Provincial Park — swimming in the lake, a picnic, a walk on the marsh walkway, and a forest hike. A wonderful family outing, far from the worries of business and production. I felt relaxed and carefree. I was reminded of a similar feeling forty-two years ago when my friends and I were driving back from the Lake District in England, after an idyllic summer outing.

And then it started. Right there, in the left lane, as I passed a truck and shared the road with many loaded vehicles returning to the city after a summer weekend. *My God*, I thought, *I'm having a heart attack.* My breathing was rapid. Sharp pains seared through my chest as both my hands tightly clenched the steering wheel. My internal voices kicked in. *Pull over, Linda. Don't crash. Check the rear-view mirror. Move to the centre lane. Breathe. Keep your passengers safe. Pull into the right lane. Breathe. Pull over.*

As the car came to a stop on the shoulder, all three passengers looked at me in confusion. Keeping my breathing as regular as possible, I asked Stephen if he'd be okay to drive the rest of the way home.

"Are you all right?" he asked.

"Just not feeling too great right this minute, but I'll be fine." I mustered a smile.

As we started up again, my breathing began to slow. My racing heart became more regular. No, not a heart attack. It was a panic attack, and as I was soon to find out, it would be the first of many. When we got home, Stephen confided he was worried about me. He was not fooled by my fake cheerfulness at the side of Highway 401. He knew my feelings of failure and tried to reassure me that everything would be okay. But even he, with his resolutely sunny outlook, didn't know how.

Now that *Riverdale* was cancelled, we were both worried about the future of our huge studio with its Mt. Everest–sized mortgage. Over the course of renovations and production, we had both fallen in love with our warehouse/shooting stage. We enjoyed how efficiently all departments could work under one roof with opportunities for casual conversations, cross-pollination, and innovative problem-solving. But what now? With no production slate, Epitome Pictures Inc. had no income stream and a mounting string of expenses and debts. We faced the obvious: we needed to put the building on the market.

And then . . . financial kismet.

Alliance Atlantis Communications (AAC), a powerhouse production company and our distributor, had just clinched a deal with Disney for a youth co-production, *In a Heartbeat*, complete with a ridiculously tight deadline. They were desperate to find a shooting space and conducted a quick recce of our studio. They immediately made an offer for a year-long lease, enough to cover the mortgage for that period. With our short-term finances secured, Stephen, who fortunately remained a practising lawyer, suggested, "Now with the studio rented, how about we spend a few weeks in the south of France? We'll take a villa in Saint-Paul-de-Vence. Max can bring Adam. We'll have a French tutor, play tennis, visit galleries, and take in the local sights."

"Fine" was about as excited as I could get. "I suppose this could be a good plan."

Stephen took that as an enthusiastic "Yes" and began to organize travel plans. I, meanwhile, stepped up my trips to my therapist — not the same one I had seen twelve years earlier while struggling with my infertility, but the one who had helped me through the painful process of my separation with Kit. I hadn't seen her for a couple of years and thought it would be good to reconnect about the annoying panic attacks that were becoming more and more frequent. My independence was vanishing as I was paralyzed by the prospect of turning onto a multi-lane freeway. Doctor K gave me two choices: I could either get to the root of my attacks or approach them from a behavioural perspective. As a practical person, I selected the latter.

"Are you sure?" she asked. "I get the feeling there could be more to these attacks than you are acknowledging."

"I'm fine, really," I replied. "I just need to get my independence back, and let the past be the past."

"Okay, you're the boss," she smiled. "But whenever you are ready to go back, we can go there. And should the past try to speak to you, please welcome it."

We started a slow cognitive behavioural therapy process. She encouraged me to enter the on-ramp of a highway (I chose the Don Valley Parkway) and stay in the right lane, then exit at the following ramp. I was to do that daily. Hunched over my steering wheel, clinging tightly as though my life depended on it, I dutifully followed the advice. Next, I was asked to repeat the same exercise, only this time to travel for two exits. The following week, I was told to continue that exercise, but between exits, move into the left lane for a short while. Bit by bit we built up my confidence. Slowly, I was regaining my ability to drive and with it, my independence.

★

Meanwhile, totally unrelated to me or any of the Degrassi team, a *Degrassi* resurgence was underway. *Jonovision*, a CBC youth reality show hosted by Jonathan Torrens (*Trailer Park Boys*), ran a *Degrassi* reunion show that attracted its largest audience ever. In addition, CBC execs programmed *Degrassi Junior High* and *Degrassi High* as an after-school event, running classic episodes daily at 4 p.m. Ratings were amazing. With the backdrop of these double successes, Stephen quietly whispered to me, "Linda, do you think we should consider a *Degrassi* reboot?"

"Are you insane?" I faked a polite smile. "I'm so done with television, broadcasters, disingenuous promises, and fractured dreams. Why would I think about TV again?"

"Because you're good at it," said Stephen, "and because I think we can make it work."

I'd been watching. I knew what was going on with *Jonovision* and the CBC after-school strip. I liked what I saw, but only with detached curiosity. Then I got a call from Yan. "The renewed interest for *Degrassi* is incredible," he gushed. "I'm ready for some development, are you?"

Did I dare allow myself to be sucked back in? Was it possible that my new coping therapy for panic attacks could help guide me back to production? Perhaps, but did I really want to return to teenagers, high school, and social issues? I thought back to my feelings when seeing firsthand the aftermath of the L.A. riots and my cynicism about the effectiveness of the media to spark social change. Then . . . I thought about the boxes of mail that *Degrassi* had received over the years: fan letters, heartfelt shared stories, gifts for Spike's baby, and thank-you notes. It had been eight years since we'd completed *School's Out*. Over that time my productions had focused mainly on entertainment. The *Degrassi* mandate was so much more. Yes, it was about entertainment, but it was also about education and reassurance, about inclusivity and authenticity. It was about creating accessible storylines around complex political and social issues. I had always known in my heart that no single show could change deep-rooted systemic problems, but I did know it could make a difference in one child's life. I thought about my student, young Angie, and how *The Summer We Moved to Elm Street* gave her the courage to talk about her dad's alcoholism and seek help. I missed my teenagers.

I agreed to meet with Yan the day before we took off for France. "I don't want to do any formal development with any broadcaster," I told him firmly. "But I am happy to engage you to do some preliminary work while we are away."

We both acknowledged that it had been almost a decade since we'd last told *Degrassi* stories and that we would need some new young writers to help us. "I can work on that while you're away," he volunteered cheerfully.

"Don't push me," I warned Yan. "Work on your own for now; we can build a team, if necessary, when I return." I knew that I needed to approach this cautiously, one exit at a time.

*

One of the oldest towns on the French Riviera, Saint-Paul-de-Vence is a medieval hilltop village snuggled between Nice and the Alpes-Maritimes. Our villa was halfway up the hill, just outside the ancient walled town. We looked down over olive groves and cypress trees and saw Mount Saint-Jeannet in the distance. This would be our home for the next five weeks.

Our swimming pool was surrounded by gardens overflowing with lavender, rosemary, sage, and thyme — the herbes de Provence. And then there was the light. Although it was a well-used cliché, it was impossible to stay in the south of France without noticing the light. The intensely bright blue sky met the soft greens of cypress and pines and caressed the deep purples from the sun-drenched lavender fields. No wonder the region has been and continues to be a magnet for painters.

The day after we arrived, promptly at 10 a.m. our French teacher knocked at our door. "Bonjour, mes amis," she cheerfully introduced herself. "Je suis Nadia, votre professeur." For the next three hours, we were allowed to speak only French — a pattern we repeated each weekday for the next five weeks.

Nadia was an engaging teacher. She believed in experiential learning and took us to the local boulangerie, fromagerie, and boucher to negotiate for our food. She planned trips to local art galleries and took us for a day trip in Nice. Here Max got a cool new spiked haircut. One day, we travelled together to the Mediterranean seaside and the boys were surprised both by the hard pebbles on the beach . . . and the lack of tops on the female sunbathers.

★

The pool and gardens at our villa, L'Olivier, in Provence provided a welcome respite from the disappointment of the *Riverdale* cancellation.

After swimming lengths one afternoon, I relaxed poolside, blissfully intoxicated by the herbes de Provence. My mind drifted to the first time I had planned to travel to France, over thirty years earlier. I had already purchased my ticket to cross the English Channel from Dover to Calais and was scheduled to make the trip a few days after my crash.

My crash. Usually when my thoughts would wander back to that moment, I would instantly shut them down. But on that peaceful summer afternoon, I allowed myself to go there.

★

When I first regained consciousness after the accident, I had no idea how long I had been hospitalized or how I had gotten there. With my eyes and head bandaged, I lay in the dark, wondering if I would ever see again. Bit by bit, I started to piece together the order of events: I remembered the lake and waterskiing; stopping for coffee; the soothing voice of a stranger who held my head in his lap. I started to recall an argument about who should sit in the front seat, yes, an argument with friends, but who were they? Whose car? . . . Simon, yes . . . *Oh my God, where is Simon? Is he here in hospital?* I started frantically calling for a nurse. When I finally got assistance, she was no help. "We have no record of others," she said gently. "But the doctor might have more information, he'll be here tomorrow."

I remembered an argument. *Something about changing seats. But who was I arguing with? I didn't think it was with Simon.* Then I remembered Simon had been angry. "Bloody hell, mate. Do as she says!" *Mate. Mate . . . who was the mate? Yes . . . he needed to get into the front seat. He was tall, too big for the back. The mate? His friend — right — the one whose girlfriend couldn't be with us . . . Elliot.*

The following morning, when the doctor arrived, I immediately asked about my friends. "I can see what I can find, but first we need to examine you."

After completing his physical exam and ordering more X-rays, he offered to inquire about the others. "I'm so sorry to tell you," he said on his return, "your friend, the driver, was brought to this hospital, but . . . there was no response from him. I'm afraid he lost his life on impact."

I thought I was going to throw up. "And, the other guy, the one in the passenger seat?"

"Yes, there was another passenger, but he was taken to a different hospital. I have no further knowledge, I'm afraid."

Simon dead? That can't be, I thought. *He was planning to open a new club in London the following month.* He was dead. And I was alive.

I wouldn't get news of Elliot's fate till much later. He lived for a few weeks with massive brain damage, then quietly passed away. His family mourned privately. *Elliot? He was sitting in my original place, the front passenger seat. When I had forced my way out of the back to exit the car, did I do additional harm to Elliot? Did I make his brain damage worse? Did I kill him?*

I sat on the edge of the pool in France, remembering the confusion and upset of being in that hospital in England, and my mind took me to a cathartic event that had happened more recently.

*

My niece Erika had been born in June 1997. This was a happy event as at this point my parents had six grandchildren — all of them boys. I decided to take a quick break from *Riverdale* production and head to Seattle to welcome the new addition to our family. A couple of years earlier, my brother Tony had been working in Ottawa for the young and ambitious telecommunications company Mitel. There he was headhunted by Bill Gates to relocate to Seattle and help lead the integration of computers and phones. At Microsoft, Tony eventually ran the team that would negotiate the $8.5-billion deal for Microsoft to acquire Skype, one of the first companies to offer video chat and voice calls across multiple digital devices. But this trip wasn't about his work, it was to celebrate the arrival of a beautiful baby girl. We spent a lovely day wandering about Seattle, shopping in the fish market, and fixing a yummy seafood meal together. Tony's exhausted but very happy wife and young Erika bade us an early goodnight as Tony and I chilled out on the living room floor. We had our backs on the furniture, our legs spread out in front of us, and a bottle of wine between us. It felt easy and safe and a welcome respite from the demanding schedule that I had just been through to get *Riverdale* up and running.

At one point, Tony asked me to tell him about my car crash. Tony was, and still is, an enthusiastic hobby race car driver and vintage car collector. He loved car stories of all sorts. *Really?* I thought. *All right.* I told him about driving back from our day in the sun, about drifting off then abruptly waking up. I spoke of the kindness of the stranger. I wrapped up with my well-rehearsed phrase, "I'm truly fortunate to be alive today."

"Yes, I know all that," my brother said, "but I want to know more."

"You know I can't have children because of that?"

"Yes, and I'm truly sorry for you, I know how much you love kids." He paused and topped up both our wine glasses. "But," he continued, "I want to know . . . what did it sound like? What were the smells? And, most importantly, how did you feel?"

No one had asked me those questions before.

Wary at first, I started to describe to him, with increasing detail, how terrified I felt when I'd woken up in the back seat to the dreadful sights and smells. I explained that I'd had one basic survival instinct and that was to get myself out of the car — in a hurry. I told him how I'd hung on every word the stranger said to me as he'd cradled my head, and how my blood had soaked his lap. I recounted how I'd never felt so alone as when I woke up in the public ward of the British hospital, fearing I had lost my sight.

The words, locked up for so long, came tumbling out.

"Whoa," said Tony, "brutal."

"But there's more."

Tony looked at me expectantly.

"I killed one of the boys," I said flatly.

There, finally, after all these years of hearing it as a repeated internal phrase, I had said it out loud. "I killed one of them."

I told him how we had changed seats not long before the crash. I then described guiltily how, after the crash, I'd exited the back seat. As the car was only a two-door, I'd had to push the front seat — hard.

"There was still a person in there. I crushed him further. I gave Elliot the brain damage that killed him."

"I'm pretty sure I'm safe in saying that it was the double-decker that did the damage," Tony said as he headed for his desk to find a pen and paper. "But let's sketch it all out."

I explained the logistics as Tony drew.

"And you're sure this is the side of the car from which you exited?"

"Hundred percent," I replied.

"And you said the driver died on impact?"

"That's what I was told."

"Then there is no way you did further damage to the passenger. You came out of the right side of the car. You are forgetting that in England, the driver sits on the right-hand side."

"Oh my God, yes . . . you're right!"

That night, safely tucked in my brother's guest bedroom, I had one of the best sleeps I'd had in a long while.

On my flight back to Toronto, I felt a sense of peace. Tony had helped me unlock a memory. However, once back in Toronto, I was immediately thrown back into the rigorous pace of production. The peace from that night fell deeper and deeper into the back of my mind to join all the other details of that fatal night.

*

Now, suddenly, here in Provence, without the constant pressures and distractions of TV production, I was beginning to unpack all the memories I'd stored away.

"And should the past try to speak to you, please welcome it."

The next morning, as we sipped lattes in the garden, I asked Stephen if he would mind if I discussed my crash. He, of course, already knew the basic facts as well as my resulting endometriosis and infertility, but I'd never shared with him the emotional side of it — the reality of being the sole survivor of a crash that had taken two lives. It was a tough conversation, and Stephen was an

Stephen and I sip Kir Royale as we watch the locals play boules at Place Général de Gaulle in Saint-Paul-de-Vence.

empathetic listener. As I dried my cathartic tears, he asked, "What can I do to help?"

"You already have," I said. "You listened."

Stephen put his hand over mine as we sat silently side by side. Then I took a breath.

"You know, people often ask me where my drive and ambition comes from? I've always answered that it comes from being the eldest child of an immigrant family. But today, I realize it is more than that. I believe I have a deep-seated need to succeed as the price I must pay for surviving."

*

A few days later, in Provence, our friends Hunter and Valerie came from England for a visit. We enjoyed exploring the famous Maeght Foundation and were dazzled by the local pyrotechnic festival on July 14. All too quickly our time disappeared. It had been five weeks of croque monsieurs, art galleries, and boules games. I had forgotten about the pain and disappointment of the *Riverdale* cancellation a few short months earlier.

For our final night, Stephen booked us for dinner at La Colombe d'Or. This beautiful hotel, known for its rustic charm and famous art collection, was the perfect place for us to entertain our tutor Nadia and her seven-year-old daughter, Josephine, for a thank-you supper. Here, surrounded by works of Picasso, Chagall, Miró, and Calder, we knew that we had added new friends and memories to our shared family history. It was time to return.

"Linda, um, we have to meet as soon as you're back," Yan stuttered on our answering machine as we checked our five-week-long load of messages. "Please call me, um, as soon as you can, you're going to love this!" I knew when Yan spoke like that he was genuinely excited. He'd certainly piqued my curiosity. I called him first thing the next morning, only to be told that he'd rather meet in person.

"So, two things," said an ebullient Yan in my office. "One, I've been doing some reading and visiting the Canadian Film Centre. I think I've found us two amazing young writers for our new *Degrassi* team."

Wait, I thought to myself. *Didn't I say before my vacation that I didn't want to go there yet?* But I couldn't get the words out as Yan was still charging forward. "And two — you're never going to believe this, but I've found a brilliant hook to kick off the new *Degrassi* series!" He paused for dramatic effect.

"Well," I said. "Do share."

"Seriously, you really want to know?" he teased.

"Yes, dammit, what's your brilliant hook?"

"Okay, it came to me in the shower. I do a lot of good thinking there."

My eyes were rolling now — *please get on with it.*

"So, if you do the math, it's been, uh, let me make sure, yes, it has been since 1987, or maybe it was 1988, we'll need to check, when the episode aired of the birth of Spike's baby. If the new show goes on air in 2001, Emma will be about twelve or thirteen. She's more than ready for junior high."

"Oh my," I mused. "This is true. So, we could kick off the new series with a reunion of the old cast and find Emma as she starts junior high?"

"Yes, you get it. It's brilliant, no?"

"Actually, Yan . . . it's *totally* brilliant!"

And then he and I started to riff — about characters, about the importance of the internet that was non-existent when we filmed the classic series, about the richness of a potential reunion. Okay, forget all those baby steps and that cautious "one ramp at a time" behavioural psychology stuff, I was all in! Stephen shared Yan's and my excitement. We agreed that we would not approach broadcasters for development money, but rather front it ourselves. We knew we had a great idea and wanted to flesh it out internally before pitching it to others. But there was one snag: Kit and I still jointly owned the rights to *Degrassi*.

The negotiations with Kit were predictably difficult. Numerous lawyers were involved, as were accountants with spreadsheets and forward multiplier projections. Eventually, we settled on a price, and I was able to buy him out. As Kit took his cheque, he couldn't resist one last jab. "Don't know why you're bothering with a reboot, you're going to fail without me. But hey, good luck, ta-ta! And thanks for the cheque."

That would be the last time I would see Kit. Wendy and Lew kept in touch with him and were invited to his wedding in Nova Scotia where he had bought a large property on the cliffs above the sea. "It reminded him of his childhood in the Isle of Man," Wendy reported back. By all accounts, Kit seemed more settled and happier than he had been for years. It was therefore a great shock when we heard of his sudden death from a brain aneurysm in January 2020.

When word of his death came out, I was bombarded with requests from the press. I told them that Kit's unique talent — his intimate style of directing, small of scale yet richly layered — was integral to the success of *Degrassi*. I was surprised how saddened I was to hear of Kit's passing. It was true, our relationship had passed its best-before date years earlier, but his legacy lived on in my shows, and in my heart, and I am eternally grateful for that.

Kit also left me with another legacy. When we were deep into production of *Degrassi: TNG*, my self-doubts would creep in. I would hear Kit's final words replayed over and over in my mind. *"You're going to fail without me."*

But, in the fall of 2000, I wasn't in my worrying stage yet. I was in that glorious phase where anything was possible. Yan and

I hired Aaron Martin and Tassie Cameron, recent graduates from the Canadian Film Centre. They were young, talented, enthusiastic, and fans of the original show. It was perfect. Simultaneously, Stephen ran a digital development agenda with Raja Khanna and his team at Snap Media Corp. Our goal was to launch the show and website concurrently. Our website was ambitious. It was to be a virtual school where our fans could enroll and engage in various school activities. In the industry, the buzzword of the day was "convergence" and that was how we developed our show. It would be a convergence of traditional storytelling on television and non-linear storytelling on the web. Our online "students" could select homerooms, use moderated email, take quizzes, participate in extracurricular events, and decorate their own lockers. We couldn't have known it at the time, but this Snap invention was actually what MySpace would become in a few more years.

★

While our virtual school evolved, Aaron, Tassie, Yan, and I worked to develop a pilot storyline that would be a satisfying reunion for the old fans and an exciting online cyberstalking story for the "next generation." We developed rich new characters, some connected to the original classic characters, some brand new, but all with raging hormones, intense curiosity, and an appetite for the internet and community. Before the end of the year, we had created an impressive glossy pitch document for both television and the web.

The night we picked up the final printed version of our document, Stephen and I had dinner at the local Italian restaurant at the top of our street. We knew we had something very special. "I'm afraid to say this out loud," I said to Stephen over a glass of Montepulciano d'Abruzzo, "but this feels like the right project at the right time." The internet had given us the opportunity for a fresh new take on teenage stories, yet we still got to explore those rich and ongoing teenage themes of sexual awakening, first-time adventures, and introspective self-analysis. "I love it!"

"I think it's exceptional," agreed Stephen. "We have to position it correctly with broadcasters. I recommend that we pitch all potential broadcasters in the same week."

"Whoa!" I gasped. "Don't you think we owe CBC the first look?" For the last two decades, with the exception of some documentaries for TVO and Global, I'd produced almost exclusively for CBC.

"They can be our first meeting if you like, but I think we would be doing the project a disservice if we didn't let all the appropriate broadcasters know about it," Stephen sagely suggested.

"Okay, it'll be just like the L.A. agent tour all over again!"

We set up four broadcaster meetings.

We gave four energetic and engaging pitches.

We waited — but not long. Within the space of a week, we had interest from all four broadcasters. "Say it isn't so," I laughed, back at our local restaurant. "Four friggin' broadcasters want our show! This never happens."

"Enjoy this point in time," Stephen counselled wisely. "It might never happen again!"

"Four friggin' broadcasters," I repeated as I twirled my seafood pasta.

Within a short time, it was clear we had only two real contenders for *Degrassi: The Next Generation*. Despite enthusiasm from all, only two had the ability to buy both the television show and the ambitious web component. We had offers from CBC and CTV. Negotiations were ongoing and culminated at the Banff Television Festival in late spring.

At the same time, CTV was negotiating a major deal with Bell Globemedia — convergence on a large scale. To ensure the deal passed CRTC scrutiny, CTV was promising the domestic production community substantial "significant benefits" such as increased licence fees and extended number of episodes per season. If the deal was finalized, it could be a great opportunity for our new show. Meanwhile, the CBC was seriously studying how they could deploy their current public funds to support more television with heavy web involvement.

At CBC, final programming decisions were being made by the same team who had cancelled *Riverdale*, while over at CTV, decisions were in the hands of my old friend, Ivan Fecan. Ivan had left the Mother Corp a few years earlier and was now moving and shaking the world of private broadcasters. He had persuaded the incredible champion of Canadian culture, Susanne Boyce, to join him at CTV. Together, they made a formidable team.

I went back and forth. Despite my huge disappointment with CBC over the *Riverdale* decision, I had a fundamental loyalty to them. They had stood by me for twenty years of production: *The Kids of Degrassi Street, Degrassi Junior High, Degrassi High, School's Out, Liberty Street,* and *Riverdale*. Plus, I'm personally a strong supporter of public broadcasting.

Negotiations with both sides continued in various spots in and around the regal Banff Springs Hotel: on the terrace with the Rocky Mountains forming a majestic backdrop (almost too perfect to be real), in the cozy bar, and on walks throughout the well-manicured and landscaped gardens. At one point, it was obvious that things were coming to a head. Difficult as it would

be to leave so many old friends at CBC, it was the right decision for our show to work with CTV. We had an established relationship with Ivan, and CTV held so much promise for new revenue sources. In the end, CTV proved to be the best broadcasting

With Ivan Fecan in New York, celebrating our third International Emmy Award nomination.

partner we could have imagined and became true champions of *Degrassi: The Next Generation.*

With our broadcaster negotiations concluded, Stephen and I talked to our agent and various distributors to firm up international rights and a U.S. deal. In the end it was our distributor Alliance Atlantis who came through. They offered an aggressive distribution deal to pick up all rights outside of Canada for a substantive guarantee per episode. Interestingly, they also saved us from what could have been an unfortunate school naming. As our new series would span Grade 7 to Grade 12, we had decided to call the school Degrassi Community School Institute. It turned out that AAC were in negotiations to distribute a new U.S. show. They couldn't talk about it yet but highly recommended that we drop the word "Institute" from our official school name. When, later that year, AAC proudly announced that they were the worldwide distributor for the new and exciting CBS show *C.S.I.: Crime Scene Investigation*, we understood why they had suggested we not call our school Degrassi: CSI!

With the ink barely dry on the Epitome-AAC deal for the distribution rights, Ken Faier from AAC attended a Kidscreen conference in NYC. On one panel was Meeri Park Cunniff, from the newly formed Noggin channel at Viacom. Noggin had a double mandate: preschool programming in the morning and adolescent programming in the afternoon. The afternoon initiative was a pioneering venture for them. At the panel, an audience member asked Meeri what sort of programming she would be considering for the new adolescent schedule. Without missing a beat, Meeri said, "A few years back, there was a great series on PBS called *Degrassi*. That's exactly the kind of show we are looking for."

"Well," said Ken in the corridor moments later to a surprised Meeri, "do I have the show for you! It's called *Degrassi*."

"Really?" queried a skeptical Meeri.

"Yes, *Degrassi: The Next Generation*. And it's everything you need — respectful storytelling, hard-hitting teenage issues, a major web presence, and a seasoned producer. What more could you want?"

"Let's take a meeting with my boss, Sarah Lindman!"

In a few months, Stephen and I had secured a major Canadian broadcaster, an innovative web partner, a tremendous storytelling team, an international advance, and an exciting new U.S. partner.

The Kids were back.

And so was Linda Schuyler.

CHAPTER FOURTEEN

Some Things Change, Others Don't

She took my hat! She walked over in her "Ashley Kerwin" way and picked it off. What does she expect me to do? Play tag? I got more important things to worry about. My mom and dad? They told me last night if my marks slip below A minus, I'm yanked off the team. That cannot happen. I'm playing basketball all the way — past junior high, past university. I don't have time for stupid games. Tell Ashley she can keep my hat.

Our casting director Nicole Hamilton, Yan, Aaron, and I were silent as the young man in front of the camera finished his monologue. "What?" he asked. "Did I do it wrong? I can do it again." We noted a certain panic in his voice.

"No, it was great," I reassured him. "We'll be in touch with your agent shortly. Thanks so much for coming in today."

He rubbed his hands together in a nervous gesture and looked at the four of us. "Right. Yes . . . I should go. Thanks for the opportunity." He leapt from the chair and was preparing to shake our hands when he accidentally nudged a light and it started to topple. Uncertain whether to catch the light or continue with his handshaking gesture, he chose the latter. Our production assistant saved the light. With hand-shakes completed, he backed his lanky body humbly out of the room while continuing to smile and nod. Once the door was firmly closed, we looked at each other, smiled, and simultaneously said, "We've found our Jimmy Brooks!"

Our new audition process was far different than when we had cast the original *Degrassi* series. No longer did a sand-wich board sit at our curbside advertising auditions. We had

Fourteen-year-old Aubrey Drake Graham at his audition for *Degrassi: The Next Generation*, 2001.

a casting director and numerous agents committed to the search. At first, I was nervous about having intermediaries involved, but I quickly learned to trust the judgment of those who specialized in child actors. The casting process might have changed, but the key criteria for selecting our young performers remained the same. We were still looking for vulnerability. Even if we were casting a bully or a mean girl, we wanted to see that behind the eyes was someone for whom the audience might eventually feel empathy. Sincerity, likeability, sense of humour, and age-appropriateness were all on the checklist. And then there was that all-important, hard-to-quantify quality of charisma.

In our search, we were looking for nine main characters to populate the student body of our new Degrassi Community School. So far, we had found eight strong leads and a rich assort-ment of recurring characters who could eventually become leads.

One of the first to be cast was Miriam McDonald as Emma Nelson, our environmental crusader and Spike's daughter. When Miriam and Amanda Stepto (Spike) did their chemistry read, Miriam had been particularly nervous. She was a big fan of the original show and was starstruck to meet Amanda. To help get herself in character, Miriam had purchased a new set of leggings that she thought would be appropriate for Emma. The leggings were soft blues and greens and had dolphins flying up and down each leg. This was a delightful take on the character of Emma and seemed to give Miriam the confidence she needed; so perfect, in fact, that she wore them in the first episode. She and Amanda nailed their reading.

The bubbly Cassie Steele had easily won the role of Emma's best friend, Manuella "Manny" Santos. Manny was known for her giggles, her gossip, and her envelope-pushing wardrobe. Forming part of Emma and Manny's friend group was the class clown, J.T. Yorke, portrayed by the mischievous Ryan Cooley, and Toby Issacs, our devilishly smart nerd, who was brought to life by the sardonic Jake Goldsbie. Ashley Kerwin, our golden girl, was a high academic achiever, president of the student council, and annoyingly (to her), the new stepsister to Toby. Melissa McIntyre was perfect for this role. Ashley's best friends included the sensitive and insecure Terri MacGregor, beautifully brought to life by Christina Schmidt, and Paige Michalchuk, our somewhat manipulative cheerleader, captured by the engaging Lauren Collins. Daniel Clarke had easily won the role of our dark and brooding bad boy, Sean Cameron.

We added two unexpected characters to our roster, Liberty Van Zandt and Gavin "Spinner" Mason, to be played by Sarah Barrable-Tishauer and Shane Kippel. Sarah and Shane had originally auditioned for other roles. Although they didn't get those parts, we were so struck by the two that we created characters just for them. (Earlier, on *Degrassi Junior High*, we had done the same thing when we created the roles of Archie "Snake" Simpson and Christine "Spike" Nelson for Stefan Brogren and Amanda Stepto, respectively.)

We were excited about our new cast. They brought an abundance of enthusiasm, diversity, and talent. But we still hadn't found our Jimmy Brooks until the day that Aubrey walked into the audition room.

No worries that his résumé was virtually nonexistent: Aubrey Graham, at fourteen, connected with the camera in a powerfully charismatic and magnetic way. It was all there — the twinkle in the eyes, the infectious smile, and the loose and easy body language. The camera loved him, and so did we.

Fourteen years later, in advance of his appearance on *Saturday Night Live*, Aubrey, now known simply by his middle name, Drake, appeared on *The Tonight Show Starring Jimmy Fallon*. When Fallon asked Drake about his *Degrassi* audition, he shared his memories of that day. He remembered an experience different than mine. "Man, it was the first audition I went on, but it was also the day I got accepted by these really cool Jewish kids at school — I mean, I finally got invited to Daniel Pearlman's house. It was the first time I had smoked, probably not the best choice! . . . Before the audition I started getting really paranoid. I thought I had completely ruined my life. I was splashing water on my face constantly — it was like a Clearasil commercial."

Aubrey admitted it was a boneheaded choice and was shocked and delighted to find out that he hadn't sabotaged himself in the audition. In fact, he had won the role. Aubrey would be with *Degrassi* for over seven amazing years until his character, held back by a devastating school shooting, would finally graduate. His character's graduation coincided with the year he released his debut mixtape *Room for Improvement*. Little could any of us have predicted where music would eventually take our talented and enchanting Aubrey Graham.

In 2013, Aubrey released his new single "Started from the Bottom." I was initially bemused by the notion. Certainly, in my mind, *Degrassi* didn't constitute "the bottom." But as I listened to the lyrics more, I started to understand where he was coming from when he sang about working all night and facing traffic on the way home.

Early in 2007, the assistant directors (ADs) had come to my office to complain that they were having some difficulty with Aubrey. He was often late for work, and when he did arrive, he was tired and ill-prepared. Aubrey and I had a brief but firm discussion about this, and he promised to be more professional. He never once mentioned the reason why he was tired and unfocused, he just volunteered to fix it.

Aubrey found the solution to his "professionalism" problem with the ADs and the security guards. When Aubrey would leave our studio at the wrap of a production day, till his call-time the following morning, unbeknownst to me he would be hard at work at the music studio and/or working the phones. He was building his own mixtapes and establishing influential connections — from the bottom up. After "working all night," he would return to our studio. The security guards would let him into his dressing room to sleep for what little was left of the night. The ADs, tipped off by security, would leave him sleeping till he was needed on set. I was blissfully oblivious to all of this. But it worked. I got my reliable actor back, and Aubrey got to push hard to position himself for the next leg of his professional journey.

And what an amazing journey that has been and continues to be. We're all so proud of Aubrey.

★

The original *Degrassi* series had been shot on location in real schools, something that I felt added to the authenticity of our show. Even though we owned a one-hundred-thousand-square-foot studio and a backlot, I was worried that this facility would limit our relatability. I insisted on a city-wide search for an underused school location. It didn't take long to realize that, one, not a lot of space was available, and two, what space might be suitable was expensive. As the independent production industry had grown, school boards had recognized that there was a lucrative business to be had, renting to film companies. I ended up making the decision that everyone knew I should have made in the first place: we started to convert our studio into a school. Once convinced, I became a zealous advocate of this idea. "We need classrooms with natural light," I asserted. "Let's blow out this west wall and replace it with windows for two classrooms. Let's remove the southwest wall and create a double glass door front entrance.

Let's build a gym, a media studies room, locker rooms, hallways, principal's office, cafeteria, and whatever else we might need!"

I was euphoric. This large space that had felt like an incredible liability after the untimely death of *Riverdale*, was now, once again, abuzz with anticipation and opportunity. To establish a style, the art department, writers, and I visited the old set of *Degrassi High*, now a vibrant campus of Centennial College. The architectural style was a good fit for our 1950s studio. We adopted their colour scheme and general look and tone.

It was now time to hire a director. Even though I had over 120 television episodes under my belt since my split from Kit, I was worried about his absence from the new series. The influence of the British kitchen-sink dramas of the 1960s had a positive impact on our ability to establish an authentic visual style for our youth show. I remembered Kit's parting threat, "You're going to fail without me."

Snap out of it, Linda, I reprimanded myself. *These are new times, with new opportunities. Don't look back.*

★

In the late 1980s, when I was deep into production of the classic series, upstart director Bruce McDonald was making a name for himself as part of a loosely affiliated group of filmmakers known as the Toronto New Wave. His breakthrough films *Roadkill* and *Highway 61* had earned him notoriety both nationally and internationally. His later film *Hard Core Logo* had screened at Cannes, where it received much buzz and was lauded by Quentin Tarantino. For some reason, I thought Bruce's irreverent style and whimsical tone might be just what we needed to launch *Degrassi: The Next Generation*. I met Bruce in his "too cool for school" cluttered office in Toronto's west end. As I climbed the stairs, I thought, *You're a crazy person, Linda Schuyler. This young, internationally acclaimed director is not going to be interested in your little school show.*

Bruce also came with a reputation. When he'd received his $25,000 TIFF award for *Roadkill*, he accepted with a smile and the acknowledgement that he was going to spend it on a "big chunk of hash." So why did I think Bruce might be a good *Degrassi* fit? I couldn't explain it but, despite logic telling me otherwise, something told me to push through with the meeting.

Although I hardly recognized him without his trademark cowboy hat, Bruce was polite and engaged in our meeting. I dutifully explained what *Degrassi: TNG* was all about and how I wanted to launch it with a fresh new look and energy. "So," I cautiously proceeded, "I'm wondering if you might be interested in directing our opening one-hour special, a reunion show? We'll catch up with old characters and introduce our new cast against the backdrop of a cyberstalker. The character being stalked is Emma Nelson, the daughter of Spike."

"Ah, Spike," Bruce mused. "I had a crush on her. Whatever happened with her and Snake?"

"Well," I replied, secretly amused that Bruce was aware of my *Degrassi* characters. "Spike and Snake are actually key returning characters, and Snake will be our new media arts teacher, Mr. Archie Simpson."

I looked at Bruce's well-worn cowboy boots and ill-fitting jeans and caught a glimpse of the roaches on his desk. I glanced up and saw dust collecting on multiple awards on his windowsill. After a considerable pause, Bruce looked at me and said, "Yup, I'm interested."

"Whoa," I said. "You've surprised me. Pleased me — but surprised me! I'm curious, why does this appeal to you?"

After more considered silence, Bruce shared: "It goes like this. My dad's been a high school principal for years. He doesn't really understand me or my films. If I do your show, I think for the first time my dad might be proud of me. So, there you have it."

With that, Bruce and I began a professional partnership and friendship. Despite our age difference and divergent styles, Bruce and I shared a love of storytelling and young people that saw us

On set, Bruce McDonald and I discuss script revisions. After directing "Mother and Child Reunion," Bruce became a regular part of the team.

through multiple episodes together. I'll never forget one capti-vating evening on set, early on in the production of "Mother and Child Reunion," the kickoff to the new series. We were preparing for a large establishing shot of the school at magic hour, as our whole cast, old and young, made their way into the school for the much-anticipated school reunion dinner and dance. I stood beside Bruce as our AD, Derby Crewe, set up the shot.

"Look at all this," Bruce said. "Take it in."

I glanced about and saw how fine the exterior of our school looked with its grand new entrance, complete with glass doors and wide steps. I admired the freshly planted trees and shrubs that lined the front wall. I scanned to the right and saw light coming from inside the windows of our new classrooms. In the parking lot were carefully placed production vehicles and extras, all decked out in their party finest. Our camera operator was on a jib arm, practising the moving shot that would take us dynamically from the front of the school and into the foyer. Grips and gaffers ran about adjusting rigs and lights.

"You made this happen." Bruce winked at me. "Be proud."

And I was proud, very proud. Proud of everything and everyone. And yes, proud of myself. *We're going to pull this off,* I thought.

"Stand by!" Derby called. "Roll sound. Roll camera. Slate. And..." Derby made a gesture to Bruce silently saying, *It's all yours.*

"And . . . action!" called Bruce.

As soon as the words were out of his mouth, Bruce doffed his cowboy hat, put his arm around my waist, and started walking me towards the school. I was wearing a red-print summer dress; Bruce was in denim. I let my head rest on his shoulder as we walked. We were playing extras in our own scene. As we reached the front steps, Bruce called, "Cut!" He and I both got the giggles. It was magic.

★

The first time we collectively knew "Mother and Child Reunion" could be magical was three weeks prior when we'd assembled the cast, writers, director, and producers for the first read-through. Holding a read-through had been part of my process since the early days of *The Kids of Degrassi Street.* This practice happened a few days before a script was published. Our young cast, who were seeing the script for the first time, had an opportunity to weigh in with spontaneous thoughts and opinions. This worthwhile process served a couple of purposes: One, we got fresh dialogue suggestions and story comments from our cast (another reason why I'm such a fan of casting age-appropriate actors). And two, with the cast having an opportunity to discuss the script at the read-through, and again at rehearsals, there should be no delays on set. Actors had ample time to understand their story and their motivation. Many times, when my production managers would sharpen their pencils to bring the budget down to a "doable" number, they'd target both the read-through and the rehearsals as "big savings" that could go into production. My answer was always the same: "No." These two elements played a critical role in maintaining the authenticity of our show.

For "Mother and Child Reunion" we needed to break one of our *Degrassi* writing rules. Until this point we had never shot a scene from the adult perspective. Even if a scene began with adults talking, the camera would pull back to reveal a young character overhearing the conversation. Now that we had classic *Degrassi* "kids" returning as adults, we needed to amend this rule to allow our classic characters to have scenes with each other, without a young character present.

The "Mother and Child Reunion" read-through was the first opportunity to see our classic and next generation cast together. I had wondered when we'd first approached some of our classic cast how they would feel about reviving their characters. For the most part, this was greeted with great enthusiasm. We did have pushback from one actor, the one who had played Emma's birth father, Shane. It was hard to get a real fix as to why he was reluctant to return, but I surmised it had something to do with the negative feedback he had received for Shane's handling of Spike's pregnancy and the character's subsequent drug use. I was sorry for this, of course. It was also a big reminder for me to re-enforce the X Factor with our new cast, to help them keep distance between their own identities and their screen counterparts.

On the day of our first read-through, the electricity in the air was palpable. There was a gasp from all our newbies as the last cast member of the classic cast entered the read-through. "It's Snake!" someone quietly whispered.

Stefan Brogren, all six-foot-three of him, cleared his throat, looked at all the fresh young new faces, and announced sternly to the room, "Okay, guys, if I'm coming back to play Mr. Simpson, your media immersion teacher, I intend to run a tight ship — no nonsense or silliness from any of you — clear?!"

The new cast was stunned.

Then Stefan broke into a wide smile. "Gotcha. Just kidding, you guys! Welcome to *Degrassi* — we're going to have a blast together!"

Everyone broke into spontaneous smiles and applause.

As the read-through started, we heard, for the first time, the blended voices of our classic characters — Joey, Caitlin, Spike, and

I look on as Stefan checks out our new digi-props with the cast of *The Next Generation*.

Snake — and the new generation. I sat in the circle with my original and new casts, my writers, my production team, and my husband/partner, and thought, *I'm blessed*. I'd left teaching twenty-three years ago, and here I was, still enjoying the thrill of working with adolescents while being my own boss. Life was good.

★

Unlike the classic *Degrassi* series, *Degrassi: The Next Generation* was a union production. Our company had become signatories not only to ACTRA, the WGC, and the DGC, but also to a number of other guilds and unions. In some ways, adherence to these various labour groups with rate cards made negotiations and budgeting easier. Even so, at times, I would glitch on various union regulations. We ran into one of these early in production of season one. With age-appropriate casting we were working with many minors with strict provisions under ACTRA. They could work for a maximum of eight hours — there was no overtime — and they must be tutored for two hours each day. All this made sense and aligned with how we'd run the original *Degrassi*.

However, there was another union requirement that I'd never permitted on the original show — parents must be within eyesight of their children when they are performing in front of the camera. This was a fine rule for younger children, but for our adolescents, it was complicated and often counterproductive.

In episode 107, "Basketball Diaries," Ashley is afraid she is going to lose her boyfriend, Jimmy, and invites him to her bedroom after school. They engage in a serious make-out session that has Ashley trying to undo the buckle of Jimmy's jeans. After the rehearsal for this scene, Aubrey and Melissa McIntyre made an appointment to see me in my office. "It's about the make-out scene," Aubrey began hesitatingly.

"You have a problem with the scene?" I asked, rather surprised. "We had a good discussion about this scene in the read-through."

"No, we love the scene," Melissa said quickly. "We just, er, we just—"

"—don't feel comfortable performing it in front of our parents," Aubrey hastily completed her thought.

"You know it's a union requirement that parents or guardians be there," I explained. The looks on their faces said they were not impressed.

"Okay, let me discuss this with the production team," I offered. "I have no idea what the solution could be, but I want to find one." I was sympathetic to their request.

An hour later, with the combined thoughts of our key administrative team, we had a plan. We emptied a storage room to convert to a parents' lounge, outfitted with coffee, snacks and, most importantly, a live video feed from the floor. Parents could watch their kids through the monitor while the actors felt they had some space. I explained to Melissa and Aubrey what we were setting up. Although they didn't think it was ideal, they were grateful that parents would not be in their immediate view.

The next day, everything went well, and we got a touching and beautifully awkward scene shot with Jimmy and Ashley. Once the scene was safely in the can, David Lowe, our production manager,

Aubrey and Melissa get into character.

felt it was prudent to tell ACTRA what we had done. The union was immediately on the defensive and swiftly dispatched a steward up to our set. By the time they arrived, we were on to an innocent scene in the hallway with bad boy Sean and our crusading environmentalist, Emma. The parents were still in the parents' lounge.

ACTRA was at first dogmatic — we had violated the proximity required between actor and parent. A lengthy debate ensued with the following compromise: we could keep the parent's lounge, but any parent or child who wanted to be closer during filming, as the rule provided, must be allowed to do so. Interestingly, over the course of sixteen years, rarely did a parent request to be closer to set. And not once did we receive such a request from an actor. Our parents' lounge would ultimately be located in a sunny room upstairs at the far end of the studio, and became a favourite spot for the parents and chaperones. Over time, we added the amenities of a telephone line, fax machine, computer, and eventually the internet.

Even if there had not been a union requirement for parents on set, I think this new generation of parents would have been more visible than those of the original cast. Unlike the original series, where parents seldom came to set, we were dealing with a new group of parents who were of a generation that had become known for having a tendancy to hover over their millennial children like "helicoptors." The millennials were also a different actor and audience cohort from our previous Gen Xers. They were the first generation to grow up as digital natives in the internet age. They had confidence and an easiness about them but could also act entitled, causing some to refer to them as Generation Me.

Despite all the handy buzzwords for a generation, we had assembled an amazing and enthusiastic group of young people who were as excited to be part of our production as were we to have them.

★

And then, September 11, 2001.

We were a few months into production and had settled into a comfortable rhythm. I was at home reading scripts for a late morning writer's meeting. An hour and a half earlier, I had received my customary call from our production manager, David. He assured me all the cast and crew had arrived on time and confirmed the time of the first shot. We were off to a good start. I sat back on my front porch and began to mark up my scripts. My PM unexpectedly called again, "Have you seen the TV?" he anxiously asked.

"Er, not watching TV — reading scripts here."

"A plane has crashed into the World Trade Center," David said with forced calmness.

"Oh," I thought out loud. "What an awful accident."

"I don't think so. Turn on your TV now, and then please get to the office ASAP."

I went to our media room, just in time to see the second plane crash into the south tower. Oh my God. Terrorists. The drive from our house to the office typically took about eleven minutes. I made it in seven.

Production had ground to a halt. There were tears in every corner of the set. Actors, crew, writers, administrators — all crying. No one could comprehend what had just happened in our time zone, on our continent — in our world. Stephen and I split our duties. We travelled around set, offering hugs of support and sharing tears. Yet we remained resolute. Production would continue. Some of our cast considered us harsh and uncaring. We empathized, but explained, "If we stop work, the terrorists win." We didn't realize it at the time, but this would be a mantra in the post-9/11 world. This attitude was influenced by the 1989 conversation Ivan and I had had on the terrible day of the Montreal massacre. In spite of the gravity of the situation, Ivan and I agreed that our episode of sexual abuse should continue to air. The misogynists and terrorists would not win.

We pushed through the production day and hastily made counselling available. When we called wrap for the day, we had not accomplished our scheduled scenes, but we had established a work attitude that we considered critical in the age of terror.

September 11 proved to be a pivotal point for Generation Me — it changed their lives. The large cohort that had been known for their overconfidence and narcissism was now confronted for the first time with fear and terror. This collective anxiety influenced a new *Degrassi* storytelling resolve. As well as reassuring our young audience that they were not alone, we felt it was increasingly important that our stories contain messages of empowerment and hope. We wanted our young audience to know that they could make a difference. And it wasn't just our storytelling that was affected. At this time, our music team, Jim McGrath, Jody Colero, and Stephen, were already working on our theme song. They doubled down after 9/11.

Whatever it takes,
I know I can make it through.
If I hold out,
I know I can make it through.
Be the best, the best that I can be.
Whatever it takes,
I know I can make it,
I can make it,
I can make it through.
Whatever it takes,
I know I can make it through.

Degrassi: The Next Generation theme song
Music and lyrics by Jim McGrath,
Jody Colero, and Stephen Stohn

Despite scripted drama, crises behind the scenes, and shocking international acts of terror, *Degrassi: The Next Generation* was ready for release in early October. Those of us on the inside were convinced that we had produced something special, but would the critics and our audience see it that way? Our publicists had been busy in the weeks leading up to our launch. As most members of our young cast were new to acting, we had conducted a series of workshops to help them with the press and various interviews. Prior to the release date, and on the day, many interviews for print, television, and radio were conducted with folks both in front of and behind the camera. I had been alerted by our publicist that the first review to come out would be on CBC Radio.

I hoped the review wouldn't be coloured by the fact that the CBC did not get the television rights to the show. With this thought in mind, and also genuine concern about whether or not people would like the new show, I decided to listen to the review alone in my office, without our publicist, or even Stephen. My biggest fear was that we would be compared, unfavourably, to the classic *Degrassi* series. I could hear people saying, "Linda Schuyler had a great show with *Degrassi Junior High* and *Degrassi High*, why didn't she just quit when she was ahead?"

I held my breath as the review began and then heard the words: "The kids are all right!" I slowly exhaled. As I listened to the entirety of the review, we didn't get crucified. There were no sour grapes. The reviewer enjoyed the show. When I opened my door, a small crowd was gathered in the hall, all with great big smiles on their faces and with "thumbs-up" gestures. I threw my arms open for a group hug. THE KIDS ARE ALL RIGHT!

As other press rolled in, there was much support of the new generation. Oh, we got some diehards who felt that we had become too glossy and too slick, but overall, it was very good.

And so were the ratings.

CHAPTER FIFTEEN

THE KIDS ARE ALL RIGHT!

Friday, the end of the week. I was happy to be home, and I was stoked. *Degrassi: TNG* was finishing its third season, and our shoot the previous night with a guest star couldn't have gone better. We hadn't even reached out to Billy Ray Cyrus about a guest appearance — he had approached us. I pulled out my heavy poolside chair to settle in with a glass of wine. Our garden chairs needed to have exceptional heft as they lived on the deck facing south over Lake Ontario. Chairs any lighter (and we have had them) would be easily picked up by strong offshore winds and deposited either in our neighbour's lawn or dropped to the bottom of our pool. As I looked out over the lake, I marvelled at how the infinity edge of our pool blended with Lake Ontario, making it appear as though our pool stretched thirty-five kilometres out from the house. I thought to myself that, in a strange way, this was a metaphor for how my company felt in that moment — a solid underpinning with an expansive reach. I'd never felt more secure as an independent producer.

Billy Ray Cyrus was in town shooting his own series, *Doc*, and one of our regular directors, Stefan Scaini, was at the helm of Billy's show. Billy Ray approached him and wondered if Stefan might be able to score him a guest spot on *Degrassi*. "Would the role as a skanky limo driver work?" we wondered. In the closing episode of season three, Jimmy is trying to impress his new girlfriend, Hazel, by renting a special limo to take them to the year-end formal dance. When the limo pulls up, the script describes it this way:

HAZEL (excited): I've never been in a limo before. Do we get champagne, too?

They stop, en masse. Horrified looks. Waiting is a DISGUSTING LIMOUSINE — dirty, rusted, sort of small, flickering under-lighting.
    It's driven by DUKE, the king of all bikers, wearing a tuxedo-printed T-shirt. Doffs his cowboy hat to the girls:

DUKE: Howdy darlins. I'm Duke — your chauffeur for the evening.

They stare at him in horror. Jimmy steps forward.

JIMMY: I think there's been a mistake.
DUKE: You Jimmy Brooks? Ain't no mistake, hound dog. So giddyup.

Billy read the script and good-naturedly agreed to the part. As he and I waited in the backlot between set-ups he asked if I'd like to sit in his truck, where it was warmer. In his deluxe black pickup, he fired up a killer sound system and popped in a CD of his latest music. "Thought you might like to hear some of my new tunes," he offered with a smile. We sat back and chilled. It was a moment. Then Billy turned the volume down and looked at me directly. "Linda, I want you to know it's an honour to be on your show. When I got home to the family and told them I was doing a gig on *Degrassi*, well — I might as well have told them I was the new president of the United States of America. My daughter Miley said, 'That's so cool!' I tempered her expectations. It ain't like I'm the new principal

Billy Ray Cyrus, our skanky limo driver, Duke, tries to convince his client, Jimmy Brooks, that his limo is a peach.

or nothing, I'm just doin' a day, as a limo driver. She said, 'Still cool, Dad — my friends will be so proud of you.'

"I have to tell you, Linda, my girl don't impress easy. So, you can see why I was happy to get your offer!"

★

I smiled to myself now as I sat beachside and replayed those words. On the beach, I heard the delighted squeals of kids at the water's edge as they built and destroyed sandcastles. I overheard dog owners throw sticks and toys into the lake. I was aware of lovers strolling barefoot in the sand. Then, the phone rang. I thought I might let it go, but, even as I tried to relax, I couldn't ignore it. I put down my glass, ran, and grabbed it on the final ring before it went to messages.

"Hi Linda, Kevin Smith here!"

"Oh my God, Kevin, how nice to hear from you!" I gathered myself and thought, *Is he still mad at me for that whole* Speakers Corner *debacle?*

As a New Jersey teenager, Kevin worked in a convenience store. Apart from tending cash, he and his buddy would "make papers."

This meant taking the various sections of the Sunday paper and assembling them ready for sale. This was boring work, so they kept the TV on in the background. The new time slot the WNET executives had selected for *Degrassi* was Sundays at 10:30 a.m. So, while making papers, Kevin Smith and Jason Mewes discovered, and got hooked on, *Degrassi*.

A few years later, when I was on location on *Liberty Street*, Kevin and Jason, fresh off the release of their first movie, *Clerks*, made a pilgrimage to our Playing With Time Inc. offices in Toronto's east end. They wanted to meet me. Our receptionist at the time had no idea who they were and would not give out any information as to where I was on location or how I could be reached. When I got back to the office a friend called and said, "Turn on your TV, *right now*, to Citytv."

There on the screen were Kevin and Jason. They were making their angry voices heard on the local TV show, *Speakers Corner*. Material for the half-hour show *Speakers Corner* came from the self-taped video pieces that members of the public could record using a video booth on the sidewalk, outside of the Citytv studio. Here people could record personal rants, raves, shout-outs, jokes, or musical numbers — it was like social media before social media. Kevin and Jason had availed themselves of this opportunity and, using straightforward and colourful language, declared their love for *Degrassi*. Then they launched into a tirade about the terrible treatment these poor American fans had received at our office.

Over the next few days, I tracked down Kevin at his New Jersey office and apologized. He was quite lovely and asked, "Would it be possible to get a *Degrassi Junior High* jacket?"

"My pleasure," I happily offered up. "What size would you like?"

"Small should do, thank you."

Oh, I thought, *Kevin is not a small man*, and discreetly tried to suggest a larger size.

"It's not for me," Kevin laughed. "I'm working on a new movie, *Mallrats*, and I want my actress, Shannen Doherty, to wear it in a scene."

We arranged for the jacket to be delivered and planned that we would meet either in Toronto or New York. As it turned out, it would take almost another decade before that meeting would happen.

★

"So, Ms. Schuyler," Kevin continued on the phone. "I've been watching your new show. Frankly, I didn't think you could pull it off — but you have."

"Oh, nice of you to say," I said, not sure where this was going.

"So, here's the deal. I want to come to Toronto and do a three-episode arc on your new show. I will write the episodes, direct them, and act in them. Are we good?"

"Oh," I muttered, frantically wondering where I put my wine. "First off, Kevin, it would be an *honour* to have you be part of our show. Truly."

"Right, then. Tell me how we'll schedule this."

"Well, before we get that far, we have some hoops. I rely on the Canadian Television Fund for a large part of my financing. This means I have restrictions as to how to hire. Meaning — all my writers need to be Canadian."

"Fine," said Smith, "I'll consult with your writers, and they can get the credit."

"Cool. Good. But . . ." I hated having to say this. "I also can't have a non-Canadian director."

"Oh, so I can't direct?"

"I'm afraid not."

"Can I at least *act* in your show?"

"Oh, most definitely," I happily agreed. "But, there's a little glitch. We have favoured nations. We can only pay you scale."

"Seriously. Hmm."

I listened to the sounds of everyday life from the beach: kids laughing, dogs barking and splashing in the lake, a passing boom box blasting music, as Kevin paused to think. "Okay, I'll do it. Let's make it happen next spring."

"Kevin, you are the best — let's *so* do this!" I returned to the pool and couldn't wait for Stephen to come home to tell him. I also couldn't wait to share the news with Aaron Martin. Yan Moore had left *Degrassi: TNG* a couple of years earlier when he got a once-in-a-lifetime opportunity for his own show, the futuristic *2030 CE*, to go into production in Winnipeg. This gave Aaron a great opportunity: four years out of the Canadian Film Centre, he was now our showrunner, and a *huge* Kevin Smith fan.

Kevin and Aaron hit it off famously and work began to incorporate Kevin and Jason Mewes into season four of *Degrassi: TNG*. Kevin, Aaron, and I were in an early script meeting when Aaron suggested, "Well, if Kevin Smith is at *Degrassi*, we gotta have ninjas."

"Ninjas! I don't think so."

Kevin and Aaron both looked at me.

We had ninjas.

The story conceit was that Kevin Smith is shooting his new movie — *Jay and Silent Bob Go Canadian, Eh?* — on location at Degrassi and is working with many of the Degrassi students as actors and musicians. This allowed us to enter into a larger-than-life

Kevin Smith and me at a 2004 press conference. I was amazed with Kevin's photographic memory. He had the ability to recall far more *Degrassi* trivia than I could.

fantasy world, yet still keep our authentic teenage stories alive. In this two-part episode, "Goin' Down the Road," Kevin hires Degrassi student Craig (Jake Epstein) to do the music for the movie. Craig, a talented musician (as Jake is in real life), is fighting his own demons as well as the imminent loss of his girlfriend Ashley.

Aaron and Kevin worked to seamlessly blend the make-believe world of moviemaking with the angst-ridden reality of our teenagers. This worked, in part, because of the beautiful personality that lurked behind Kevin's dark trench coat and fake mullet. Despite his irreverence and potty mouth, Kevin is one of the warmest and most empathetic men I have met. His script sensibility and that of Aaron's pulled off what I thought would be impossible. Kevin even convinced Alanis Morissette to play herself as the fictional school principal. We closed out season four with a preposterous movie shoot, a love story gone bad, a poignant story of loss and depression, and . . . ninjas.

This took us to a total of eighty-one episodes since we'd begun the new series with "Mother and Child Reunion." And what story we had packed into these episodes! Apart from much fun and hijinks, we'd tackled some very serious and moving topics. During that span, we finally told the story of a gay bashing, the story I had wanted to tell since my friend Bruce had been so rocked by the death of librarian Kenneth Zeller in High Park on a summer night in 1985. It had taken me over twenty years to tell this story from the teenage perspective. I needed the climate to be accepting and the deft hand and sensibility of Aaron and team to make it work.

*

Aaron grew up as a closeted gay Armenian-Canadian in the blue-collar town of Brantford, Ontario. I knew Brantford well — it was only eleven kilometres away from my hometown of Paris — and I understood Aaron's need to move to the city. By the time he and I met, Aaron was living in Toronto, newly out and a recent graduate from the prestigious Canadian Film Centre's writing program.

He was ready to make his mark. Aaron and I were both lucky to have found one another, although at times it wouldn't appear that way. In six years of working together, we fought, we laughed, we argued. When our relationship was at its rockiest, Aaron would vow never to return. "I can't work for you anymore," he'd assert. "You don't know how to produce."

Usually, we solved our differences on our own, recognizing that it was passion that drove us both. One time, though, it got to such a fever pitch that it took his agent and my lawyer (husband) to sit us down in a room and not let us leave till we patched up our dispute. And thank goodness they did. I can't imagine how I would have produced our LGBTQ+ storylines without Aaron's talent and passion.

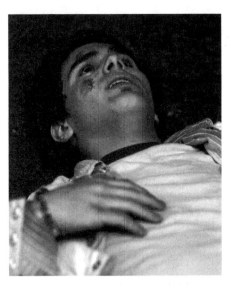

Marco (Adamo Ruggiero) gets gay-bashed. It took me eighteen years after the death of Kenneth Zeller, in 1985, to be able to tell this story.

"Pride" (written by Aaron Martin with James Hurst and Shelley Scarrow) is a two-parter about a young teenage boy, Marco, beaten in a park for no reason other than his sexuality. We took a long view of this storyline and planned it out over numerous episodes. Marco's coming-out would happen first to his best girlfriend, Ellie (Stacey Farber), then to his buddies Jimmy and Spinner, next to his mom, and lastly — in a later season — to his father.

Casting of this role was critical and in some ways a bit random. We had originally cast Adamo Ruggiero, a day player, as a break-dancer. After watching him in his bit role, we thought, *Looks like we might have an actor who could play Marco!* In a funny way of life imitating art (or vice versa?), we had no idea that young Adamo was actually living his own real-life version of Marco. Adamo would eventually have a series of "coming-outs" culminating on his eighteenth birthday. He invited the whole cast and crew to join him and his friends and family for his "I'm out" party at the Drake Hotel. It was a joyful occasion, and, of course, my mind went to my dear friend Bruce. If only he could have had the opportunity to celebrate his sexuality rather than be trapped in his double life, caught between truth and self-denial.

Throughout production, I kept a variety of black binders behind my desk called "Why I Do What I Do," which became known affectionately as "WIDWID." They were overflowing with letters, emails, and later, tweets and blog comments. In one binder was a heartfelt email from a mother who'd felt compelled to write after watching the first Marco episode.

> Thank you for the Marco storyline. My son is gay. Once my husband and I found out, we stopped talking to him. I watched the Marco episode on *Degrassi* the other night. When it was over, I picked up the phone and called my son. It was the first time we have spoken in ten years. Thank you.

Others wrote to say:

> When I started to look at *Degrassi* I saw someone just like me. Marco, thanks to you, I came out to myself and my friends. (Jorne, Belgium)

> I am gay, and watching *Degrassi* made me somewhat more proud of myself, or easier for me to accept myself. (Tim, U.S.)

> When I see episodes that look like my real life, I start to cry . . . Living my kind of life is not easy . . . everyone knows I'm Homosexual. You made a way through my life. Now I can see more clear. (Marc, Quebec)

It was gratifying to know our stories were connecting with people of all ages. This confirmed what I had known for a long time: that with intimate and personal storytelling, we were able to make large political statements accessible to our young audience. This was captured poignantly in "Accidents Will Happen." Written by Shelley Scarrow, this story explores Manny's journey to make a tough choice when she finds out she is pregnant with Craig's child. In this script, we structured a similar balancing technique as we had in our first abortion story, "A New Start." Emma — Manny's best friend and Spike's daughter — is a strong pro-lifer who tells Manny, "My mom was your age when she got pregnant with me. I wouldn't be here today if my mom had had an abortion." Regardless of Emma's compelling arguments, Manny knows abortion is the right choice for her. Unlike Erica in *Degrassi High*, Manny does not face protesters at the clinic. She has made this decision along with her mother, and we see mother and daughter enter the clinic together. Our final shot is Manny opening the door to the procedure room. With the slightest of smiles on her face, she knows what she's doing is right for her. Manny is a third-wave feminist.

Close to the air date for "Accidents Will Happen," in April 2004, a massive demonstration was organized in Washington to protest various restrictions on abortion and other anti-women policies. Women walked through downtown Washington to support the right to abortion and access to birth control as well as scientifically accurate sex education. But also, many pro-life demonstrators lined the route.

With the abortion debate back in the headlines, our American broadcaster started to get nervous. Initially supportive of this storyline, they were sensitive to the climate and believed the responsible thing to do was hold the episode off the air. In Canada, "Accidents Will Happen" aired as scheduled and garnered our highest ratings of the season.

The chatter from our American audience on our website was intense. They were furious and demanded they get to see the show.

Degrassi's third-wave feminists.

Even though it was geo-gated, some got their hands on bootlegged copies. The N (formerly known as Noggin) finally aired the show a couple of years later. The show was accompanied by wrap-around discussions with experts. Even though I was initially disappointed that the episode was delayed, it reminded me that our stories had to walk a delicate balance to find the right message for the right times.

Finding balance was how we approached development of our strong storyline for "Time Stands Still" (written by Aaron Martin with Brendon Yorke).

Prompted by the shock of the Columbine shooting of 1999 — the year before we began development of *Degrassi: TNG* — and remembering the terrible Montreal massacre at the École Polytechnique in 1989, we developed a school shooting story that would be personal and have long-term reverberations for our characters. We chose our character Jimmy Brooks to be the victim of the shooting. By season four, Aubrey's character was immensely popular with our fans. We had positioned his character on track to get a basketball scholarship for university. We chose the troubled character Rick Murray (Ephraim Ellis) as our shooter. Rick had a problematic past, and had been a bully and an abuser of his girlfriend Terri. In turn, he was picked on and bullied by many of the *Degrassi* regulars, including Jimmy. Using the Barbara Coloroso paradigm from her book *The Bully, the Bullied, and the Bystander*, we positioned a number of our characters as bystanders.

I found this episode particularly difficult to produce. It's one thing to tell stories about teenage sexuality, abortion, and mental illness. All these issues are multi-faceted and allow for much story nuance. The problem with a school shooting is that the whole premise is just wrong. A gun in a building dedicated to youth and education? It's wrong. A gun in the hands of a misguided youth? Wrong. I was uncomfortable with this story but also committed to getting it as right as possible. All the decisions leading up to production were difficult — what kind of gun will it be? How many bullets will be fired? How much blood will be shown? Each question sent chills down my spine. On the day of production for the actual shooting, our set reflected the title of the episode: time stood still. All cast and crew were particularly hushed throughout the day. Our school set was so authentic that the gun looked hideously out of place.

I continued to be haunted by questions throughout postproduction. I watched with our editor, Stephen Withrow, over and over again, forward and backwards, as Jimmy slumped to the

A gun in the school — so wrong.

floor, got up, slumped once more, got up again. How long should we linger on the bullet entering Jimmy's back? How many frames of the blood do we show? The task was to get it right, to respect the gravity of the situation without glorifying it, to be neither sensational nor trivial. At one point, I found it all too much.

I headed out of the editing room into the main hallway that connected our administrative offices with our studio. The long corridor was empty as I leaned back, took a breath, and let my eyes close. As I opened my eyes, I saw a lone figure coming towards the set. I recognized Aubrey, dancing obliviously down the hall to the music in his earbuds. As he got closer to me, he pulled out the earbuds and gave me a great "how-are-ya?" smile. He looked so healthy, so happy, compared to the gruesome images that were currently filling my head. I instinctively gave him a hug.

"Whoa," said a surprised Aubrey.

"I'm just so grateful to see you whole and healthy," I explained. "The shooting story is very hard to work on, it's such a tough topic. But you're brilliant. Thank you for such an honest and moving performance."

Aubrey smiled; he now pulled me in for a hug — a big Aubrey Graham bear hug.

"Thank you," he said, "for the amazing opportunity. I'm so grateful you had confidence in me, and my character, to pull this off."

Aubrey's earbuds went back in, and I returned to editing, reinvigorated. I'd just been reminded of another reason why I do what I do. It wasn't just about the stories, but the ability to provide a supportive yet challenging environment for young people. What a pleasure it was to watch them grow in confidence and expand their talents.

I reminded myself that the "kids" in my life were not just the ones in front of the camera; they were my crew, my production staff, and my corporate staff. All of them were hardworking, dedicated to our vision, and, well, just awesome. They were all my "big kids." And then there were the other kids — the fans.

By this point in the series, our fan base was growing exponentially. Weekly, thousands of new students enrolled in our virtual school and the television ratings continued to climb. To capitalize on this forward energy, The N, in partnership with a number of corporate sponsors, organized mall tours throughout the U.S. where fans could meet and greet actors from the show for autograph signings. Cast members would travel in pairs to various cities throughout the U.S. When they returned, they would share stories of vast lineups and hysterical fans, some who had travelled miles to attend, often camping overnight to secure a spot.

Hearing these tales, Stephen and I decided to observe, firsthand, this mall tour phenomenon and travelled with Lauren Collins and Adamo Ruggiero to the event in New Jersey at the Woodbridge Center Mall. As we waited in the green room with our cast and the publicity team, a crackling voice came over the walkie, "Prepare to travel the cast. We're live in five." With a quick check of hair and makeup for Lauren and Adamo, we were on the move — swiftly escorted through a labyrinth of back hallways to a set of double doors. Here the security guards stopped us. "Stand by," said the walkie. We heard, from the other side of the door, the local radio personality give an upbeat introduction to our two stars and then — the double doors were thrown open. Huge screams filled the air as thousands of fans waved signs — "We love you, Lauren!" and "Marry me, Adamo!" They clutched their hearts and tried to breathe, tears rolling down some cheeks. Lauren and Adamo looked back to us as if to say "Is this for real?" Then, they gathered themselves and strutted out, smiling and waving at the fans as they took their places. Towards the end of the afternoon, the numbers were so large that the fire marshall, much to the annoyance of our fans, had to close the event. He estimated that close to eight thousand kids had been in attendance.

The *New York Times Magazine* described the mall tours as "the kinds of events that record labels use to stoke interest in teen-pop musicians like Avril Lavigne. With only the N's on-air and online promotion — and some local coverage — fans swarmed the food courts. In Atlanta, Boston, Los Angeles, and Dallas, teenagers lined up for hours to get autographs from cast members. In Honolulu, shrieking kids wearing homemade "I Love Ashley" T-shirts gave

Lauren Collins and Adamo Ruggiero with excited fans at a New Jersey mall.

Stacey Farber and Melissa McIntyre engage with some next–*Next Generation* fans in Honolulu.

Melissa McIntyre candy leis they had strung themselves . . . During one mall appearance, fans told Stacey Farber that they were dressing up as Ellie for Halloween." This feature-length article, complete with multiple pictures, ran with the Sunday paper under the title: "DGrassi Is tha Best Teen TV N da WRLD!"

Yes, my kids were all right — the ones in front of the camera, and those behind. And those in our extended audience, the ones who camped out to secure a spot at mall tours, and who engaged earnestly and regularly in conversations at our virtual *Degrassi* school. Everyone seemed all right.

And, so was I . . . I thought.

CHAPTER SIXTEEN

Insight, Oversight — No Sight?

From the bedroom, I heard routine sounds as the day slowly sprang to life. Stephen sang "Catfood in a Can" to Oscar, our cat, as he opened a fresh can of Fancy Feast. The hum of the milk frother on the cappuccino machine and the clink of china mugs signalled that my morning latte was in the works. In my closet was the new outfit I'd laid out the night before: white pants, pale yellow linen jacket, white T-shirt, gold jewellery, and strappy high-heeled sandals. Perfect for a June day. My speech notes were printed and waiting on the hall table by my purse. I just needed to shower, and I'd be good to go.

As I sat up, I screamed.

Overnight, someone had driven a meat cleaver through the centre of my skull. The top left side of my head was on fire. I leapt from the bed and almost knocked Stephen and my latte over as I dashed into the bathroom. "Can you see it?" I shouted at him. "I've got to get this thing out of my head!"

Bewildered, Stephen followed me into the bathroom as I stared in disbelief at the mirror. "How can this be? I look perfectly normal?"

"Well, you certainly don't sound that way!"

"Stephen, seriously, half my head has flames coming out of it. My skull has been cracked down the middle by a meat cleaver, or an axe. It really hurts."

Stephen handed me my latte and meekly suggested, "Maybe the coffee will help?"

Along with the caffeine, I popped a couple of Advil Extra Strength caplets and took another glance in the mirror. Something was really *not* right, but I couldn't see it and I couldn't linger in the bathroom. Today, I needed to be "on." Today was CTV's 2005 fall launch.

CTV always threw an amazing annual bash for their advertisers to create excitement and buzz for the upcoming new fall season. Actors, writers, producers, and various creative types were on tap to mingle with the sponsors and contribute to the atmosphere of celebrity and celebration. It was a particularly important day for us as we were commemorating the twenty-fifth anniversary of the airing of the first-ever *Degrassi* episode, "Ida Makes a Movie." Ivan and Susanne had asked me to be on stage with twenty of the *Degrassi* cast, representing past and present, to pay tribute to the sponsors, advertisers, and press for their support. Susanne, Ivan, and the whole CTV team had been so supportive of *Degrassi: TNG*, I knew I couldn't let them down. I showered, dressed, and, with Stephen, set out for the Hummingbird Centre.

As I hung out backstage with my cast, waiting for our cue, I checked my face in my compact mirror. I could feel the meat cleaver and the flames. *Why couldn't I see them?* I heard our theme song and applause from the audience — we were on. I made my way to centre stage, surrounded by cast members. As the bright lights obscured the capacity crowd, I looked to my cast for reassurance, convinced I might spontaneously combust in front of two thousand people. Yet, surprisingly, I didn't. I made it through my speech. Then exciting clips from the upcoming fifth season of *Degrassi: TNG* season filled the oversized screens. More applause. We smiled and waved as we exited the stage. Next came the mingling part at a lush and extravagant party. The party was held in a number of interconnected white tents, each with its own signature specialty bar and elegant hors d'oeuvres, yet all tents had the same fake Astroturf. And each area of turf was being "mowed" by a shirtless, buff young man with a hand mower. Yes, we were also celebrating the upcoming second season of *Desperate Housewives.* Despite the lavish surroundings and the excited buzz, I whispered to Stephen, "Can we please leave as soon as is politely possible?"

I don't know how I fell asleep that night, but when I awoke in the morning the pain had intensified. The cleaver was still there, and the flames now leapt to a height of two feet above the left side of my head. I waved my hand above them and could feel an intense force field. The right side was normal. Walking to the bathroom mirror, I expected once again to see nothing extraordinary, but today was different. In a neat inverted "V" was a series of small spots, running from inside my hairline, down and across my eyelid. The pain was excruciating.

"Let's get you to a doctor right now," Stephen calmly said.

My doctor was off that day, but his office suggested I go directly to the closest walk-in clinic. I grabbed my cell phone and script. Aaron, Tassie, and I had a script meeting scheduled for early morning, and I planned to take it from the clinic waiting room. "Hang on," I said to Aaron partway through our meeting, "I'm heading into the doctor now, I'll see you at the office shortly."

With absolutely no bedside manner, the overworked doctor flatly said, "You have shingles, here's a prescription, take them all, and it'll clear up in two weeks."

"Okay, fine, thank you, I guess."

I went to the pharmacy next door and dutifully filled my prescription for horse pill–sized, heavy-duty antivirals and realized the pain was too intense. I couldn't go to the office.

The next day, my own doctor was able to see me. Within thirty seconds, he said, "Get to emergency immediately, you need an ophthalmologist. You're in imminent danger of losing your eye."

Not again.

★

Waking up after the crash, even though I couldn't see, my twenty-year-old self knew I was in a hospital. There were the sounds of clanging metal carts, the soft moaning of others in pain, muted professional conversations, and the ubiquitous smell of disinfectant. Nights turned into days. Days into nights. I began to wonder what my life would be like without sight. *I'll probably get myself a dog,* I thought. *One of those large, well-trained, and loyal seeing-eye dogs. But, because I'm young, the dog will die before me. I'll probably have to go through a bunch of dogs in my lifetime, and it will be so sad to repeatedly lose my best friend.*

Of course, I wouldn't be able to drive. Growing up in a small southern Ontario town, I had meticulously counted down the days to my sixteenth birthday. At 9 a.m. sharp on February 12, 1964, I was the first customer at the licence bureau, and a short time later proudly walked out with not only my beginner's permit but also a scheduled appointment for my driving test. But now, even if I could drive again, would I ever want to? In fact, would I ever want to get into a car again?

As I was drifting off, I heard a thud beside my bed. "Right, then, let's see what we have here." Slowly, the doctor began to unwrap the bandages. As the layers were unpeeled, I became aware of a faint presence of light, at least in my right eye. As the unwrapping continued, I sensed more and more light in my right eye. With professional gentleness, he removed the gauze.

Yes! My right eye is working!

Removing the gauze from my left eye was a more delicate matter. It was stuck in places, and the doctor tried not to exert unnecessary pressure. When he finally got the stubborn gauze off — nothing. No light. No shapes. Zero in the left eye. "I'm blind in this eye, aren't I?"

"It's too early to tell," he said matter-of-factly. "It remains swollen and shut. I cannot examine it with so many stitches on your forehead and eyelid. You need patience. But I want you to know you're a fortunate girl."

Fortunate? Did he not realize that I might not have sight in my left eye, that I had internal bleeding and maybe organ damage, that friends of mine had died in the crash? He and I obviously didn't have the same understanding of the word *fortunate*.

The nurse handed me a small mirror and asked if I were ready to have a little look. "Oh my," I gasped. If I hadn't known it was me, I wouldn't have recognized myself. My whole face was grotesquely swollen and covered with lacerations and bruises. I saw the line of stitches that marched into my scalp and down across my swollen left eyelid. The stiches formed a large inverted "V" pattern. The doctor again used the word *fortunate*. Evidently, the night I had been brought to emergency after the crash, I was seen by a visiting, world-renowned plastic surgeon from India. He was there as a mentor and advisor, but when he saw how young I was, he offered to do the surgery himself.

The doctor covered both my eyes with fresh bandages. "We need to keep your eye movement to a minimum," he explained. I was back in the dark but knew I had some sight. It would be a few more days till the doctor was able to reassure me that I miraculously had sight in my left eye as well.

★

After hours of waiting in the downtown Toronto emergency department, I eventually saw the ophthalmologist. He confirmed that my eye was threatened, and prescribed steroid eye drops and daily visits to his clinic. The shingles rash followed the fault line where my head had been cracked open. I tried to figure out why I might have contracted shingles. It was true, I'd had chicken pox as a child, which was a prerequisite for shingles, but not everyone who had chicken pox got shingles. I researched that it can be from a compromised immune system, which I didn't have. Another theory was that it can be stress-related. *Ah, that made some sense.* In the past couple of years, we not only had been producing twenty-two episodes of *Degrassi: TNG* per season, but also, in 2004, had added a second series to our slate: *Instant Star.*

I had been sitting in the audience of *Canadian Idol* with Stephen and was struck by how young all the contestants looked. I turned to Stephen and said, "They look like *Degrassi* kids. I wonder what it's like to be a normal teenager, then find yourself the winner of a high-profile show, get a record deal, and have your life change overnight?"

"Well, there's a good premise for a new show," smiled Stephen.

"Yes, I think I'll put a writer on that!"

In fact, I put many writers on development of this new show. I started to believe that perhaps it wasn't meant to be. Then writer James Hurst submitted a killer script — he had cracked it. We offered it to CTV and The N, who both bought it immediately. So, simultaneously with *Degrassi: TNG*, we were producing an additional thirteen episodes of our new show. We hired a second writing team but, for efficiency, kept the same crew and shared our studio with *Degrassi*. My production team was amazing. We developed a whole new way of scheduling production by interweaving the two series. While one block of *Degrassi* was shooting, a block of *Instant Star* was being prepped.

While I was juggling our two series, Kevin Smith and I were also exploring a new partnership to produce our *Degrassi* feature — not a TV movie, but a real feature with a big-screen release backed by a major studio. Yes, I had been busy, and admittedly, quite stressed at times.

Even though shingles was excruciatingly painful, the good news was that the rash cleared up in a couple of weeks. The bad news was — I had postherpetic neuralgia. Described by the Mayo Clinic as "damaged fibers that send confused and exaggerated pain messages from your skin to your brain," postherpetic neuralgia is an agonizing condition that a very small percentage of shingles patients develop. It can linger for years after the shingles rash has disappeared. I was one of the small percentage of people to get this condition. My scarred head and damaged nerves from the accident provided the right environment for postherpetic neuralgia. This pain, starting in 2005, would remain with me for over fifteen years. Even today, when the weather pressure is low or I'm feeling particularly stressed, there's a buzz and slight fire over my left eye.

I experimented with all kinds of pain relief: a variety of pain-killers (all gross), hypnosis, acupuncture, yoga, and eventually, the most successful, nerve blockers, which were injected into the base of my skull into my occipital nerves. It felt similar to getting your gums frozen before dental work. The nerve blockers provided a numbing effect on the left side of my head that dulled the pain but needed to be repeated every six to eight weeks.

Meanwhile, the shows had to go on. Stephen, Aaron, Stefan, and I travelled to L.A. where we had dinner at Kevin Smith's house (steaks cooked beautifully by the man himself). It was the night before we were scheduled to pitch the *Degrassi* feature on the Paramount lot. We were all pumped for this heavy-hitters meeting. In the morning, Stephen drove our gang in our rented car (not a pink Mustang), and I rode with Kevin in his intim-idating black Cadillac Escalade. When stopped at the security gate, the world-weary guard asked, "Name?"

"Kevin Smith and Linda Schuyler for a meeting in Building C."

The guard flipped pages on his clipboard. "Right. Here you are. Carry on, driver."

Kevin nodded his head and dutifully carried on. When we got a respectable distance away, I burst out laughing. "Kevin, he thinks you're my driver!"

Kevin smiled. "Well, technically, Ms. Schuyler, I am!"

Our meeting went very smoothly, with much laughter and encouragement. We buoyantly left the lot knowing we were 95 percent of the way to a green light with Paramount. The execs had confirmed they wanted the movie shot that fall so it would be ready for a late spring, early summer release. "All right, we can do that!"

But could we?

Once back at the office, the daily pressures of production for two series continued while Aaron and Tassie wrestled with the feature script. The challenge they faced was caused by our own series.

Our TV show was so darn ballsy — "It Goes There!" was the tagline that our American broadcaster used. And we did go there on a weekly basis. This was part of the *Degrassi* DNA: "If the kids are talking about it in the schoolyard, at the mall, on social media, we should be talking about it on our show. We will go there." The writers wanted to find a way to up the ante in the feature yet still be on *Degrassi* brand. As they continued to brainstorm, Kevin Smith got an opportunity he couldn't refuse. He was offered a lead role in *Catch and Release*, a romantic comedy to star him alongside Jennifer Garner, Juliette Lewis, and others. Great news for Kevin, not so much for us. With no viable script and no director, our hopes of a fall shoot faded daily. Within a few weeks, our 95 percent chance of a green light rapidly dropped to 50, and soon became zero.

It would take another four years before we'd be able to make a feature-length movie happen.

*

As Stephen and I sat on our veranda at the end of our long production week, we took a collective breath and quietly admitted to each other that, even though we could have pulled off the feature, it would have been a huge workload. We also acknowledged that producing a feature could have compromised our two series. Fortunately, production on both shows was continuing well and both broadcasters remained happy. In fact, that very afternoon, Sarah Lindman, our broadcast executive and champion from The N, had called us with exciting news. We had been invited to the ballroom at The Beverly Hilton in L.A. in July 2005 to receive a Television Critics Association (TCA) award for *Degrassi: TNG*. I loved visiting L.A., and to do so for a prestigious award was doubly exciting, but I was nervous about flying. The previous L.A. trip had been particularly painful. The pressure from the cabin made my aching head felt like an inferno, ready to explode at any minute. My doctor assured me that flying would do no further damage: it would just be unpleasant. For a moment, I thought maybe I'd leave Stephen and the gang to go, but a TCA award was a big deal. *Suck it up, Linda, and travel!*

As we entered the opulent ballroom in search of our seats, we realized that our table was beside Hugh Laurie. (It was 2005 and he was receiving his first TCA award for *House*.) I loved that show and thought Hugh Laurie was brilliant. I allowed myself a small fangirl gasp. I was staring at him a bit too long before I realized who our tablemates were — Bob Newhart and family. Another fangirl gasp. Bob was delightful and an excellent dinner companion. When he realized we were from *Degrassi*, he told us he wished his granddaughter were here to meet us, as she was a huge fan of our show. Wow, could this night get any better?

It did.

Me accepting the TCA Award.

At the afterparty in the adjacent Hilton ballroom, I was aware of someone approaching me. "Linda Schuyler," he said in a soft English accent, "it is an honour to meet you. I grew up watching *The Kids of Degrassi Street* in the UK. I loved it." This was Dominic

Monaghan, who was at the TCAs representing *Lost*, also an award winner that year. Without hesitation, Dominic began to recite to me a scene from *The Kids of Degrassi Street*, one where Martin Schlegel threw plastic vomit on the table and tried to convince his mother that he was too sick for school. I glanced around the glittering star-studded L.A. ballroom and realized that I was having my own script privately performed for me by a hobbit!

On the plane home, I thought about what a wacky business television production is — it's hard work, with ridiculous deadlines and impossible demands, yet, it's also magical and addictive. It's challenging to retain a balance, as my shingles had so sharply pointed out. I then started to think about our young cast. They too had been enjoying special nights of glitz and glamour as well as heady promotional tours. They'd been to the Teen Choice Awards, the MMVAs, the Emmys, the Geminis, and been guests in numerous major cities. *How can I help them to keep some balance in their lives?* I wondered. I remembered back to the classic *Degrassi* series when we had partnered with UNICEF to produce a video to celebrate the UN's ratification of the Convention on the Rights of the Child. It had been a win-win situation, with our cast enjoying the glow of volunteering for a cause in which they believed, and UNICEF having the cachet of teaching materials with recognizable stars. The *Degrassi* cast continued as UNICEF ambassadors throughout the run of the series. I also recalled when the *Degrassi* gang had been invited to participate at the launch of a new initiative, Kids Help Phone, in 1989. At the opening cocktail event, we met the larger-than-life, warm, and gregarious Wes Williams — a.k.a. Maestro Fresh Wes — Canada's first hip-hop artist (and years later a lead on our own *Instant Star*). The night was full of promise for a new service that would be there on call for kids, 24/7. The initial focus of the charity was to support young people experiencing abuse, but almost immediately young people let them know they needed more from the service. Over the years, the charity would grow to address a continuum of young people's emotional and mental health needs. During the COVID pandemic, they served young people over 9.5 million times. *Degrassi* has enjoyed a long-term, evolving symbiotic partnership with both Kids Help Phone and UNICEF. In the spirit of encouraging our young performers to "give back," we were open to a new opportunity when it presented itself to *Degrassi: TNG*.

Through one of my writers, I had become aware of the Canadian charity called Free the Children (FTC). Founded by Toronto-based Kielburger brothers Craig and Marc, the mandate of the charity, simply put, was to empower youth through education. And, to encourage youth to "be the change." *Hmm*, I thought. *The FTC mandate sounds similar to that of Degrassi. Craig, Marc, and I should meet.*

The cast of classic *Degrassi* embraced their roles as ambassadors for UNICEF.

As a twelve-year-old in 1995, Craig Kielburger was searching the *Toronto Star* for the comics section of the newspaper. Before he could get to "the funnies," he was jolted by the main headline, one that would change his life forever: "Battled child labour; boy, 12, murdered."

That defining moment moved Craig to activism. He started motivating his classmates to be aware of injustice, to become advocates, and to fundraise. In a short time, he was travelling to South Asia to see firsthand what slums, sweatshops, and child labour were really about. From this experience, with the help of his older brother Marc, Craig launched the charity Free the Children.

"Jambo!" Craig and Marc called out their hello and welcome as they entered our cast meeting. "Jambo. And please have one of these." The two young men passed out handmade wooden boxes to our assembled cast. Inside each box was information on FTC, with specific reference to Kenya, and a beautiful handcrafted, multi-coloured beaded necklace. Our young cast and their parents were enthralled with the brothers, their gifts, and their stories. Our cast knew that if they wanted to get involved in any level of participation with FTC it would be strictly voluntary, no expectations attached. Craig and Marc, while talking over one another, cutting each other off, and laughing at each other's bad jokes, gave us a spirited, brief history of FTC. They outlined their particular initiative in Kenya. Their lively and enthusiastic talk was contagious. Many questions followed from both cast and parents. After a few days, several cast members came to us and said, "We've had a cast meeting and we'd like to build a *Degrassi* school in the Maasai Mara. Is that okay?"

"Okay?" I looked at their eager faces. "It's more than okay, it's terrific! Let's see how we can make this all work."

Some of them wanted to travel in person and be part of the building project. Others committed to fundraising. They needed to raise $20,000 for the building supplies. Hearing their enthusiasm, Stephen and I promised to match dollar for dollar the monies they raised. For those planning to go to Kenya, they would be responsible for paying the cost of their own transportation and, once there, would physically work daily to help construct the school while staying at the FTC base camp.

The fundraising efforts were quickly successful, thanks in part to great generosity from our crew, broadcast partners, and other cast members. And, thanks to the ingenuity of our ADs, a summer production schedule was built to allow time for the Kenya trip. As this was our first partnership with FTC, I had offered to meet up with our group. I did this, despite my ongoing postherpetic neuralgia, so I could reassure parents and cast, for the future, that FTC trips were safe and conditions were good. I knew these trips were intended to be all about the kids, and I assured Marc and Craig that if we did future trips, I would not tag along.

Prior to leaving for Kenya, I excitedly explained our trip to my friend Cathy Dunphy, a journalist. She did not share my same enthusiasm. "Sounds to me like a bit of white saviourism," she mused.

I was quick to defend our plan. I told Cathy that, growing up, I had been exposed to a lot of "do-good missionary work" through our church. Even though many worthwhile works were accomplished in developing countries, the ultimate aim was to preach the gospel. FTC seemed to have none of the missionary zealousness of the church. It was a secular organization looking to educate children and communities to become self-sufficient. It also promised to be a positive and grounding experience for our cast. "I'm good with this," I told Cathy, but her caution stayed with me.

I flew from Nairobi to the Maasai Mara as the only passenger in a small Cessna aircraft with a knowledgeable pilot. As we cruised at a low altitude above the beautiful windswept Mara, he pointed out herds of elephants, some running zebras, and a group of giraffes munching on treetops. He also told me, although I couldn't make them out, that in the large watering hole below, several hippopotami were bathing. Stephen, Max, and I had been on safari a few years earlier at the Sabi Sabi Game Reserve in South Africa and on the Okavango Delta in Botswana. That expedition had been an amazing bonding experience for our recently blended family. Seeing the vastness and the grandeur of the Mara brought back so many of our incredible memories. However, I reminded myself, I'm not on holiday this time, I'm here to fact-find and to work.

As our plane drew to a stop at the end of a bumpy, makeshift runway, I was met by a small group of singing FTC staff, including Maasai warriors in their traditional red-checkered cloth blankets. The refrain of the song was "Jambo" (hello and welcome). Together, as they danced and sang, they led me to the base camp for Free the Children.

The main building was simple in design yet beautiful. I later found out, when talking to the local architect who had designed it, that he had taken his influence from the style of the traditional Maasai homes (enkaji, or huts) but in much larger proportions. This circular structure was the centre of the base camp and acted as the dining room and common area. Dotted around the circumference were the individual sleeping tents. I was just about to be shown to my sleeping area when the bus from the building site pulled up and my excited *Degrassi* team rushed over to greet me. Talking over one another, they told me how amazing it was there and what a great day they had

had on the construction site. Over supper that night, I heard more about the daily trips to the school building site, but also about their community interaction. Our cast told me how they shared stories and songs alongside the local schoolchildren. They performed plays with them and played endless soccer. Easy moments were shared learning beading and some Swahili words under the sycamore trees. They were learning as much from the local kids as the local kids were from our team. I couldn't have been happier.

Craig Kielburger and I walk with some local kids to visit the mommas at the community centre.

Construction on the school site was slow but steady, and our gang proved to be very dedicated workers. However, a few days into the project, we had a "white saviourism" moment. It didn't come from FTC, but from our own *Degrassi* team. We were nearing the end of our first week of construction when some local residents arrived and started to work alongside our team. I became vaguely aware of some disgruntled voices. Then suddenly, two of our team threw down their tools in anger and marched away from the site. I caught up with the boys as they leaned defiantly against an acacia tree staring disdainfully at the working group.

"What's up?" I asked.

"What are they doing here?" the one boy asked, pointing towards the local villagers.

"Yeah, we're here to help *them*. This is *our* project, not theirs," the other angrily agreed.

Whoooaaa. We needed a group meeting. I asked the group facilitator if we could assemble our gang for a discussion. The FTC facilitator was excellent. It was obviously not the first time she had experienced this situation. We engaged in an open and frank discussion about aid, empowerment, education, and the road to self-sufficiency. This was perhaps the most important part of our whole journey. After the discussion, we all returned to the site, including our two agitated young men. I'm not convinced they totally changed their attitude, but their anger dissipated, and they continued as team players alongside the locals for the rest of the project.

The two weeks passed quickly.

Our final day was particularly memorable. We were invited, in groups of twos and threes, into the villagers' homes for tea. I went with Nina Dobrev (who'd joined the show in season six as Mia), and Jake Epstein to one of the mud huts. Both of these actors would become tireless ambassadors for FTC and *Degrassi*. We were welcomed with a tin mug of chai-type tea. "Pssst," said a young girl, Sharon, as we drank our tea. "I want to show you something." She looked at her parents to make sure it was okay, they nodded their approval, and she grabbed our hands. Sharon excitedly took us out back into the field. Here they had constructed, out of planks and plants, an outhouse. It was new for them. They, like other locals, were responding to the FTC educational push to improve sanitation. Sharon was proud of her family's accomplishments. Nina, Jake, and I were touched. We knew this was a positive result of "aid" and education.

Nina and Jake enjoy their chai. They were given the heads-up not to drink it all. Rations were tight in the village and any tea we left behind would be reused.

When we arrived back in Toronto, we found the city abuzz with preparations for the 2007 TIFF, the Toronto International Film Festival. The next night was opening night, and Nina Dobrev would be walking the red carpet for the premiere of her new film, *Fugitive Pieces*. When I opened the *Toronto Star* the morning after the gala, the front page featured our beautiful Nina, glowing in a vibrant red Brian Bailey dress. I took out my camera and looked at photos from two days earlier. There was Nina, beside Jake, drinking tea at a mud hut. I was so proud of my *Degrassi* kids. Little did we know that Nina would soon shoot to international stardom as Elena on *The Vampire Diaries*, with multiple film and television roles to follow. And — Jake would soon be flying over Broadway as Spider-Man and channelling Gerry Goffin in *Beautiful: The Carole King Musical.*

★

In our original FTC orientation meeting, the Kielburger brothers, Marc and Craig, had promised that our cast would not just be enriching the lives of others, but their own as well. I was happy to report back to the *Degrassi* team and parents that the Kielburgers over-delivered on both accounts. Our initial trip was so successful that FTC trips became a regular part of *Degrassi* life. After Kenya, we partnered on many more building trips, including India, Haiti, and Ecuador. The *Degrassi* cast became regular speakers at conferences and events for ME to WE (the new name of the Kielburgers' organization). Our partnership came to a natural end with the end of production on *Degrassi: TNG* in 2014. I was proud of our *Degrassi* kids, our local Kielburger boys, and our shared message of empowering youth to be agents of change.

It was therefore shocking, in the summer of 2020, when the following headlines hit the news:

> From me, to we, to what next? How the Kielburgers went from charity rock stars to embroiled in a political scandal. (*Toronto Star*)

> The Kielburgers struggle to salvage their brand. (CBC News)

> The WE Charity scandal and the arrogance of Canada's progressive establishment. (washingtonpost.com)

> Scandal pushing WE Charity to lay off staff. (CP24)

Since our initial trip with FTC to Kenya, I'd been aware of the exponential growth of the WE Charity. New entities had been formed, each with its own raison d'être — WE Charity, ME to WE Foundation, ME to WE Social Enterprise, and so on. Some of these entities were not-for-profit; others, for-profit. The lines often got blurred. WE had offices in Canada, Britain, and the U.S. They ran WE celebrations in major cities around the world. So what brought them to that critical moment in the summer of 2020? Hubris? Lack of transparency? The cult of celebrity? Lax board oversight? I was certainly in no position to judge, I could only piece together what I knew.

During COVID, after giving support to individuals and businesses, the federal government planned a $900-million relief program for students. Without going to tender, they enlisted the WE Charity to be the delivery arm of this program. Immmediately, controversy swirled. Ties with the Kielburgers and the prime minister's familiy were revealed, and the finance minister was discovered to have a daughter who had worked for WE. As the allegations of conflicts of interest grew, the ME to WE Foundation was pulled off the extensive relief program and became a target for the media. There were no winners in this scandal, but there were certainly losers — thousands of Canadian university students would not receive badly needed financial support during a devastating pandemic, and school students across the country would no longer be able to participate in WE's programs supporting volunteerism and community activism.

My original impulse to partner with FTC was to help my young cast keep a healthy and balanced perspective about their lives. Was my friend Cathy right — had this been a flawed initiative from the beginning? Had I inadvertently gotten myself and others caught up in celebrity white saviourism?

I thought back to the pride on Sharon's face as she showed Nina, Jake, and me their newly constructed outhouse. I remembered the eagerness with which villagers embraced our school-building project, the welcome tea we'd shared in their homes. I don't think we meddled. I can certainly say that my *Degrassi* cast, and my team, were made stronger for the experience they were able to realize through FTC. I don't regret the relationship, and I hope my cast feels the same way.

*

The swift downfall of the Kielburger brothers reminded me how quickly life can change. I've certainly lived through dramatic and instant change with my car crash: one minute I was a healthy, carefree, twenty-something hippie pursuing world travels; next, I was a crumpled bleeding mess on the British pavement.

At a recent university lecture, a student made the following observation at the end of my talk.

"I find it fascinating," she said, "that your accident stopped you from travelling around the world, yet the stories you have subsequently told have made their way across the globe."

After the accident, I was so grateful to be alive that I abandoned all thoughts of further adventures and risk-taking. I settled for a conservative lifestyle, afraid to put myself "out there" for fear of being slapped down. As time went on, I started subconsciously, and then consciously, to push back against those thoughts. I started to own the reality of the crash within the larger context of my life. Despite it being responsible for my endometriosis, post-herpetic neuralgia, survivor's guilt, and of course, my infertility, I realized it was the accident that had ultimately allowed me to reboot my life. The crash led me to teacher's college. During my years of teaching, I learned the importance of empowering young people, and became compelled to tell their stories. The stories I've had the opportunity to tell have travelled the world and impacted the lives of many young people. Reflecting on this throughline of my life leads me to the unanswerable question that has haunted me for years — would *Degrassi* have existed without my head-on collision?

CHAPTER SEVENTEEN

WHEN LESS BECOMES MORE

There were hugs, air kisses, and laughter as Stephen and I left the executive boardroom of CTV. "Thanks for everything," shouted Ivan. "We'll see you soon."

Susanne smiled, a little apologetically, but reinforced the sentiment: "Looking forward to the next steps."

As Stephen and I made our way to the elevator, our backs to our hosts, our smiles faded. Once safely inside the elevator, I turned to Stephen. "Did we just get cancelled?" I asked.

"I think we did," replied a bewildered Stephen.

It was all a bit confusing. The tone of the meeting had been quite jolly, as Ivan was very complimentary about our movie of the week, *Degrassi Goes Hollywood*. A few weeks prior, it had aired to great ratings and good press coverage — the perfect ending to season eight. We were now deep into production of season nine. The show just kept getting stronger — or so we thought.

Degrassi Goes Hollywood was the feature-length story we hadn't cracked a few years earlier. The key was to heighten reality yet still create a believable environment for our *Degrassi* characters. We borrowed from the tone that had made the "Goin' Down the Road" episodes so successful, and we'd asked Kevin Smith and Jason Mewes to return. The conceit was that Jason Mewes is making his first movie — *Mewesical High* — in L.A., mentored by Kevin. They put out an open call for auditions and of course, the *Degrassi* kids, having been involved in Kevin's earlier show, hear of the call and are determined to give it a shot, which means getting to L.A. by whatever means necessary. The story was larger-than-life, and a great opportunity for our own Stefan Brogren to make his debut as a television director. Stefan, apart from his continued role as Mr. Simpson, had been writing and directing many of the *Degrassi Minis*, fun two-to-five-minute episodes produced exclusively for the web.

Stefan and I began working together in 1986 when he was a lanky fourteen-year old enrolled at the Claude Watson School for the Arts. Stefan had known from an early age that he wanted to pursue the arts and had the full support of his parents who, in turn, became great champions of *Degrassi*. His mom would often help out on set organizing craft projects for the actors who were between scenes. Over the years, Stefan has been the only actor to have appeared in every season of all series in the *Degrassi* franchise. When discussing scripts, Stefan and I have developed our own unique shorthand as we are both so deeply steeped in *Degrassi's* DNA. In 2008, I knew Stefan was more than ready to make his prime time directing debut.

Stefan's style, coupled with the fun script penned by Sarah Glinski, Matt Huether, Vera Santamaria, and Sara Snow, turned in a great *Degrassi* romp. Our cast was stellar, and we sprinkled in some fun cameos: Perez Hilton, Pete Wentz of Fall Out Boy, Cassadee Pope, Kelly Carlson, Vivica A. Fox, and Canada's own Jessi Cruickshank and Dan Levy. For Dan, now of *Schitt's Creek* fame, this was his first foray into scripted material. When Stefan was shooting for two days on location in L.A., the California crew were impressed by his laid-back style and easy manner. They compared his MO to that of Clint Eastwood — a great tribute to a then-neophyte director.

Ivan had loved the movie. And this was why our meeting was so confusing. He wanted the new *Degrassi* season to be a spinoff of

Stefan, the director, on the set of *Degrassi: Next Class* with Amanda Arcuri (Lola), Reiya Downs (Shay) and Sara Waisglass (Frankie).

the movie: young Canadian kids trying to make it in L.A. Hmm, we were already halfway through shooting season nine, and it was not like that. Once Ivan realized it was too late to turn the current season around, he mused, "After this season, maybe we don't want any more of our old-style *Degrassi*. Perhaps we want a new show, set in L.A., developed by a whole new writing team." I think in Ivan's mind, it really was a positive meeting. For, although he didn't want more of our current show, he wanted a new one. Hence the upbeat tone and our conflicted attitude.

Now, we were no strangers to cancellation. The death of *Riverdale* had almost estranged me from the industry altogether. I'd put my heart and soul into that show, and its cancellation left me wondering about my self-worth and my abilities. We'd also been cancelled the year before, after four seasons of *Instant Star*. With its innovative style and unique music component, we loved our show. Our lead in *Instant Star* was an extraordinarily talented singer, songwriter, and actor, all in one — and age appropriate.

However, she wouldn't help publicize our show. She felt that by helping to promote the music of Jude Harrison (her character) she would detract from her own music. This was a disappointment to both broadcasters, who felt let down, knowing the opportunity they had provided. In the end, they exercised their right to cancel, and we were not surprised.

This latest cancellation felt different. Stephen and I continued to dissect the tea leaves of our afternoon meeting as we ordered a meal at our local Italian restaurant. The message became increasingly clear: *Degrassi* was tired; the movie was fresh. Strangely, I wasn't insulted or angry. We'd already had nine seasons of *Degrassi: TNG* — a tremendous vote of confidence from both broadcasters in our show and our team.

One of the reasons *Degrassi* had stayed alive for nine seasons was that we had overcome our fear of graduating characters. In the classic *Degrassi* series, once the main characters graduated, there was no new student population left. We were quick to rectify that for *Degrassi: TNG*. Each year we introduced new characters into the younger grades, many of them related in some way to existing characters. However, when our first tranche of *Next Generation* characters — including Marco, Paige, and Ellie — graduated at the end of season five, our broadcasters, particularly The N, were concerned that our audience loyalty would wane as their favourite characters left the show. To ease this fear, we developed some storylines to follow them at an off-campus house at Toronto University. The next year, we sent graduating students Emma, Manny, and Liberty away to a dorm room in fictional Smithdale University. We still played the majority of our storylines at Degrassi with the rest of our cast, but were able to continue with beloved characters, assuming the audience would want to follow them beyond the halls of high school. After three seasons of experimenting, and various audience testing, we learned we were wrong.

Matt Huether, a long-time *Degrassi* writer and pop culture guru, summed it up this way when he spoke on *The Imposter* podcast for the episode "Degrassiland":

We were not the only show experimenting. When this happened on *90210*, they sent most of their characters to "California University." *Dawson's Creek* fumbled through higher education and into adulthood; *Saved By the Bell* spun off a whole new series, *The College Years*. But, in every case, the post-graduation years paled in comparison to the high school years. But why does high school make for better TV storytelling than university? . . . It's because high school is kind of like prison. Once you've graduated and you're in university, you're basically free to do whatever you want. If you want to skip class . . . nobody's going to call your parents. But, in high school, if you skip class . . . they hunt you down and make you go.

Our focus testing supported Matt's theory — our audience preferred the high school storylines to the post-secondary ones. However, with our latest broadcaster meeting, it seemed that CTV would prefer all our characters bust out and leave high school behind. I was trying to digest this along with my chicken parmesan, when Stephen said, "There's something else you should know." His tone made me feel as though I was about to be called into the principal's office.

"Yes. I'm all ears."

"Well, I've been having some phone calls with The N, and they have some interesting thoughts about *Degrassi* going forward."

Silence on my end.

"I've been waiting for the right moment to tell you this," he proceeded cautiously. "I know it's been challenging, producing both series, developing the feature, and working with FTC, all while dealing with your health issues."

I nodded, curious about what he'd been withholding for my sake. "True, but I love what I do."

"Well, that's good then, because you need to know that The N would like to order forty-four episodes of *Degrassi* for season ten."

"You're kidding me?!"

"Nope. It's true. On The N, *Degrassi* is far from tired! They had great ratings successes last summer and want to explore new and innovative ways to keep building the audience. They'd like to try to run a daily strip Monday to Thursday during July and August, and return to a weekly schedule in the fall. Also, they are rebranding themselves as TeenNick. Our summer telenovela, as they are calling it, will be an important part of that rebrand."

"That's awesome." I smiled. "But how can we finance this? We just lost our Canadian broadcaster."

"We'll just have to find another one." Stephen gave me a wily smile.

For the next few days, as I continued to monitor the production of season nine, Stephen had further discussions with TeenNick. He got them to confirm not only the increased number of episodes, but also a substantive increase in the licence fee for each episode. Eventually, he had a plan that would allow a Canadian broadcaster to acquire the expanded series at a price far less than the original licence at CTV. The next thing I heard from Stephen was "YTV is interested. Really interested." Many meetings followed with much enthusiasm and excitement. Then YTV went quiet.

We were close to crunch time when we needed to apply to the appropriate funds to secure our financing. With apologies, YTV asked for more time, but it was running out. Using a "Hail Mary" tactic, Stephen reached back out to CTV. He explained to Corrie Coe, senior vice-president of independent production, how the new financing would work. As *Degrassi* would now be classified as a children's show, CTV would be able to pay a smaller licence fee than the premium they'd paid when *Degrassi* was in prime time. "This is timely," Corrie mused. "We are looking to reinvent and rebrand our cable channel, MuchMusic, with greater youth appeal. Let me run this by Ivan."

Within twenty-four hours, Corrie got back to us.

"Yes, it's a go. We'd love to be back in business with you under these new terms," a delighted Corrie reported to Stephen.

Season ten was a go with an order for forty-four episodes, more episodes than we'd ever produced in a single year. Our new reality was "more episodes at a drastically reduced budget." Stephen and I started a series of meetings with all our key departments, explaining that we needed to produce faster, better, and cheaper. "We know that common wisdom will tell you that you can have any two of the above. Well, that's not good enough for us, we need all three!"

Just as with *Instant Star*, where we had created a whole new paradigm for the production of two series in a leap-frog pattern, our teams worked to find cost and time efficiencies without sacrificing the show quality. Our solutions came fast and furious. We would stop shooting on Super 16mm film and move directly to shooting on the RED digital camera. By doing this, we'd skip the need for overnight dailies and various other costs associated with film. This would also streamline the whole post-production process, allowing for further savings of both time and money.

We planned to block-shoot four episodes at a time. To achieve this, the writers would develop the stories in blocks of four, being mindful to minimize the need for location moves, limit the number of characters per block, and reduce calls for costume and hair changes. However, to achieve this, our story department needed to grow rather than shrink. We doubled the size of our writing department so two teams could work simultaneously, a successful model we had used when we ran two series. Even though we had two teams, there would only be one head writer/showrunner for both, and that would be the indefatigable Brendon Yorke. Brendon, who ten years earlier was a writer for our virtual online school, had worked his way up through the story department and would now run the department with our largest volume ever.

Despite all the emphasis on savings and efficiencies, as producers and writers, we couldn't lose sight of the fact that it was story and character that were the heart of our show. We also needed to be mindful that the times around us continued to change and evolve. When *Degrassi: TNG* had started ten years earlier, young people's access to the internet was in the early stages. Within a few short years, new avenues had opened up and the term *social media* was ubiquitous. Kids were using their phones for Facebook, YouTube, and Twitter. This expanding digital universe offered new story opportunities.

"What?" I found myself exclaiming as my writers pitched me a new idea. "You can't tell me kids are really doing that."

"Yup, Linda. Junk pics — penis shots — and there's a lot of them going around."

"Really," I mused.

"And there are boob shots, ghosting, rainbow parties, catfishing, and so much more." Sexual fluidity was moving into the conversation as a more inclusive LGBTQ+ community emerged. The rich and complex digital era called for new dating protocols and hookup opportunities as well as providing a home to scams, schemes, and fake news.

"Well," I said to my team, "seems like we won't have trouble filling forty-four episodes with interesting story!" And it was true. We were able to create bold and lively stories for all our great characters: Sav (Raymond Ablack), Holly J. (Charlotte Arnold), Drew (Luke Bilyk), Chantay (Jajube Mandiela), Bianca (Alicia Josipovic), Declan (Landon Liboiron), Dave (Jahmil French), Connor (A.J. Saudin), and more. It was in this block that we introduced Adam as our trans male character, Alli's (Melinda Shankar) escapades in the boiler room, Jenna (Jessica Tyler) and K.C.'s (Sam Earle) pregnancy, Anya's (Samantha Munro) mom's cancer, and Fiona's (Annie Clark) abusive boyfriend. We continued the epic relationship between Clare (Aislinn Paul) and Eli (Munro Chambers), or "Eclare" as the fans called them. There was also a Vegas night gone bad, a shot at a Guinness record for pogo jumps, and an eligible bachelor auction.

An additional challenge facing the writing department was the fact that the rollout schedule was in two sections. The first twenty-four episodes would be aired Monday to Thursday for six weeks over the summer. The remaining episodes would air weekly starting in the fall. This meant slightly adjusting the rhythm in which story and character development rolled out.

Drew (Luke Bilyk), Bianca (Alicia Josipovic), Dave (Jahmil French), K.C. (Sam Earle), Jenna (Jessica Tyler) and Chantay (Jajube Mandiela), with Jenna and K.C.'s new baby.

Over the years, our format for storytelling has constantly needed to evolve. In the early days of *The Kids of Degrassi Street* and *Degrassi Junior High*, our shows ran as children's television and could not contain commercials. Once we moved to prime time, we had to lose about five minutes of story time to make room for commercial messages. We also needed to construct the stories in such a way that there would be a dramatic high point at the commercial break to ensure that the audience would come back. We learned about not only the structure of individual stories, but also the shape of story arcs throughout the season. The rhythm of these changed with the broadcast schedule depending if we aired once a week or four times a week. And then, it would change again when, in 2015, we moved with *Degrassi: Next Class* to Netflix, a streaming service. We needed to adjust to binge-watching.

The new rhythms of binge-watching initially took us by surprise and caused audience pushback. Interestingly, the small stories needed the most adjustment. In a traditional broadcast schedule, one episode airs each week. If we'd had an on-again, off-again romantic relationship, the audience would enjoy the roller-coaster ride over a

Our new studio was originally a warehouse printing and storage facility that didn't require windows. To turn our building into a believable school, we blew out large pieces of wall, inserted classroom windows, and added large double doors and wide steps.

Me with some of the early cast of *Degrassi: The Next Generation* in front of the new facade.

DEGRASSI BANDS

The Zit Remedy, 1987.

Hell Hath No Fury, 2003.

Whisperhug, 2012.

Downtown Sasquatch, 2003.

Janie and the Studs, 2009
(formerly Stüdz).

DEGRASSI TEST RESULTS

Erica, 1988.

Manny, 2003.

Lola, 2014.

On set with
Chaz Bono, 2012.

Chillin' with Aubrey
in Vegas after a 2007
publicity event.

Two proud grads,
Jason Mewes and
Kevin Smith, from
Kevin's *Degrassi*
movie *Jay and Silent
Bob Go Canadian, Eh?*

A pre-party gathering with friends from The N, on the roof of the Viacom building in New York City.

My breath was taken away when, in 2006, I saw our name in bright lights on the Hard Rock Cafe in Times Square.

Cast and fans at the "Ultimate Degrassi Party" thrown by The N.

Holly J. and Fiona. In season 10, after events spiral out of control at Vegas Night, Degrassi is locked down. Principal Simpson, in an effort to regain order, introduces mandatory school uniforms.

The cast of *Degrassi: Next Class*. Uniforms have long been abandoned.

Stephen and me on the red carpet at the 2015 Primetime Emmy Awards in Los Angeles.

Cast, crew, and broadcasters on the steps of Degrassi celebrate the shooting of the 500th episode of our franchise, 2015.

ONCE UPON A TIME, A YOUNG GIRL WANTED TO MAKE A MOVIE . . .

Ida T. Lucas (Zoe Newman),
age nine, in *Ida Makes a Movie*.

Me, age five.

number of weeks. However, when all the episodes were streamed at once, our audience found the relationship arcs moved too quickly and seemed "fake." We needed to course correct — quickly.

★

Throughout the bustle of preparation for a challenging and exciting new *Degrassi* season ten, we had not forgotten Ivan's request for a new show about "young Canadians trying to make it in L.A." Stephanie Williams, one of our producers and head of development, was working with agents to find an appropriate writer. Ivan was clear: he wanted a fresh voice, not someone who had written on either *Degrassi* or *Instant Star*.

"I think you should take a look at who I just found," Stephanie said one day shortly before production started on *Degrassi* season ten. "He's represented by Glenn Cockburn, an agent we respect. He's not long out of Ryerson [now Toronto Metropolitan University], but he's worked on *Stargate* and has written and produced his own feature, *Young People Fucking*."

He sounded promising.

That night, Stephen and I watched his show, read a sample of his work, and knew we were ready to meet Martin Gero. Martin was a young, explosive, and talented force, exactly what we were looking for. And, it turned out, exactly what Ivan was seeking. We quickly entered into a broadcast deal to develop the new series.

Partway through the *Degrassi* production schedule, Martin delivered the first draft of *The L.A. Complex*. Stephen and I both had a read and came to the same conclusion: "It's brilliant!" Martin had captured the romance and the desperation of young Canadian dreamers living in the rundown Deluxe Motel ("the Lux"), who all knew their big break was "just around the corner." The script was funny, poignant, and just crazy enough. We were excited to present it to Ivan. With a smile, he ordered five more scripts.

★

On the *Degrassi* front, there was growing excitement about the upcoming release of season ten. With both MuchMusic and TeenNick in the process of rebranding, *Degrassi* played an important role in these exciting initiatives. To help hype the first twenty-four episodes of season ten, the ones that would play as the telenovela, TeenNick called the block "Degrassi: The Boiling Point." They planned a bold marketing campaign and created innovative promos. Using as a soundtrack the song "Shark in the Water" by British singer and songwriter VV Brown, they produced the first-ever *Degrassi*/TeenNick musical promo. The saucy video teased storylines for the upcoming summer premiere and garnered much audience attention. We loved the thought and creativity our broadcasters were bringing to our show. The launch of season ten was a huge success. Broadcasters were happy with the ratings and the press coverage, and the digital response from our audience was overwhelming.

Season ten also received some attention from an unlikely source: the Florida Family Association. David Caton, founder and CEO of the association and a self-professed Christian fundamentalist, sent a letter informing me, "Your show is hateful. It's a sin against God . . . Your stories will turn young people across the country into homosexuals . . . Your story of Adam is false and sick." I was reminded of a letter we'd received during production of *Degrassi High*. A minister from Georgia was extremely offended by our opening sequence, where we included a shot of B.L.T. (who is Black) kissing Michelle (who is white). He told us, "Shame be heaped upon you. . . . Maybe, the buzzards laid you on a log and the Sun hatched you to cause such terrible sins."

The latest *Degrassi* hate mail from Caton was not only directed at me and my company, but a barrage of letters had also been sent to various executives at TeenNick and to every advertiser in our show, requesting them to pull their ads. For a moment, Caton celebrated a victory when it appeared that Kodak had pulled its ads in *Degrassi*. But his triumph was short-lived, as in a follow-up statement, Kodak clarified that stopping its ads had been part of a "planned break." The following week they had spots back in the

B.L.T. (Dayo Ade) and Michelle (Maureen McKay). This shot ran in the generic opening that started each episode of *Degrassi High*.

body of our show. We were very grateful for the solidarity shown by our broadcaster and our advertisers.

We responded to David Caton and his ilk by simply ignoring them, knowing that if someone this closed-minded was incensed by what we were doing, then we were doing it right. I hoped David would "stay tuned" and watch our upcoming new series. Here, along with exploring the lives of young Canadians trying to make it in L.A., we would also take a deep dive into the often misogynistic, homophobic world of hip-hop culture. Here we would follow Kaldrick King, a closeted, self-hating rap star, on his journey to come to terms with his sexual identity and find inner peace.

Yes, it was now a confirmed fact. CTV had placed their production order for the first season of the *The L.A. Complex*. Once again, we would be shooting two series simultaneously with a higher volume than ever before.

Our company was *on fire!*

CHAPTER EIGHTEEN

No More Playing with Dimes

"The bank called," Stephen said as he entered my office and closed the door.

Usually those three words would send chills down my spine. But not today. I knew that last week we'd closed our financing for the season. Our diligent director of finance, Dave Shippel, had been working with the lawyers for the last few weeks to secure all the letters of assignment from our funders and broadcasters, along with "second-place" assurances from our suppliers, adequate insurance, and a detailed spreadsheet of cash flow requirements for the next twelve months. (A far cry from the documents provided by my fake husband for my first business loan in the late 1970s!) I knew all this paperwork must be satisfactory as we'd received our first drawdown on Monday.

As Stephen took a seat on the other side of my desk, I thought maybe the call from the bank could be a fun one. Perhaps they were going to offer us tickets for the opening night of TIFF, or maybe a preview of the latest exhibition at the AGO, or courtside seats for the Raptors. We'd been fortunate to be their guests many times at such prestigious events.

"So?" I asked. "What do they want?"

Stephen hesitated for a moment, then said, "They want us to change accountants."

"Not happening," I quickly responded and returned to reading my current script. Leonard Cappe had been my accountant since the early 1980s, over thirty-five years. Stephen sat patiently, then offered, "I know how important loyalty is to you, and it is to me as well, but you have to listen. It's really a good news story."

Oh right, here goes Stephen, I thought. *Always finding the positive in every situation.* Stephen is my Pollyanna optimist. He calls me a pessimist. I tell him that if I sound that way, it's because I'm a contingency planner, seeing all potential outcomes. As such, I like to think of myself as a realistic optimist. We agree to disagree. Agreeing to disagree was actually the secret of our joint management style, and it wasn't really a secret. When our staff needed to come to us for a special request or consideration, they carefully weighed which one of us to approach first. They were well aware that two very different responses could come their way.

I threw my script down. "Okay, Pollyanna, how is terminating a thirty-five-year working relationship a good news story?"

"It's because our company has reached such a significant volume of business, the bank considers us on a level with publicly traded companies. With that comes additional requirements for due diligence. We need a larger accounting firm."

"I've never wanted to be a publicly traded company." I was petulant.

"You're missing the point, Linda. They have put us in this bracket because," he spelled it out slowly, "We. Are. Doing. Really. Well. The company is hugely successful. Be proud."

"Hmm, now you put it that way, I suppose I can see the point."

"I'll make the call," Stephen volunteered.

"No, I should do it," I said. "I've worked with Leonard longer than you. It's only appropriate I deliver the news."

I could feel my heart rate rise as I waited for Leonard's secretary to get him on the line. This was one call I would prefer not to have to make. To my surprise, Leonard was extremely accommodating. "This is not the first time I've been in this position," he graciously offered, and like Stephen had added, "You should be delighted with yourself for the company you have built, Ms. Schuyler!"

I was reminded of the evening at magic hour, twelve years earlier, when Bruce McDonald encouraged me to look at all my cast, crew, and equipment gathered for the start of production on *Degrassi: The Next Generation.* "You made it happen," he said. "Be proud." And truth be told, I was incredibly proud of our company and our entire team, but right now I had to get back to work: there was a lot of reading to do.

★

For season eleven, *Degrassi* had been ordered for another forty-five half-hours and season two of *The L.A. Complex* had found a U.S. home with The CW. Not only had The CW ordered thirteen more hours of our new show, but the network wanted them delivered twice as fast.

"That's ridiculous," I had said to Stephen when he'd told me, a couple of weeks earlier, about this request. "I'm happy to do thirteen, very happy, but we can't do them in that timeline."

"Well," Stephen proceeded carefully, "I've spoken to Martin, and he thinks we can." He confessed to me that Ella Schwarzman, our meticulous and enthusiastic post producer, was still working on the schedule but was confident she could figure out how to make it work.

"Have you just done an end run around me?" I asked.

Stephen smiled, faintly. "Guilty as charged, Your Honour."

Once again, we pulled in our team and explained the unique opportunities we had. In order to make this wild delivery, it would require not only double shooting, but sometimes triple — three crews running simultaneously. In total, we had seventy-one dramatic half-hours to produce. It was this volume and accompanying budgets — totalling just over $40 million — that had caught the eye of the bank and made them require a change in our accountant.

It was also this volume that attracted the interest of Michael Donovan.

★

I hadn't seen much of Michael since, in the late 1990s, we were conspiring together to buy more Showcase shares. In that time, Michael had grown his company, DHX Media (now called WildBrain), to become one of Canada's largest integrated entertainment companies, complete with live-action production, animation, distribution, merchandising, and a television channel. Oh, and he rented a yacht in the Mediterranean where he entertained grandly at various film and TV festivals. It was to this yacht that Stephen was invited when he attended the 2013 MIPCOM television trade show in Cannes.

With Stephen away, I continued to supervise the production of both our shows. There were many moving parts to manage as well as some big egos and unique challenges. Both shows had storylines that required characters travelling to other places. In *Degrassi*, for a few episodes, we followed a class trip to Paris, France. To create the illusion of France, we converted the street in our backlot to a Parisian boulevard, complete with a boulangerie, bibliothèque, and outdoor café. For *The L.A. Complex*, as the name suggested, we actually needed to shoot some scenes on location in L.A., as well as grab various establishing shots from a helicopter. *Degrassi* featured several specific sets: a car crash in a texting and driving story, a beach party, a science fair, a semi-formal, and more. As well, both shows were starting to use a fair amount of green screen, which required much coordination with on-set personnel, editors, and the lab. Time went by quickly.

On his arrival home, Stephen once again walked into my office and closed the door. He sat across from my desk and fished out a wine-stained paper napkin from his pocket, uncrumpled it, and slid it across my desk.

"What do you think?" he expectantly asked.

Our backlot is transformed into a Parisian street.

"I'm not sure." I looked at the stains. "Is it a pinot noir or a cab?"

"No, not the wine — the number."

I looked more carefully and saw double digit numbers in the millions, two or three scratched out, but one with a circle around it and a star.

"It's a big number," I offered.

"It's what Michael is prepared to pay for our company," a somewhat hesitant Stephen explained.

My jaw dropped.

Since Stephen and I had both turned sixty-five earlier that year, we had engaged, somewhat casually, in discussions about an "exit strategy" and if there might be a possibility, down the line, for someone to buy our boutique mom-and-pop shop. Now, suddenly, the conversation was no longer idle. It was real, with a serious player and a respectful offer.

I'd been working in television since 1976, and for almost forty years I had seen changes in the industry, business, and government. With industry peers, I'd negotiated for tax credits. I'd hired many women in executive positions and mentored others. I'd created an environment for storytelling for racialized youth, the marginalized, and the LGBTQ+ community. I also knew there were still so many stories to be told. Was I really ready to sell?

★

That night, I stayed late at the office, long after the crew had wrapped for the day, and took a private tour of my studio. I headed down the executive corridor past the offices of Melinda Sutton, our executive assistant, and our two vice-presidents, Stephanie Cohen and Dave Shippel. This stellar triumvirate provided the corporate glue, moral support, and sage advice that Stephen and I counted on to run our business. We had great respect for them and, more importantly, trusted them implicitly. I entered the main foyer where I had a cheery discussion with "Little Dave," working the night security shift. He wanted to show me the new laser toy he had bought to entertain the cats. He called Noggin and Panther and got them to repeatedly leap at the narrow red laser beam. The cats and Dave always gave me a laugh.

I turned down the production corridor, past the empty offices of the ADs, the production manager, and production staff. Tomorrow at 7 a.m. these offices would be abuzz with activity as the new production day began. On my left, I looked through the glass doors of the production boardroom and paused. So many wonderful moments had transpired in this large and versatile space. All our casting happened here. Every script was read through in this room with actors, writers, directors, and producers. It was the hub for production meetings and occasionally was used as a shooting set for a location such as a community centre or counselling office.

Looking through the glass, I saw hundreds of auditions of hopeful young actors. I heard the gasps from the cast as they read through the script and found out that Jane (Paula Brancati) had been sexually abused as a young girl by her father. I remembered the tears of numerous cast members as they read the scripts where their characters would graduate.

I continued on to the corridor that led to the art department. For the last thirteen years, this had been the domain of Stephen Stanley, our brilliant, unflappable genius production designer, who had designed his way through hundreds of episodes, never repeating himself and being a firm but encouraging boss to all his department heads and interns. Colour palettes, floor layouts, sample logos, and random sketches adorned the walls.

Onward, I peeked into the women's washroom. This was a functioning washroom with multiple stalls and sinks. It also doubled as the location for the *Degrassi* girls' washroom. Here, Manny and Paige had an epic fight, Ellie's self-harm was revealed, Lola took her pregnancy test, and various meaty gossip sessions transpired. With a quick addition of urinals, this space then became the shooting stage for the boys' washroom. Here, secretly in a stall, J.T. tried to understand the Chinese instructions to his newly acquired penis pump; Rick overheard Jimmy and Spinner's bullying plans; and Adam, our trans male character, had been callously beaten up and thrown out the door.

My solo walk took me farther down the corridor to the door that led to the post-production and editing area. *Oh my*, I thought. *How I love the editing process.* So many hours I'd spent here with Steve, Gillian, Jason, Nick, Mike, and others, dealing with the realities of the production material. Forwards, backwards, forwards again, relentlessly massaging the footage to create the final draft of the script.

Even farther down the hall, my next stop was the cafeteria. I paused at the upper level and imagined the caterers efficiently bringing in the hot and assorted lunch for the day. For logistical purposes, we would always serve two lunches — one not governed by the production schedule and a second for the cast and crew six hours after crew call. Stephen and I would usually eat at the early lunch. Here we'd stand in line at the buffet along with all our writers, editors, staff, and interns, and take random seats with our gang. I loved these lunch sessions. It was here that my team shared stories from their own lives: moving out to escape an impossible roommate, coaching their kid's soccer team, buying a new car. They also shared their latest YouTube finds and, of course, cat videos. Sometimes, when I'd eaten at the first lunch, it would be necessary for me to attend the second lunch. Here, I'd huddle with the director, ADs, and production manager when we were running behind schedule on our morning to look at the upcoming afternoon scenes and see what we could simplify or delete if necessary.

The cafeteria also had an administrative function. Every year, this is where we gathered our actors and their parents for orientation. We'd explain what was in store for the new season, how they could keep their own social media safe, PR expectations, and the opportunities to participate with Free the Children. The cafeteria, like every other nook and cranny of our building, doubled as a set. It was *Degrassi's* cafeteria and had been home to many lunchtime scenes, including our famous food fight. Before I left the caf, I glanced at the ceiling and smiled. This was the same ceiling that Stephen and I had looked at in despair the night we'd taken possession of the building when streams of melted snow poured into overflowing garbage cans.

I went towards the actual studio, where a severe warning hung over the door: "DO NOT OPEN WHEN RED LIGHT IS FLASHING." With nobody about, I opened it confidently. It was dark, and I had to remember how to reach for the lights. On my left were two very realistic classrooms, complete with black and white boards, versatile furniture, and real windows that let in the sunlight and a view of the parking lot. It was in these classrooms where Emma had her first period, and Spinner, his embarrassing boner.

On my right was the very authentic science room. On one occasion, actor Matthew Gray Gubler from *Criminal Minds* visited our set. In the science classroom, he looked at the shelves on which we had jars of real pig brains, formaldehyde frogs, and various pickled animal parts.

"Gross," was the response from Matthew.

The art direction, set dressing, and props give our science classroom an unnervingly authentic atmosphere.

"Seriously," I said, "you guys deal with sooo much worse."

"But," he said, "on our show, we know it's all props. This reminds me so much of my real high school. You guys have brought back my old high school angst!"

Behind the classrooms was a corridor to the outside. It was here that Maya proudly strutted wearing her newly acquired "chicken cutlets" and where a few years earlier, Manny had saucily sported her new thong. Around the corner was where Jimmy got shot.

I walked on towards the gym. Oh my, the gym. What *hasn't* happened here? Marco's blood drive, Holly J. and Declan's first dance, Adam's nose being broken during a volleyball match, Drew winning as school president, ex-lovers Tristan and Miles in a sexually charged debate, Mr. Simpson presiding over graduations, a hoedown, multiple proms, and so much more. I looked down at the gym floor. Back in 2001, I had the art department paint the concrete floor with a trompe l'oeil hardwood finish, complete with markings for basketball, volleyball, and badminton. I wasn't

Without the bustle of our cast and crew, our hallways feel eerily hollow.

a hundred percent satisfied with the work and thought we would change it in the next year or two. Now, fourteen years later, it was still servicing us.

I entered the foyer, remembering so many scenes from first days of school as anxious newbies collected maps and schedules while seasoned seniors smirked. It was through this foyer that Eli ran naked wearing nothing but a superhero cape, where Goldi received a junk pic from Winston, and where, from the upper balcony, Cam contemplated a suicide jump.

I opened the double glass doors and ventured into the cool night air. I remembered how proud I was the day we installed these doors. The front steps brought so many scenes to mind. It was up these steps that Bruce McDonald and I walked arm in arm as extras in the first episode of *Degrassi: The Next Generation.* Here J.T. crashed his car after Liberty told him she was pregnant and Downtown Sasquatch played their charity carwash gig. Down these steps was where Connor snuck out of school to

Anya, Holly J., and Chantay leave an indelible mark on *Degrassi* as they say goodbye to their high school years.

meet LoveQueen16. It was on this sidewalk that Holly J., Anya, and Chantay, dressed in their fancy prom outfits, put their handprints and initials in the wet cement.

So many stories have been told from this building. So many careers launched. How could I possibly sell the business?

CHAPTER NINETEEN

AN ENGLISH GIRL IN PARIS (ONTARIO)

November 1956.

"Ouch, you're hurting me," I cried out.

"Don't be daft." Mum gave my tie a final yank. "There. Perfect." Not only was my tie tight, but my mum had put extra starch in my shirt. "You need to make a good first impression," she insisted. "Chop, chop. Let's go."

My younger brother Tony and a nervously excited eight-year-old me gathered around my baby sister, Barb, sleeping soundly in her English pram. Mum pushed as Tony and I each grabbed a side handle. We walked briskly to my new school. Once there, I saw the other children on the playground and looked down at my grey tunic, white shirt, striped tie, navy knee-high socks, and Oxford shoes, standard issue from my previous all-girls' school in England, St. Mildred's. I was suddenly self-conscious. I looked at Mum. She and I both realized that no other children were in uniform.

At the bell, I automatically straightened my tie as we approached the office for registration. By the time I was admitted to Mrs. Harrison's Grade 3/4 class, my new classmates were hard at work on an Uncle Funny Bunny phonics assignment. Mrs. Harrison gave me a warm smile as she asked for her students' attention. "Class, I'd like you to meet our new classmate. She has moved all the way from England to join us. Would you like to introduce yourself?" she asked, looking at me.

I stared out at twenty-five or so students, all wearing an assortment of colourful clothes, very mindful of my drab uniform. I took a breath and started. "Good morning, class. My name is Linda Bawcutt and I'm eight years old."

Before I'd even finished my sentence, I could hear snickers.

"Ohhh, she's got an accent," a voice called from the back of the room. "Say something else." "Yeah, we wanna hear you toolk." "Heh! Heh!"

"That's quite enough," Mrs. Harrison said sternly. "Welcome to Grade 3, Linda, and to the home of Uncle Funny Bunny." She put a protective arm on my shoulder and gently guided me to my desk, where I tried to make myself invisible.

★

It was hard to believe that just four short days earlier, we had been at Gatwick Airport just outside of London, preparing to say goodbye to our relatives. It was November 5, Guy Fawkes Day in England. There was a large contingent wishing us well as we set off on our transatlantic adventure — both sets of grandparents plus various aunties and uncles. My mum had little to say. She was thirty-three and clutching two things dearly: my six-month-old sister, Barb, in one arm and her purse in the other. The purse contained all our travel documents and immigration papers.

My mother had been preparing for this day for months, ever since my dad had left for Canada to find a job and a new home for his family. She and her mum had planned our going-away outfits as meticulously as Guy Fawkes had plotted to blow up the British parliament buildings. My homemade, long-sleeved crew neck sweater of coarse worsted wool was royal blue. The homemade woolen skirt was a herringbone design, in grey and white. Four-year-old Tony wore a matching royal blue sweater, grey herringbone shorts, knee socks, and Oxfords.

Outside Buckingham Palace, November 5, 1956. Uncle Geoff took Tony and me on a sightseeing tour of London before we boarded our transatlantic flight to Canada.

As we took off from Gatwick, London as seen from the air was an unexpected treat. All over the city, countless bonfires were burning with effigies of Guy Fawkes going up in flames. Mum quietly recited:

Remember, remember the fifth of November,
Gunpowder treason and plot.
I see no reason why gunpowder treason
Should ever be forgot.

Quickly, the fires of London vanished, and we looked forward into the dark of night. My girlish recollection of our flight was that we completed our epic transatlantic trip on a prop plane. Years later my brother corrected me. We did, in fact, land in Toronto on a prop plane, but that was after we had fuelled up in both Glasgow and Gander and had cleared customs in Montreal. The bulk of our journey had been on one of the first passenger transatlantic jets.

Arriving in Toronto by prop plane was spectacular. We were weary from hours of flying, crowded airport waiting rooms, and officious customs officers. But, as our plane taxied to a stop, there on the tarmac was Dad. As we had already cleared customs in Montreal, and as Malton airport was pretty much a farmers' field in those days, Dad had, officially or not (perhaps he pulled some old Air Force strings, who knows), made his way to the bottom of our gangplank. Elbowing each other, and most likely other passengers as well, Tony and I raced down the stairs screaming one word over and over again. "Daddy! Daddy!! Daddy!!!" Simultaneously the two of us were lifted up by the strong arms of our dad. We hadn't seen him in almost six months.

After his stint in Dauphin, Manitoba, as a British Royal Air Force pilot-in-training during WWII, Dad had vowed to one day return to Canada. It would take almost ten years, a marriage of romance, many odd jobs, and three children for that pledge to eventually become a reality. But here we were, a product of my dad's dreams, my mother's belief in those dreams, and their combined determination to provide well for their kids. It seemed like an eternity that we stood at the bottom of the airplane stairs, nestled in Dad's arms as the other passengers disembarked.

"I've got so many wonderful places to show you. There are huge lakes here, so big you can't see the other side," Dad told us excitedly. "And wait till you see what we can do with our car. We can go to a drive-in restaurant and order cheeseburgers and hot dogs — footlong ones! — and eat them in our car. We can go to a drive-in theatre and watch a movie without leaving our car. We can travel to the country and go horseback riding and fishing. You're going to love Canada!"

Finally, Dad's eye was drawn to the top of the stairs. There stood the last passenger off the plane, our mum. She still clutched her precious cargo in either hand and was surrounded by stewardesses helping with various baby bags, blankets, sweaters, and paper bags — all remnants of our epic journey, so thoughtlessly left behind by

Tony and me. And then time stood still. My dad and mum locked eyes. Even though Tony and I had never doubted the love that our parents had for each of us kids, we knew it was in a different class from the love they shared for each other.

In July 2020, we celebrated our folks' seventy-fifth wedding anniversary. We had their wedding photo from 1945 blown up to life size. The photo poetically captured their moment of sheer joy and love. That same look, still there at their milestone anniversary, was unmistakably there on the airplane steps in 1956.

Mum and Dad, July 28, 1945.

Mum and Dad had met in London in September 1940. It was the middle of the night and the all-clear had just been sounded after an onslaught of German bombs. My mum and her family, who had been sheltering under the stairs, came out from hiding to serve hot tea and biscuits to the firemen and air raid wardens, one of whom would eventually become my dad. Evidently, it was love at first sight (even though, as my mum remembers, she was wearing her dad's old dressing gown and had her hair in rollers). From that day forward to the present, the two have dedicated their lives to each other and to their families. Apart from love, they've both shared a sense of adventure. Over the course of their lives in Canada, they've jointly opened and closed many entrepreneurial endeavours, including a knitting mill, various retail outlets, and a wholesale warehouse, all in the textile-related field. As such, I got much firsthand experience with the family businesses, working the floor as a labourer in the mill and as a salesperson at various stores.

I often did banking, some inventory control, and the odd bit of bookkeeping. The thing that bothered me about my parents' efforts was that they both worked very hard and would be successful for a bit, then eventually the businesses, for various reasons, would fizzle out. I saw how much they invested of themselves in each new start-up and vowed to myself that I would never start a business of my own.

The one job that Dad did enjoy — and stuck with for almost twenty years — was his elected role as the mayor of Paris, Ontario. This position was only part time and certainly didn't pay very much, but it provided him with rich rewards in terms of job satisfaction. He took great pride in serving his constituents. With Mum by his side, they tirelessly gave back to their community, their church, and their adopted country.

★

On our November drive to our new hometown of Paris — headquarters of Mary Maxim, the knitting company that had hired Dad (whose fond memories of this job include the day he presented a Mary Maxim sweater with a large bison to then–prime minister John Diefenbaker) — Dad introduced us to a new traffic phenomenon: the cloverleaf. In England, traffic was all about the roundabouts, but this cloverleaf was something quite intriguing. As Dad explained how the traffic flow worked, I imagined myself floating above it, looking down at the overall total pattern of the moulded asphalt cloverleaf and intricate guardrails. With my overview-vision, I could see what he was talking about.

The house that Dad had rented for us was modest. There was one bedroom on the main floor for Mum and Dad, and a small attic space that would serve as the bedroom for the three of us kids. It was almost a mile walk from my new home to school, and I walked it four times a day. Sometimes it seemed particularly long, as there were bullies along the way. My fellow classmates laughed at my foreign accent, my British school uniform, and my

Mum, Tony, and me in Mary Maxim sweaters. Mum became a master knitter and tested many patterns for the company that employed my dad.

protruding front teeth. That plummy English accent of mine was mimicked constantly by many of my Grade 3 classmates.

I'd storm home, hot tears on my cheeks, and rush to the privacy — well, semi-privacy — of our shared attic. Here, for hours on end, I would practise speaking Canadian English. Every pavement, lorry, loo, and bobby was banished from my vocabulary and replaced with sidewalk, truck, bathroom, and policeman. And the pronunciation had to change and change quickly. I was determined to fit in.

The bullies ridiculed me on a regular basis. My mother tried to help by coming, with my sister in the pram, to meet me after school and walk home with me. The bullies would sneer at me the next day. "Limey Linda needs her mama" and "Sucky, sucky, Mommy's girl." And, making bad-smell faces, they'd brush pretend cooties off their fingers. I had to ask Mum to stop meeting me.

My parents advised me, "Keep your head high. Remember: sticks and stones." I started to employ my overview-vision. I'd stand at my front door and imagine an aerial map of my route to school. The school was the goal. I'd walk sternly and deliberately to that goal. When bullies got in the way, I'd nimbly shift to an alternate route provided by my mental map. My determination did not stop the bullies, but they didn't stop me. I would head on, through their taunts, keeping my focus clearly on my goal. I had no idea, at that time, how far my steely eight-year-old resolve would take me.

CHAPTER TWENTY

Made in Canada

On April 3, 2014, at 2:15 p.m., Epitome Pictures Inc. was officially sold to DHX Media.

"Your company is a coral reef," DHX CEO Michael Donovan graciously reiterated to Stephen and me once the paperwork for our sale was complete. "The two of you have a unique way of energizing your cast and crew while keeping fresh and innovative stories alive. We will protect you as an endangered species."

Stephen and I were both grateful to be selling to someone who respected our work. In fact, Michael's reassurance was the final piece of our decision-making process. When we weighed the pros and cons of selling our company, many variables were considered. Both Stephen and I were fortunate enough to have all four of our parents alive and in their early nineties, but their various health issues were starting to require our attention. Our son Max was also battling a severe illness and needed our support. When family responsibilities permitted, we both knew we would like to travel more. We were also well aware that few companies would be in a position to make an offer such as the one we'd received from Michael and DHX Media. It was a fair deal, and we decided to take it. As part of the transaction, Stephen and I agreed to continue on as producers for at least the next three years.

When we announced our sale to the cast and crew, we shared with them Michael's message that there should be no appreciable change in the rhythm of daily production. Season fourteen of *Degrassi* was already in prep and would begin production as scheduled. We also had a new series ready for production, *Open Heart* (YTV and TeenNick), a teen mystery drama, set in a hospital, run by *Degrassi* veteran Ramona Barckert. Our staff and crew, many of whom had been with us for years, responded warmly to our news and to our reassurance that it would be "business as usual." However, for reasons unrelated to the sale of the business, at the end of that year we learned that neither *Degrassi* nor *Open Heart* would be renewed by our current broadcasters.

Josh Scherba, head of distribution at DHX Media, immediately set up meetings with several streaming services for us to pitch the continuation of *Degrassi* as *Degrassi: Next Class*. In short order we secured a Netflix deal for forty episodes over two years. Not only did our new title indicate a fresh start with new partners, it also reflected the fact that our audience had changed. Our cast and our audience for *Degrassi: Next Generation* had been the millennials.

With *Next Class* we were now talking to Generation Z, the kids who had grown up alongside the internet and had never known a world without mobile devices. They were our neo-digital natives, nimble in adapting to new apps, such as Instagram, Snapchat, TikTok, and more. On the whole, Gen Z was more hopeful than their predecessors and more likely to get involved with social issues and activism. However, they were also a generation with growing anxiety — social anxiety, eco-anxiety, and internet anxiety. They were crushed when they got a "downvote" or an "unfollow" on their socials.

The rise of social media had also ushered in the fourth wave of feminism. Women and young girls had a new, equal platform to speak out about abusers of power, their right to control their own bodies, and to demand equal opportunities for all ethnicities as well as for the acceptance of gender fluidity.

Against this multi-layered and rich societal backdrop, we enthusiastically developed stories and characters for what would become a four-season run on Netflix.

Our stories saw Maya (Olivia Scriven) push back against microaggressions as she made a debut singing appearance in a night club. Hunter (Spencer MacPherson) couldn't understand why his Gamer Club was shut down due to misogynistic content. Yael (Jamie Bloch) came to terms with their gender fluidity, and Zig (Ricardo Hoyos) and Maya engaged in consensual "yes means yes" sex. We welcomed new Syrian refugee families into the community; enjoyed the Tristan (Lyle Lettau) and Miles (Eric Osborne) on again, off again relationship; followed Goldi (Soma Chhaya) as she wondered about her Muslim faith; saw the impact of Grace's (Nikki Gould) cystic fibrosis on her relationship with Zoe (Ana Golja); and watched racism tear best friends Shay (Reiya Downs) and Frankie (Sara Waisglass) apart. We also enjoyed the wacky antics of Baaz (Amir Bageria), Vijay (Dante Scott), and Yael with their earnest yet comical podcasts.

Parham Rownaghi (Saad), Jamie Bloch (Yael), Richard Walters (Tiny), Sara Waisglass (Frankie), and Reiya Downs (Shay) take a break from filming beside the Hollingsworth's pool.

During production, Netflix adopted an attitude similar to that of Michael's "coral reef" and stayed mostly hands-off. Over this period, DHX Media changed its upper management, and Michael Donovan was no longer CEO. By the time we had produced all forty episodes of *Degrassi: Next Class*, all our execs at both DHX Media and Netflix had either moved on or been fired. And, politically in the U.S., even bigger changes had happened: Donald Trump had been elected the forty-fifth president of the United States of America.

At the end of our Netflix production run, we found ourselves facing a void. Netflix shared no data or feedback on the performance of *Degrassi: Next Class*; its audience algorithms were a closely guarded secret. We did, however, receive encouraging feedback through the press. A few days before Donald Trump's inauguration, *Bustle* ran an article by Jamie Primeau with the following headline: "What *Degrassi: Next Class* Gets Right About Social Issues That The GOP Can't." It was a lengthy piece, critiquing our various storylines, and said in part:

> Though *Degrassi* takes place in Canada . . . its messages still resonate. *Degrassi: Next Class* addresses subjects ranging from the Syrian refugee crisis to abortion, in a way that's accessible, eye-opening, and informative. I'd argue that we all could learn a thing or two from this show — especially representatives of the Republican party. . . . *Degrassi* is fearlessly educating the next generation about difficult topics, and in the face of a Trump presidency, that is more important than ever.

In addition to discussing the Syrian refugee storyline and abortion, Primeau went on to talk about how we handled LGBTQ+ relationships, religious intolerance, and mental health. This article reassured me that after all these years, and despite the fact that the company had been sold, *Degrassi* still had a relevant voice.

However, the reassurance didn't seem to be shared by Netflix. I tried to deconstruct the company's silence. Aware that we had been given wide creative freedom, I started to wonder. Did we push too far with our stories? Was the Syrian refugee story too much in a U.S. climate where the president was talking about a Muslim ban and had campaigned to build a wall at the Mexican border? Did our gender-fluid character who identified as "they" demand too much of our young audience? Were we too liberal? Was our voice advocating for fourth-wave feminists too bold?

Soma Chhaya (Goldi) and director Eleanore Lindo prepare to shoot the scene where students rally around Maya, who has been trolled for her feminist stance.

Lola's episode was certainly our most courageous abortion story yet. The episode "#IRegretNothing," written by Sarah Glinski, was all about normalizing abortion. Not trivializing, but normalizing. At the mid-point of the show, we enter the doctor's sterilized room with our character, Lola, and are with her as her procedure begins. The second part of the episode is about Lola resuming her regular school life. When some students discover her truth, she is shamed. Eventually, she makes a vlog and transmits it to the whole school, publicly and proudly owning her choice: "Yesterday, I was pregnant and now I'm not. And I'd like to talk about it. There's so many things I wanna do in high school and being a mom isn't one of them. It might not be everyone's choice, but it was mine. And I'm not ashamed."

It was a critical time for us to tell this story, as abortion was once again on the national agenda. Many states, including Arkansas, Georgia, Kentucky, Missouri, and Ohio, had recently passed the so-called "heartbeat" bills, basically overruling the *Roe v. Wade* decision that permitted abortion up until the time the fetus is viable; in other words, until it can live outside the womb. I was proud of the episode "#IRegretNothing," but we weren't getting any response from our partner, Netflix. Had we pushed too far in the current political environment?

After much internal debate, I finally reached a conclusion: at that point in American history, our show was probably just "too Canadian."

★

During our partnership with The N/TeenNick we would have annual "feel-good" dinners where together we would enjoy fine food and imported wines. At one of these meals, our execs offered up a toast to our show and said, "We are so grateful for you and your voice for youth empowerment. It's a voice that couldn't have been produced in the States." We drank to that, then started to drill down on why we all thought that was true. We mused about age-appropriate casting and how that would never happen in the U.S. We discussed our style of storytelling that allowed young characters to make choices, good and bad, and live with the consequences. This was a departure from traditional television for young people, which would always end with a strongly reinforced lesson. I shared with them the story from the development days of *Degrassi Junior High* when Kate Taylor from WGBH wanted our show to wrap up with a cat lady dishing advice on the topic of the day. As we chatted, I realized that Kate's instinct to include the cat lady was rooted in a societal consciousness that held a protective attitude towards young audiences. It's not that there weren't lessons to be learned from *Degrassi* — there were lessons in every episode. But for perhaps the first time in children's television, the lessons weren't neat or pat or summarized by an adult.

As the conversation continued, I shared with my American partners my experience with a UCLA student a few years earlier. She was writing a paper comparing *Degrassi* with *Beverly Hills 90210*. She talked about age-appropriate casting that would never have happened in the American show and she examined the differences in our generic openings. *90210* featured individual beauty shots of each of the stars with their names attached. *Degrassi* depicted shots of community and student interaction without singling out particular stars. Our Canadian opening sequence suggested the power of community and the collective rather than that of the individual.

"That makes me think of something else," I offered up at dinner. "When I received funding for my first documentary, *Between Two Worlds*, it had come from a federal initiative to promote multiculturalism. This Canadian initiative was in contrast to that of the States at the time, where their federal initiative was towards the melting pot."

Putting it all together, we extrapolated that while Canadians believed in celebrating the richness of the diversity of our population, we also believed in the power of community — our universal health care being a major example. In the U.S., it was less about diversity and more about "melting in," while achievements of individuals were celebrated.

"Interesting," we all agreed.

Of course, this analysis is overly simplistic. But at the time, it served our conversation and made me realize how proud I am to be Canadian.

As a Canadian, I am well aware that my country, like my family, is not perfect. Far from it. Trying to come to terms with Canada's historic systemic racism and the genocide of our Indigenous people is gravely challenging. For these deep wounds to heal, we need two things: truth and reconciliation. I know this on a small and personal level. I was only able to come to terms with the trauma of my car crash, and its far-reaching ramifications, once I stopped pretending it didn't happen. When I opened up and embraced my emotional truth, the healing started. Our country will heal, but we need to acknowledge the atrocirites of the past: the unmarked graves, the dehumanization inflicted by the Indian Act, and our systemically entrenched colonial attitudes. It will take a tremendous amount of patience, goodwill, and determination on all fronts.

The one truth I hold on to is that, regardless of the work we still need to do as a nation, Canada remains the country I'm most happy to call home.

*

A number of years ago, friends of my parents were travelling in China. When they were introduced to their interpreter as Canadian, he smiled and respectfully bowed his head saying, "Ah — Bethune . . . and *Degrassi*." Upon their return to Paris, Ontario, the couple couldn't wait to tell this story to my mum and dad, saying they were so proud of me and the reach of my show. Then, unbeknownst to me, they submitted my name for the Order of Canada.

A couple of years later, in 1994, I was invited to Ottawa to become a Member of the Order of Canada, which I accepted with honour and humility, from then–governor general Ray Hnatyshyn. My citation read: "Linda Schuyler has brought credibility and respect to Canadian programming with her multi-award-winning television series *Degrassi Junior High*. Her candid productions of real-life dramas have touched millions of viewers around the world, encouraging them to contact outreach programs and opening lines of communication between adults and youth."

It was an indescribably special night, sharing the spotlight with so many accomplished Canadians. As we sat having dinner in Rideau Hall, I looked at my dad, dressed in his fancy tux, and mum with her tasteful black dress and pearls, and thought how proud I was of them. What courage it had taken to leave their families behind and travel across the ocean to start a new life with three young children. I also thought about how much they had given back to others. I made a toast to them: "Thank you," I said, "for your courage, your convictions, and your unconditional love. Thank you for the room you gave us as children to find our independence, to fall down and scrape our knees. And thank you for showing, by example, that mistakes can be admitted, and closed minds changed. You are my inspiration."

In addition to being there when I received the Order of Canada, my family celebrated with me as I received the Order of Ontario in 2012.

★

When the Netflix run of *Degrassi: Next Class* ended in 2017, Stephen and I had been working for DHX for three years. With our contractual obligations fulfilled and no new production orders for *Degrassi*, Stephen and I bid adieu to the offices and studio that had been our home for the last twenty-one years. Thirty-eight years earlier, Kit and I had started production of *Ida Makes a Movie*. It was satisfying to look back and realize that *Ida Makes a Movie* had become the pilot episode of *The Kids of Degrassi Street*. *The Kids* became *Junior High*, then *High*, followed by *Next Generation* and finally *Next Class*. *Degrassi* had had the opportunity to become a franchise with over five hundred episodes. It was time to say goodbye.

In early 2022, five years since we wrapped on the final episode of *Degrassi: Next Class*, Stephen and I got a call from Josh Scherba, now president of WildBrain (formerly DHX Media). "I thought you'd like to know," said an excited Josh. "We're putting a new *Degrassi* into development!"

I wasn't surprised. My Google alerts were telling me that a next generation of fans was finding *Degrassi*. New audiences were watching old episodes on multiple platforms, responding to Manny's abortion, Jimmy's shooting, Spinner's cancer, Alli's blow jobs, and Fiona's coming out. New discussions were springing up on social media, and long-time *Degrassi* superfan Jocelyn Claybourne was releasing her in-depth podcasts, reaching thousands weekly. There was an energy in the zeitgeist similar to the one that followed classic *Degrassi* once reruns started, and *Jonovision* ran a reunion show. Josh was right. It was time for *Degrassi* to come back!

Every time there has been a new reboot of the *Degrassi* franchise, accommodations have been made to acknowledge changing times and evolving circumstances. One such adjustment, when we moved from the classic *Degrassi* series to *Degrassi: The Next Generation*, was to give ourselves permission to graduate cast members. Now, as we head into a new reboot, I need to accept the fact that I have graduated. No longer *Degrassi*'s mom, I'm about to become a grandmother! I'm looking forward to the day I can cozy up on the couch with Stephen, a cup of tea, and our Scottish Fold cats, turn on the television, and welcome the grandkids into our living room.

Television production is a team sport. It takes a large team effort to get a television series on the air, and I've been blessed with great team players. To manage these teams, and to be able to tell my stories, despite my earlier pledge to the contrary, I needed to start my own company. A few weeks after the Harvey Weinstein sexual harassment and alleged rape stories broke in the fall of 2017, I was giving a lecture at Innis College (yes, my old alma mater). In the Q & A portion, I had the following exchange:

> Student: "During your career, were you ever the victim of Harvey Weinstein–type sexual harassment?"
> LS: "No, can't say I was."
> Student: "With this type of harassment so prevalent in the entertainment industry, how did you avoid it?"
> LS: "Well, I think probably because I've been my own boss for almost forty years."

It's true: by having my own company and creating my own corporate culture, I've never had to encounter the indignities of such sexually inappropriate behaviour. However, that doesn't mean I wasn't reminded from time to time that I was a woman in a traditionally male industry. Over the years, I've been called dear, sweetie, bitch, sweetheart, chick, slut, and more. I've been told I'm overly ambitious, manipulative, pushy, and too naïve. Bankers have insisted I have a husband, and a broadcast executive once suggested I sounded "half-pregnant." That was particularly painful as it happened at a time when I was trying to come to terms with my infertility. When I was looking for international representation, I asked one industry leader to explain the intricacies of international distribution to me. He kindly suggested that I needn't worry, he would look after me. He didn't want to overwhelm me with information, for that would be "like teaching a baby to drink champagne." We did not do business together.

"You're a tall girl, Linda Mary Bawcutt. Stand tall. Shoulders back. And, walk across the room with purpose." That was my paternal Victorian grandmother speaking. She didn't bark those orders; she simply imparted them in a manner that you could not ignore.

"Linda, don't be such a bull in a china shop." That was my mum's voice. When I thundered home from school and burst in the door saying, "Guess what happened today?" or when I dashed across the living room to be the first to answer a ringing phone, I would get the "bull-in-a-china-shop" note. For the longest time, I found these two pieces of well-intentioned advice incompatible. Should I hold my shoulders back, my head high, and walk with purpose? Or should I keep myself back lest I'm perceived as bullish — too ambitious? It has taken me many years to realize that these two distinct pieces of parental advice can not only co-exist, but *must* co-exist, particularly for a woman making her uncharted way in the entertainment world as an entrepreneur. I've come to learn as a leader that nuance, empathy, and patience need to work hand-in-hand with ambition, vision, and determination. I might have started my business out of necessity, but over the years it became much more than a means to an end. It's been a remarkable opportunity to create a healthy, safe, and inclusive corporate culture where world-class shows could be produced and high-quality jobs provided.

*

I now think of myself as an educator by nature, a storyteller by nurture, and an entrepreneur by necessity. That combination has allowed me to have a singularly enriching professional life. Through my work, on a regular basis, I've been invited into people's homes and allowed to tell them stories. And that is magical.

But magic doesn't happen in a vacuum.

There have been many amazing collaborators along my journey, people who have deeply enhanced my life and helped my work soar higher and further than I ever could have imagined. To all my cheerleaders and supporters; to my cast and crew; to my friends, family, and fans; and to *all* my surrogate children — thank you for your part in helping to reassure young people around the world that they are not alone.

When I looked out at the audience at Wilfrid Laurier University and told them that I thought *Degrassi* was the world's longest running anti-bullying campaign, it was not only an acknowledgement of the stories I'd been telling for forty years, but also a personal catharsis. I realized that I had been plagued by bullies and impediments throughout my life. At times, they had the ability to get the upper hand and paralyze me; but ultimately, and thankfully, they didn't stop me. To all the bullies in the schoolyard and in corporate hallways; to my naysayers, detractors, and thoughtless executives; and to countless other obstacles, both real and imagined — including twenty-eight thousand pounds of bright red metal; my bitchy inner voices; and my barren body — I have one word: *Degrassi.*

KIDS HELP PHONE

Since the launch of Kids Help Phone in 1989, *Degrassi* and Kids Help Phone have enjoyed a symbiotic relationship — a mutual commitment to support the mental health and well-being of young people across Canada. For over thirty years, Kids Help Phone, like *Degrassi*, has evolved to stay relevant to youth and address a continuum of their emotional and mental health needs. Today, Kids Help Phone is Canada's only 24/7 e-mental health service offering free, confidential support to young people in both English and French.

Through *Degrassi*, I tried to reassure young people that they are not alone. In that spirit, I'm pleased to direct my proceeds from *The Mother of All Degrassi* to Kids Help Phone. ECW Press will also contribute a portion of its proceeds to the organization.

ACKNOWLEDGEMENTS

As someone who thrives in a team atmosphere, I found writing this memoir to be a particularly lonely experience. Over time, as the project has grown, so has the number of people who have given me camaraderie, support, and much-needed feedback.

There is, of course, one person who had my back right from the beginning — my amazing Zen-bull husband. Stephen never doubted that I would finish this. Even on days when I threw my hands up in despair, claiming, "My life is bullshit, nobody cares," or crying, "My computer is impossible, it has a mind of its own." His response was always a variation on "I believe in you. You can do it." Thank you, Stephen, for the confidence, reassurance, and the love. (Not to mention endless hours of IT support!)

Finishing this book was only possible with the support of my multi-talented executive assistant, Melinda Sutton Downie. More than once she retrieved my writing files (and on one occasion, my entire Dropbox) when I erroneously erased them from my computer. Melinda has the wonderful ability to help me organize thoughts, conduct research, and source pictures. In addition, her thoughtful response to various drafts and attention to detail has been invaluable.

My agent, Sam Hiyate, and his editor Diane Terrana of the The Rights Factory, were early believers and brutally honest. When I submitted my second draft, they told me they loved it . . . then suggested I lose the first six chapters. "What!" I cried in disbelief. "Do you know how many words that is?" Then the producer in me saw their rationale, and I realized that their instincts were not only right but brilliant.

My team got bigger once Sam introduced me to Jack David of ECW Press. I consider Jack to be my brother from another mother. Our shared background as teachers, passionate entrepreneurs, and champions of our own industries ensured that Jack and I became instant friends. Through Jack, I had access to his amazing ECW team, who have given this project great love and attention. I'm particularly grateful for the guidance, sage wisdom, and understanding from my substantive editor, Jen Hale. She enthusiastically embraced the *Degrassi* world. As she worked on this manuscript, she and her thirteen-year-old son watched *Degrassi* episodes together every night.

I'm grateful to all the folks who patiently delved through photo albums, files boxes and archives to help compile the many photos in this book. My thanks go to Phil Earnshaw, Sari Friedland, John Bertram, Colleen Norcross, Stephanie Cohen, Garry Toth, John Thompson, Nancy Sinclair, Carl Knipfel, Barb Graham, Tony Bawcutt, Michael Bawcutt, and my mum, Joyce Bawcutt. I also appreciated the help from Ben Weststrate at Innis College, Rachel Beattie at Media Commons Archives at the University of Toronto Libraries, and all the folks at WildBrain, in particular Rose St. Pierre and Krista Legault.

My early readers included my trusted friend and supporter, Iain Christiansen, Ryerson professor Michael Coutanche, Cathy Bruce, Vice-President of Research and Innovation at Trent University, and my long-time collaborator Yan Moore. Their insightful comments and wise notes gave me what I needed to keep going. Yan Moore and Kathryn Ellis then read an almost-final draft and helped fill in certain gaps, and corrected some of my faulty memory. They also cleverly suggested the title of the book.

I also received early supportive comments from Max Stohn. I'm not only grateful to Max for his feedback but also for the important place he holds in my heart. Over the years, I've received numerous television credits, but the credit that means the most to me is being Max's "belle-mère."

AWARDS

1981

- Best Canadian Production, Canadian Association for Young Children's Film Festival: *The Kids of Degrassi Street*

1983

- Best Independent Producer, Children's Broadcast Institute: Linda Schuyler and Kit Hood, *The Kids of Degrassi Street*

1985

- Award of Excellence, Children's Broadcast Institute: "Griff Makes a Date," *The Kids of Degrassi Street*
- Best Instructional/Educational Broadcast Program, Canadian Film & Television Awards: "Griff Makes a Date," *The Kids of Degrassi Street*

1986

- International Emmy Award, Children & Young People: "Griff Gets a Hand," *The Kids of Degrassi Street*
- Best Drama, Prix Jeunesse International: "Griff Makes a Date," *The Kids of Degrassi Street*
- Best Children's Program, Gemini Awards: "Griff Gets a Hand," *The Kids of Degrassi Street*

- Gold Medal, Best Series for Teens, International Film and Television Festival of New York: *The Kids of Degrassi Street*

1987

- International Emmy Award, Children & Young People: "It's Late," *Degrassi Junior High*
- Award of Excellence, Children's Broadcast Institute: "Griff Gets a Hand," *The Kids of Degrassi Street*
- Best Children's Series, Gemini Awards: *Degrassi Junior High*
- Best Direction in a Dramatic or Comedy Series, Gemini Awards: Kit Hood, *Degrassi Junior High*
- Best Continuing Series, Rockie Awards, Banff Television Festival: *Degrassi Junior High*
- Personal Achievement, Canadian Film & Television Awards: Linda Schuyler and Kit Hood, *The Kids of Degrassi Street*
- Silver Apple, National Film Festival: "The Cover Up," *Degrassi Junior High*
- Chris Bronze Plaque, Columbus International Film Festival: "The Cover Up," *Degrassi Junior High*

1988

- Outstanding Achievement in Children's Programming, Television Critics Association Awards: *Degrassi Junior High*
- Best Dramatic Series, Gemini Awards: *Degrassi Junior High*
- Best Direction in a Dramatic or Comedy Series, Gemini Awards: Kit Hood, *Degrassi Junior High*
- Best Performance by an Actor in a Leading Role, Gemini Awards: Pat Mastroianni, *Degrassi Junior High*
- Multiculturalism Award, Gemini Awards: *Degrassi Junior High*
- Chris Statuette, Columbus International Film and Video Festival: "Best Laid Plans," *Degrassi Junior High*
- Chris Statuette, Columbus International Film and Video Festival: "A Helping Hand," *Degrassi Junior High*
- Ruby Slipper Award, Adult Jury, Children's Film and Television Festival: "What a Night!" *Degrassi Junior High*

- Gold Medal, Best Series for Teens, International Film and Television Festival of New York: *Degrassi Junior High*
- Silver Award, Houston International Film Festival: "The Great Race," *Degrassi Junior High*
- Blue Ribbon, American Film Festival: "It's Late," *Degrassi Junior High*
- Achievement Award, "A stimulating TV series on adolescents in action," Action for Children's Television: *Degrassi Junior High*
- Gold Apple, National Educational Film and Video Festival: "Best Laid Plans," *Degrassi Junior High*
- Bronze Apple, National Educational Film and Video Festival: "It's Late," *Degrassi Junior High*
- Media Award, National Epilepsy Association of America: "Stage Fright," *Degrassi Junior High*
- Teen Dilemmas Portrayed with Honesty & Humour, Parents' Choice Award: *Degrassi Junior High*

1989

- Best Dramatic Series, Gemini Awards: *Degrassi Junior High*
- Best Performance by an Actress in a Leading Role, Gemini Awards: Stacie Mistysyn, *Degrassi Junior High*
- Best Human Relations, Electra Certificate of Award, Birmingham International Educational Film Festival: "It's Late," *Degrassi Junior High*
- Bronze Apple Award, National Educational Film and Video Festival: "Bottled Up," *Degrassi Junior High*
- Silver Plaque, Chicago Film Festival: "Great Expectations," *Degrassi Junior High*
- Certificate of Merit, Continuing Series, Chicago Film Festival: *Degrassi Junior High*
- Gold Award, Houston Film and Video Festival: "He Ain't Heavy," *Degrassi Junior High*
- Toronto Arts Medal, Media Arts Category: Linda Schuyler and Kit Hood, *Degrassi Junior High* and *Degrassi High*
- Most Entertaining Canadian Show, TV Guide Readers' Choice Award: *Degrassi Junior High*

- Channels Magazine Excellence in Television: Linda Schuyler and Kit Hood, *Degrassi Junior High*
- Chris Statuette, Columbus International Film and Video Festival: "Bottled Up," *Degrassi Junior High*
- Chris Statuette, Columbus International Film and Video Festival: "Big Girl Now," *Degrassi Junior High*
- Ollie Award, American Children's Television Festival: *Degrassi Junior High*
- Teen Dilemmas Portrayed with Honesty & Humour, Parents' Choice Award: *Degrassi Junior High*
- Award of Excellence, Children's Broadcast Institute: "He Ain't Heavy," *Degrassi Junior High*

1990

- Chris Statuette, Columbus International Film and Video Festival: "Nobody's Perfect," *Degrassi High*
- Chris Statuette, Columbus International Film and Video Festival: "A New Start," *Degrassi High*
- Best Youth Episodic, SHINE (Sexual Health in Entertainment) Awards, The Media Project: *Degrassi High*
- Award of Excellence, Children's Broadcast Institute: "A New Start," *Degrassi High*
- Nancy Susan Reynolds Award, Center for Population Options, Los Angeles: "A New Start," *Degrassi High*
- Successors Award for Outstanding Leadership in Business, *Canadian Business*: Linda Schuyler and Kit Hood

1991

- Teen Dilemmas Portrayed with Honesty & Humour, Parents' Choice Award: *Degrassi High*
- Chris Statuette, Columbus International Film and Video Festival: "Bad Blood," *Degrassi High*
- Chris Statuette, Columbus International Film and Video Festival: "Crossed Wires," *Degrassi High*

1992

- Best Drama, Prix Jeunesse International: "Bad Blood," *Degrassi High*
- Award of Excellence, Children's Broadcast Institute: *School's Out*

1994

- Order of Canada: Linda Schuyler

2002

- Outstanding Achievement in a Television Series — Children's, Directors Guild of Canada (DGC) Awards: "Mother and Child Reunion," *Degrassi: The Next Generation (Degrassi: TNG)*
- Best Ensemble in a TV Series (Comedy or Drama), Young Artist Awards: *Degrassi: TNG*
- Most Innovative Website Competition, Gemini Awards: *Degrassi: TNG*
- Entertainment Website, International New Media Awards: *Degrassi: TNG*
- Best Technical Achievement, International New Media Awards: *Degrassi: TNG*

2003

- Best Children's and Youth Program or Series, Gemini Awards: *Degrassi: TNG*
- Best Direction in a Children's or Youth Program or Series, Gemini Awards: Bruce McDonald, "Weird Science," *Degrassi: TNG*
- Best Performance in a Children's or Youth Program or Series, Gemini Awards: Jake Epstein, "Tears Are Not Enough," *Degrassi: TNG*
- Best Interactive, Gemini Awards: *Degrassi: TNG*
- Most Popular Website, Gemini Awards: *Degrassi: TNG*
- Outstanding Achievement in a Television Series — Children's, DGC Awards: "When Doves Cry," *Degrassi: TNG*
- Outstanding Achievement in Direction — Television Series, DGC Awards: Bruce McDonald, "White Wedding," *Degrassi: TNG*
- Outstanding Achievement in Picture Editing — Short Form, DGC Awards: Stephen Withrow, "When Doves Cry," *Degrassi: TNG*

- Best Performance in a TV Comedy Series — Leading Young Actor, Young Artist Awards: Jake Epstein, *Degrassi: TNG*
- Best Family Television Series, Young Artist Awards: *Degrassi: TNG*
- Silver Plaque, Best Children's Program, The Hugo Awards: *Degrassi: TNG*
- Silver Screen Award, Best Children's Programming, U.S. International Film and Video Festival: *Degrassi: TNG*
- Award of Excellence, Alliance for Children and Television (formerly Children's Broadcast Institute): *Degrassi: TNG*

2004

- Best Children's and Youth Program, Gemini Awards: *Degrassi: TNG*
- Best Direction in a Children's or Youth Program or Series, Gemini Awards: Phil Earnshaw, "Pride," *Degrassi: TNG*
- Outstanding Team Achievement in a Television Series — Family, DGC Awards: "Holiday," *Degrassi: TNG*
- Best Writing in a Youth Program or Series, WGC Screenwriting Awards: Aaron Martin, James Hurst, Shelley Scarrow, "Pride," *Degrassi: TNG*
- Best Youth Episodic, SHINE Awards, The Media Project: *Degrassi: TNG*
- Best Family TV Series, Young Artist Awards: *Degrassi: TNG*

2005

- Outstanding Achievement in Children's Programming, Television Critics Association Award: *Degrassi: TNG*
- Outstanding Team Achievement in a Television Series — Family, DGC Awards: "Time Stands Still, Part 2," *Degrassi: TNG*
- CBC Television Gemini Special: Top Canadian Show for the Last 20 Years: *Degrassi*
- Best Writing in a Youth Program or Series, WGC Screenwriting Awards: James Hurst and Miklos Perlus, "Mercy Street," *Degrassi: TNG*
- Best Children's Series, Shaw Rocket Prize: *Degrassi: TNG*
- Choice Summer Series, Teen Choice Awards: *Degrassi: TNG*
- Best Performance in a TV Comedy Series — Supporting Young Actress, Young Artist Awards: Christina Schmidt, *Degrassi: TNG*

2006

- WIFT Crystal Awards, International Achievement Award: Linda Schuyler
- Best Original Music Score for a Dramatic Series, Gemini Awards: Jim McGrath, "Our Lips Are Sealed," *Degrassi: TNG*
- Children's Live Action Episode or Special for TV, The EDGE Awards: "Time Stands Still," *Degrassi: TNG*

2007

- Choice Summer Series, Teen Choice Awards: *Degrassi: TNG*
- Best Performance in a Children's or Youth Program or Series, Gemini Awards: Shenae Grimes, "Eyes Without a Face, Part 2," *Degrassi: TNG*

2008

- Best Children's and Youth Program or Series, Gemini Awards: *Degrassi: TNG*
- Outstanding Team Achievement in a Television Series — Family, DGC Awards: "Pass the Dutchie," *Degrassi: TNG*
- Best Performance in a TV Comedy Series — Leading Young Actor, Young Artist Awards: Jamie Johnston, *Degrassi: TNG*

2009

- Best Direction in a Children's or Youth Program or Series, Gemini Awards: Eleanore Lindo, "Fight the Power," *Degrassi: TNG*
- Webby People's Voice Award, Best Sound Design, Webby Awards: "The Curse of Degrassi," *Degrassi* Webisodes
- Award of Excellence, Alliance for Children and Television: *Degrassi: TNG*

2010

- Peabody Award: "My Body Is a Cage," *Degrassi*
- Favourite Television Program from the Last 25 years — Fan Choice, Gemini Awards: *Degrassi*
- Academy Board of Directors Tribute, Gemini Awards: *Degrassi*

- Academy Lifetime Achievement Award, Gemini Awards: Linda Schuyler
- Best Direction in a Children's or Youth Program Series, Gemini Awards: Stefan Brogren, "Beat It, Part 2," *Degrassi: TNG*
- Best Performance in a Children's or Youth Program or Series, Gemini Awards: Charlotte Arnold, "Somebody," *Degrassi: TNG*
- Brand of the Year, *Strategy Magazine: Degrassi: TNG*

2011
- Outstanding Children's Program, Primetime Emmy Awards (nomination): "My Body Is a Cage," *Degrassi*
- Order of Ontario: Linda Schuyler
- Citizenship Award, Mark S. Bonham Centre for Sexual Diversity Studies (University of Toronto): Linda Schuyler
- Best Children's and Youth Program or Series, Gemini Awards: *Degrassi*
- Best Performance in a Children's or Youth Program or Series, Gemini Awards: Jordan Todosey, "My Body Is a Cage," *Degrassi*
- Best Direction in a Children's or Youth Program Series, Gemini Awards: Pat Williams, "All Falls Down, Part 2," *Degrassi*
- Special Anniversary Outstanding Achievement Award, Youth Media Alliance (formerly the Alliance for Children and Television): *Degrassi*

2012
- Outstanding Children's Program, Primetime Emmy Awards (nomination): *Degrassi*
- Best Children's and Youth Program or Series, Gemini Awards: *Degrassi*
- Best Direction in a Children's or Youth Program Series, Gemini Awards: Phil Earnshaw, "Scream, Part 2," *Degrassi*
- Innovative Producers Award, Banff World Media Festival: Epitome Pictures
- Best Performance in a TV Series — Lead Young Actress, Young Artist Awards: Cristine Prosperi, *Degrassi*

- Best Performance in a TV Series — Lead Young Actor, Young Artist Awards: A.J. Saudin, *Degrassi*

2013

- Best Children's or Youth Fiction Program or Series, Canadian Screen Awards (formerly the Gemini Awards): *Degrassi*
- Best Teen or Children's Program, PRISM Award: *Degrassi*
- Best Direction in a Children's or Youth Program or Series, Canadian Screen Awards: Stefan Brogren, "Time of My Life," *Degrassi*
- Best Writing in a Children's or Youth Program or Series, Canadian Screen Awards: Ramona Barckert, "Bitter Sweet Symphony, Part 2," *Degrassi*
- Best Performance in a Children's or Youth Program or Series, Canadian Screen Awards: Dylan Everett, "Bitter Sweet Symphony, Part 1," *Degrassi*
- Award of Excellence, Grand Prize for Best Production — All Categories, Youth Media Alliance: *Degrassi*

2014

- Outstanding Children's Program, Primetime Emmy Awards (nomination): *Degrassi*
- Best Children's or Youth Fiction Program or Series, Canadian Screen Awards: *Degrassi*
- Best Direction in a Children's or Youth Program Series, Canadian Screen Awards: Phil Earnshaw, "Hypnotize," *Degrassi*
- Best Writing in a Children's or Youth Program or Series, Canadian Screen Awards: Matt Huether, "Unbelievable," *Degrassi*
- Best Performance in a Children's or Youth Program or Series, Canadian Screen Awards: Aislinn Paul, "My Own Worst Enemy," *Degrassi*
- Best Television (Ages: 13 and up), Parents' Choice Award: *Degrassi*

2015

- Outstanding Children's Program, Primetime Emmy Awards (nomination): *Degrassi*

- Best Children's or Youth Fiction Program or Series, Canadian Screen Awards: *Degrassi*
- Best Direction in a Children's or Youth Program Series, Canadian Screen Awards: Phil Earnshaw, "Finally, Part 2," *Degrassi*
- Best Writing in a Children's or Youth Program or Series, Canadian Screen Awards: Matt Huether, "Give Me One Reason," *Degrassi*
- Best Performance in a Children's or Youth Program or Series, Canadian Screen Awards: Aislinn Paul, "Give Me One Reason," *Degrassi*
- Award of Excellence, Youth Media Alliance: *Degrassi*
- Parents' Choice Award, Television (Ages: 12–17): *Degrassi*
- Best Performance in a TV Series — Lead Young Actor, Young Artist Awards: Eric Osborne, *Degrassi*

2016

- Best Direction in a Children's or Youth Program Series, Canadian Screen Awards: Eleanore Lindo, "#ThisCouldBeUsButYouPlayin," *Degrassi: Next Class*
- Best Writing in a Children's or Youth Program or Series, Canadian Screen Awards: Alejandro Alcoba, "#YesMeansYes," *Degrassi: Next Class*

2017

- Best Writing for Tweens & Teens, WGC Screenwriting Awards: Ian MacIntyre, "#TeamFollowBack," *Degrassi: Next Class*
- Best Series Regular or Leading Actress in a TV Series 16 Years & Over, Joey Awards: Dalia Yegavian, *Degrassi: Next Class*

2018

- Best Non-Animated or Mixed Series, Kidscreen Awards: *Degrassi: Next Class*
- Children's Live Action Humanitas Prize: Matt Huether, "#ImSleep," *Degrassi: Next Class*

IMAGE CREDITS

The following images are courtesy of:

CHAPTER ONE
Innis College, p. 5
Robert Lansdale, courtesy of University of Toronto Archives, p. 2
WildBrain / Media Commons Archives, University of Toronto Libraries, p. 16

CHAPTER TWO
WildBrain, p. 22, 27

CHAPTER THREE
Phil Earnshaw / WildBrain, p. 37
Sari Friedland, p. 34

CHAPTER FOUR
Bill Dunn, p. 55
Kay Chorao / HarperCollins, p. 56
Phil Earnshaw / WildBrain, p. 63
WildBrain / Media Commons Archives, University of Toronto Libraries, p. 68
WildBrain, p. 58, 65, 71

CHAPTER FIVE
Sari Friedland, p. 77
WildBrain, p. 74

CHAPTER SIX
WildBrain / Media Commons Archives, University of Toronto Libraries, p. 88, 92, 99

CHAPTER SEVEN
Collection Dolores Olmedo Museum, p. 114

CHAPTER EIGHT
The Globe and Mail, p. 115
WildBrain / Media Commons Archives, University of Toronto Libraries, p. 121
WildBrain, p. 125

All other images are courtesy of the author. Every effort has been made to contact the holders of copyrighted material. Omissions will be corrected in future editions if the publisher is notified in writing.

INDEX

Characters are listed under the series they appear in, alphabetized by first name. Characters played by actors are noted in parenthesis following the actor's name. Illustrations indicated by page numbers in italics. For a full list of awards see 314–323.

Arthur (character), *121*, 121–122
awards, 304
Benjamin (character), 93
better resolutions requested by Kate, 81
broadcasters concerns over storylines, 96, 97, 98, 100
bullying storyline, 95, 294–296
Caitlin (character), 25
cancellations, 146, 147
Casey (character), 68–69, 93, 116
casting process, 88–91
CBC (Canadian Broadcasting Corporation), 107, 115, 117, 199
celebrations, 100–101
character names, 91–93, 116
commercials, 274
debut, *115*, 115–116
Derek "Wheels" Wheeler (character), 76
developed with Kate Taylor, 81
in development, 78
distribution deal, 86
drugs storylines, 95–96, 116
financing, 84, 86
gay and lesbian storyline, 25, 116
Heather (character), *131*
inspiration for Stephanie Kaye, 11
jacket for *Mallrats*, 234
Kit Hood, 87, 89
links to *Degrassi: The Next Generation*, 96, 115, 116
list of storylines, 95–96
locations, 87–88, *88*, 126–127, 128–129, *130*, 131
Lucy (character), 91, *92*, 151
move to prime-time, 118–119
Neil Hope, 76
new DOP, 93–94
number of episodes of, 139
parental abuse, 95
Phil Earnshaw (DIR), 37, 93, 95

racism, 25
Sari Friedland, 87, 95
Shane (character), *99*, 100
suicide, 25
teen pregnancy, 25, 95–96, 97, 130
teen sexuality storyline, 25, 96
theme song for, 94–95
Toronto Star review, 117
Trish (Danah-Jean Brown), *171*, 171–172
underage drinking, 95
Vincent Massey Junior School, 87–88, *88*
wrap of season three, 124–125
Yan Moore, 87
Yick (character), *121*, 121–122
The Zit Remedy, 96
Degrassi Minis (web content), 267
Degrassi reunion show on *Jonovision*, 199, 306
Deiseach, Angela (Erica), 130, *131*
Deiseach, Maureen (Heather), 130, *131*
de Lint, Robert, 79
Denmark, 123–124
Desperate Housewives (series), 249
DGC (Directors Guild of Canada), 169, 224
DHX Media, 281, 297–298, 300, 305. *See also* Donovan, Michael; Scherba, Josh; Wildbrain
Directors Guild of Canada (DGC). *See* DGC (Directors Guild of Canada)
Disney, 197. *See also* Walt Disney Productions
Dobrev, Nina (Mia), 261, *262*
Donovan, Michael, 184, 281, 282, 297, 300. *See also* DHX Media
Downs, Reiya (Shay), *268*, 299, *299*
Drake. *See* Graham, Aubrey Drake
drugs. *See* Hood, Kit; storylines
Duckworth-Pilkington, Peter, II, 66, 67, *68*

Dunphy, Cathy, 258–259

Earle, Sam (K. C.), 273, *274*
Earl Grey Senior Public School, 4, 6–7,
    8–10, 11, 15–16, 48, 50, 140–141. *See
    also* White, Mack
Earnshaw, Phil
    Blue Mountain Crude
        (documentary), 36, 40
    Ida Makes a Movie (DOP), 61, 62, *63*
    involvement in *Degrassi*, 37, *37*, 72,
        93, 95
EastEnders, 179–180, 188
Eastwood, Jayne (Gloria Wilkes), *193*
Eaves, Ernie, *186*
École Polytechnique massacre, 143–144,
    242
Elliot (Simon's friend), 109–110,
    202–203, 205
Ellis, Kathryn, 64, 67, 116, 146
Emma Nelson (character)
    abortion storyline, 240
    birth father, 223
    casting, 215–216
    inspiration for *Degrassi: The Next
        Generation*, 207
    menstruation storyline, 285
    name origin, 100
    at Smithdale University, 269
    stalking storyline, 220
Emmy Awards, 27, 81, 82–83, *83*, 84,
    100, 154, 256
Epitome Pictures Inc.
    distribution deal, 212
    formation, 169
    funding/income shortages, 189, 197
    legal representation, 173
    new accountant needed, 279–280
    sale to DHX Media, 297
Epstein, Jake (Craig), 237, 261–262,
    262, 263
Erika (Linda's niece), 203

The Fabulous Sixties (series), 38–39
Faier, Ken, 212
fan mail. *See* mail received
Farber, Stacey (Ellie), 238, *246*
feature-length movie. *See* Smith, Kevin
Fecan, Ivan, *211*
    and Angela Bruce, 148
    CBS, 161, 165
    CTV, 211, 248, 266
    on *Degrassi Goes Hollywood*, 266,
        267–268
    desire for show about Canadians in
        L.A., 267–268, 275
    École Polytechnique massacre,
        143–144, 228
    entertaining Jeff Sagansky, 161
    feature-length finale, 146
    MuchMusic, 271
    prime time slots, 117–118, 136–137
    School's Out ratings, 150
feminism, 240, *241*, 298, 301, *301*
Ferron, Glen, 52–53, 54
financing. *See also* budgeting
    Between Two Worlds (documentary),
        8, 34, 40
    Blue Mountain Crude (documen-
        tary), 34, 35, 40
    Degrassi: The Next Generation, 271,
        278
    Degrassi High, 126, 146–147
    Degrassi Junior High, 84, 86
    Ida Makes a Movie (film), 63
    The Kids of Degrassi Street, 66–67
    Riverdale, 183, 189–191, 193
    tax benefits, 66–67, 174, 176, *186*
Fofo (Linda's student), 11
Fox, Beryl, 39
Fox, Vivica A., 267
Free the Children (FTC), 257, 285
French, Jahmil (Dave), 273, *274*
The Fresh Prince of Bel-Air, 119, 137

This book is also available as a Global Certified Accessible™ (GCA) ebook. ECW Press's ebooks are screen reader friendly and are built to meet the needs of those who are unable to read standard print due to blindness, low vision, dyslexia, or a physical disability.

At ECW Press, we want you to enjoy our books in whatever format you like. If you've bought a print copy just send an email to ebook@ecwpress.com and include:

- the book title
- the name of the store where you purchased it
- a screenshot or picture of your order/receipt number and your name
- your preference of file type: PDF (for desktop reading), ePub (for a phone/tablet, Kobo, or Nook), mobi (for Kindle)

A real person will respond to your email with your ebook attached. Please note this offer is only for copies bought for personal use and does not apply to school or library copies.

Thank you for supporting an independently owned Canadian publisher with your purchase!